BE BETTER, NOT BITTER:

SHARING THIRTY LIFE LESSONS
I LEARNED FROM PRISON

Dakota Decker Jr.

Library of Congress Control Number: 2017907905
ISBN: Hardcover   978-1-5434-2415-7
                 Softcover   978-1-5434-2414-0
                 eBook   978-1-5434-2413-3

Print information available on the last page.

Rev. date: 12/26/2017

To order additional copies of this book, contact:
Xlibris
1-888-795-4274
www.Xlibris.com
Orders@Xlibris.com
753863

CONTENTS

FOREWORD

I met the author seven years ago when he joined the Buddhist group at the prison where he was housed. I watched as he learned the tenets of Buddhism and then put them into practice in his positive relationships with others. Over time, he accepted a leadership role within the Buddhist group, and he began to share the teachings and experiences that he had learned. I observed that he became a more compassionate person who helped others regardless of their religious affiliation.

The author shares thirty life lessons he learned as a result of being incarcerated. He begins with the premise that the opposite of love is not hate but fear and that every situation in life is either love-based or fear-based. The author believes that every life situation can be understood by these two opposing factors. Later, he introduces the reader to a concept that he calls his love-based insight, in which he states, "Unconditional love is hard to do, but it's attainable and lasts."

I have watched as the author has developed a life devoted to being of service to and helping others. Regardless of your religious affiliation, this book will better help you understand yourself and your relationship with others.

Lama Dorje
February 7, 2017

INTRODUCTION

My story begins around eleven thirty on a Friday night at a beginning of a long Autumn holiday weekend. After the longest week of my entire life, I was taken from the courtroom, where minutes earlier, my middle daughter was begging the military police officers, "Please don't hurt him." Ironically, she has long since abandoned me, hurting me much worse than the police officers ever could. As we left the building, the police officer asked me, "Do you promise not to run?" I promised him, so he did not put on the ankle cuffs. I was, however, handcuffed, which was cinched with a body cuff (that went around the waist and pulled the cuffs on the wrist to the waist), and then I was loaded in the back of the black police suburban. I remember the discomfort as the police officer had to jostle me to get my seat belt on because of the body cuff. I also remember feeling very distant, even though my life was about to change from being free to becoming one of the United States's millions of incarcerated persons. It all seemed very surreal as the emotional trauma and pain of the trial started to subside a little, and the sadness started to set in.

In the pitch-black of midnight, where the dark dread was palpable, I was driven to the military hospital, where they drew blood to enter me into the nationwide DNA database. I was then reloaded and jostled into place in the vehicle and driven to the military police's headquarters before being "locked up." I was taken in to an office (still wearing my body cuff) and questioned as to my mental state. (Was I thinking of escape or suicide? etc.) While sitting at the officer's desk as he typed out the required paperwork, I closed my eyes, hoping for sleep, but none came.

Finally, after hours of waiting at the police station, I was reloaded in the police vehicle for the long drive to the county jail. About 4:00 a.m., we arrived, and I was placed in a garage-type waiting area. My heart had been in my throat the whole drive there. In those early morning hours, it was very cold and drafty as the garage room seemed to have no heat source. Everything around me was plain, beige, and awash in fluorescent yellow light. Yet it was stark and surreal. I knew, however, my startling new reality was still just starting. After sitting there for an hour, too cold to sleep, about 5:00 a.m., a loud, obnoxious, drunk man was also brought in cuffed and placed on the steel bench next to me. I remember I could smell the alcohol exuding from his pores and, of course, his noxious breath. His eyes were wild, and his hair was standing on end like the infamous photo of Nick Nolte and other famous people when they were arrested. The drunk began to rant and rave at the top of his lungs, yelling at the guards through the glass-and-steel door to our left. I did my best to get some sleep through his wild antics and despite the noise and cold. I'd been up for almost twenty-four hours and had not slept well in many days as I'd been facing the hardest test of my life. I was exhausted but unable to rest or sleep because of the cold and noise. Finally, at about 7:00 a.m., I was processed in and placed alone in a two-man cell, where I finally slept a fitful sleep. I woke up a few hours later to wander alone in the cold and bleak and empty pod. (A pod consists of a group of cells surrounding a common room with a TV, tables, pay-type phones, and showers.) Thus began my life in the "Incarceration Nation." Thus began being alone . . . being truly alone!

You may think it's unreasonable for me to compare my incarceration to death; however, that is pretty much what happened to me in those dark, early hours on that bleak Saturday morning. To me, it definitely felt like I'd died. I was literally stripped of everything and figuratively left for dead. Like the biblical Job, I'd lost the everything: my children (save one), my military career, my rank, my community status, my belongings, my homes, my vehicles, my good name, and my reputation (not listed in any order of importance). Eventually, just a few years ago, as if my heart had not broken into a million miniature pieces already after the trial, I'd even lost the woman whom I felt was "the love of my life." My heart has exploded into a billion more pieces of fine, powdery dust. Life has been my teacher, and coming to prison has taught me and reinforced many more of life's lessons. That's the subject of this book. I'll be sharing my life's lessons with you, the reader.

I've died many deaths since coming to prison. When you're standing there naked to be strip-searched with nothing but your body and mind, again, it feels like you have died. Over these many years, everything that I'd associated as me has been taken or has departed, and my ego has been laid bare again and again. I state this having gone through two very tough military basic training regimens as a comparison, where I was taken down to nothing. However, unlike the military training, no one was or has been there to build me back up. What's left when this happens to a person? We'll be discussing that too in the many chapters that follow. We'll be discussing the toxic incarceration environment and its effects on individuals and societies.

Like the mystics have testified to for millennia, near-death experiences bring about spiritually profound insights and deep wisdom . . . if one chooses to let the lessons go in that direction, though I can tell you I've watched it go the other way too for many of my fellow incarcerated, broken people. However, this book is about my profound insights and the deep wisdom I've gained through the process of being in prison for many, many years now. My objective in the book is to share the deep life lessons I've learned and to testify to you very meaningful insights that this process of destruction has brought to me. All this, after clearing away all that I was, except what was hidden deep down inside myself. Because of my limitations, some things really aren't expressible.

Some of my insights can only be learned while in prison. For example, having the new title of "convict" or "inmate" has brought with it all sorts of garbage that didn't and do not apply to me. However, by me making very serious mistakes, all my positive, service-related, good, heartfelt, and selfless efforts *of* my entire forty-six-year life were figuratively discarded; and I have been treated like I'm dirt or worse. Even now, I'm constantly treated as if I'm a liar and cheater, and I'm considered 100 percent untrustworthy, or that I'm trying to get over on someone or the institution. The government was even able to take away my honorable, restitution, and amelioration efforts for my crimes from many years before my trial when I came forward, confessed my grievous actions, and sought and got treatment (put myself in "rehab") for what caused my poor decision-making, which led to my grievous actions. This all with a stroke of pen, so to speak, was erased as if it never happened. So, one does not only lose his/her good name and reputation but is also given someone else's bad name and reputation. I guess I should say I'm given every convict's bad name and reputation. Everyone is lumped together and, like *Lord of the Flies*, is left fending for themselves.

Though my insights were learned in prison, they exist everywhere else as prison is a microcosm of society. The lessons and experiences I've had in prison are unique to prison, but not unique to life in general. The reason why is the things that are in prison exist in the wider world on a daily basis. Actually, I don't think I've changed from characteristics of the person before that fateful pen stroke. I'm still at my core, the honorable man of integrity I was, with the same goals and priorities to serve my fellow men and society. The government institutions and many people in society, of course, don't consider me in that way . . . I'm "bad and will most likely remain that way unless forced to be otherwise." That was the reason the system put me here, despite my honorable efforts to pay restitution. Additionally, prison is expected to turn me into a hardened criminal like all other criminals . . . That's how I'll likely be treated when I'm finally released. I'm expected to be bitter.

However, for me specifically, what's really changed is my knowledge, insights, and wisdom. The unique experience of prison has given me a new perspective that I'll be endeavoring to share with you, the reader—my insights that have revealed a whole new world . . . yet are a reflection of the one you live in too. My intent is to share these lessons without the reader having to learn them from the perspective of a prison cell. As I write this, I've been locked up for over seven years. I likened my time here to the movie *Seven Years in Tibet* based on a book by Heinrich Harrer. In Heinrich Harrer's story, he was imprisoned in India for two years; and after escaping, he traveled a very long way on foot to Tibet. There, he was introduced to Buddhism and was mentored by a very young Dalai Lama, as he himself exposed the Dalai Lama to the wider world. I, like Heinrich Harrer, have been exposed to Buddhism's mindfulness training; and I have a Tibetan Buddhist Lama who ministers to my prison. Also, I've met a real high Tibetan Lama named Phakyab Rinpoche, who was imprisoned and tortured in Tibet by the Chinese (more about him later in chapter 5 of the book). There is more of a link to Heinrich Harrier's book than just the seven years in the title. Like the book and movie, I've been exposed to Eastern philosophy; and it's changed many of my thinking methods, attitudes, and paradigms. Accordingly, I've learned many lessons I never would have, had I not been imprisoned. Prison has changed the direction of my life and my thinking processes.

In this book, I'll share with you the thirty insights that have revealed themselves to me as I, and my ego, have been laid bare upon the altar of life. Each chapter title will provide a hint of the chapter's general topic, and within each chapter, you'll find two insights: a Fear-based insight and its counterpart, a Love-based insight. One of the tools I'll be using to explain my insights is what psychologists call our *Cognitive Traps* or *thinking errors*. The *Cognitive Traps* are many times what keep us from realizing these insights. Another tool I'll be using is quotes from many wise people. I've been collecting these quotes in the past seven years with the many, many publications that I've read. As I read, their profound wisdom made me pause and write the quote down for my own introspective search of myself. Now, I'll share those wise people's wisdom with you. To understand the flow, in each chapter, there will be an exposition that leads up to the Fear-based insight. Then, with the further exposition of the Fear-based insight, I'll lead the reader to the Love-based insight and the wisdom it reveals. Then, I'll expound on the Love-based insight to close out the chapter. While each chapter's Fear-based insight is important and has much to teach us (they've been very important lessons to me), the Love-based insight is each chapter's real takeaway, for both the reader and myself. The Love-based insight is my waypoint to life's journey.

I'll mention now that the overall thing that I've learned from my prison experience is there really is no such thing as "good" or "bad." Those are just "duality" labels, perspectives, and perceptions we use to judge ourselves, others, and everything in between. Knowing that there is really no "good or bad," I struggled with what to call my "point; counterpoint" insights, and the answer came to me in the form of our two basic emotions: love and fear. More on that specific subject in chapter 1 of the book. While both the Fear-based and Love-based insights are very valuable, the reason the Love-based insight is the real takeaway is this: though it's hard to see and understand most of the time, as daily life passes by, love will conquer fear. I truly believe this to be life's truism . . . Love is the solution to every problem and every difficulty we can face. Using my trial and prison experiences as the main backdrop, I'll reveal my insights and thus bare my soul and my philosophy to you. Whenever you read the word "we," know I'm first speaking to me. My wish is this book helps someone without having to go through the ego-busting experience of prison or other extremely painful experiences. Penultimately, I seek to follow Benjamin Franklin's advice when he said, "Either write something worth reading or do something worth writing about." This book endeavors to fill both aspects of wise Ben's guidance. Thank you for letting me share myself, my experiences, my insights, and my philosophy with you. Ultimately, I want to tell my children, my family, and my friends I've looked my deepest fears in the eye, so to speak; and I'm fighting every day, with love in my heart, to be the best person I can be . . . to be Better, not Bitter.

SECTION ONE:

MY INSIGHTS EARLY ON

LOVE VERSUS FEAR

In early February 2005, over eleven years ago, I committed my last ever criminal act. I was shocked by my lack of control over myself. I'd always been able to overcome any challenge I'd put my mind to, and at the other times of my hurtful actions, I'd previously promised myself I'd never make the same mistake again. Yet there I was, committing my crime again, and I was very upset and disappointed with myself and concerned for my victim. That fateful day, I admitted to myself that I couldn't overcome the destructive cycle all by myself. I knew I had to do something . . . I *had* to get help! There was no question in my mind. I knew I'd hurt my victim, and my penitence was very great. My penitence drove me to confess my crimes within a few months of my last criminal act. My remorse motivated me to come forward to bring my actions into the light of day because I believed (and still do believe) what Supreme Court Justice Louise D. Brandeis reiterated, "Sunlight is said to be the best of disinfectant,"[1] and what Henry David Thoreau taught, "Humility like darkness reveals the Heavenly lights."[2] With my crimes, I'd jeopardized my marriage and my relationship with my children, my livelihood and career, my homes and possessions, and my reputation and position in society. By confessing, I'd become extremely vulnerable. Doing the right thing put everything on the line, but I *had* to make things right for my loved ones' sake. My remorse and my love for my loved ones gave me the courage to seek and get help. Within the week of my confession, I was in professional yearlong treatment, starting my rehabilitation and restitution efforts. My penitence has enabled me talk about my grievous misdeeds over and over, year after year, to many different people. My repentance has and will continue to be the reason I seek opportunities for restitution. I should have never made those terrible mistakes in the first place. I say all this to help the reader understand my deepest, heartfelt intentions and to emphatically state, even now, knowing the outcome as it turned out . . . my coming to prison, I'd confess all over again!

I'll also tell you my story to state I was sorely afraid, and it took all my courage to confess and to start treatment. Fear was telling me to keep my mouth shut, but my love for my family drove me to reveal the truth. My fears were well founded and very logical. Keeping my crimes a secret was safe; confessing was scary. I knew if my crimes were ever revealed, I'd be in trouble. Fear was telling me to deny, deny, deny if my actions were ever discovered. We all know life is full of fear, and there are various types. The fear I'm describing was highly palpable to me. It was both the physical fear of going to prison and losing job and home, the emotional fear of losing my loved ones, and the intellectual fear of showing the world my flaws. This was fear on every level and in any way imaginable. Richard Sine taught, "If you let fear guide you, you'll spend the rest of your life looking back and wondering what could have been."[3] I couldn't let that happen . . . I felt love!

As stated, I started treatment with three big questions: why did I act against everything I believe, why could I not control myself as I always had been able to do during my adult life, and how could I control myself in the future to prevent any more hurtful actions? My counselor, Greg, really helped me delve deeply into these questions. Seeing that fear was the driving factor in my hurtful actions, he recommended a book by Dr. Gerald Jampolsky titled *Love Is Letting Go of Fear.* Serendipitously, I mentioned my counselor's book recommendation to my father, whom I'd already informed of my amelioration efforts; and he bought me my own copy and sent it to me as a motivational gift. He also sent an old cassette tape from a radio show from the 1970s. This cassette recording was of a radio interview with Dr. Jampolsky on his then recently released book. Interestingly, the seventies recording was made by my mother, who'd passed away five years before my confession. To me, it was an amazing coincidence that my mother would tape the radio interview for my use decades later. Jampolsky's book will be the underlying theme of this chapter.

I read Dr. Jampolsky's book very quickly as it's a very easy read and took to heart its very powerful message. For a year, I would listen over and over to the cassette tape of the seventies radio interview as I drove the forty minutes each way to and from my weekly treatment sessions with Greg, my clinical social worker. Luckily, the vehicle I was driving had a cassette player—another coincidence—as almost all vehicles had CD players at that time. I drank up the book's message, letting it soak into my very soul.

While it was meaningful to me, it was not so for my wife. Our marriage was struggling, so I asked her to read it, and she quickly dismissed it as "psychology gobbledygook." She was not ready for its powerful message. Still, I was undeterred because the book's simple message helped me answer the three questions mentioned above. The first answer was I was living in fear; and I was letting fear drive my thoughts, attitudes, and actions. I was letting fear guide me. Though around a dozen years ago, I was not yet in prison, my journey to uncover this chapter's insights began. I learned fear caused my inappropriate, mistaken actions. Thus, **my Fear-based insight** can be summed up as follows: *fear is very, very powerful and scary!*

Former U.S. president Richard M. Nixon is quoted as saying, "People react to fear, not love. They don't teach that in Sunday school, but it's true."[4] Even today, politicians like Nixon use fear to sell themselves as problem solvers. This is happening currently in the most recent presidential election process. They are trying to differentiate themselves from the other candidates, but in the process, they create a *culture of fear.*[5] This is not only done by politicians. The journalist, the police, the military, the Homeland Security personnel, and many others have jobs that depend on fear—the fear of something or someone. It's painfully obvious, literally in many cases, that bad things do happen. People do hurt one another; and Mother Nature or God causes natural disasters that hurt, maim, and kill human beings. This is inevitable. It's not by accident that fear is part of being alive, being human, and has been for over two thousand generations. Rational fear serves an important evolutionary purpose for the whole of humanity.

Fear is an evolutionary advantage when we're concerned about the lions, tigers, and bears, etc. If we humans ignored predators, rising floodwaters, or what food made our cave-mate sick and die, we too would die. Most likely, archaic people who did ignore dangers didn't live on to pass their genetic makeup to their descendants. Though President Nixon was not only talking about physical threats when he was speaking of fear's motivational capabilities, fear's influence and possible control over all of us is nonetheless true. Fear creates an immediate response, often before we even cognitively realize there is danger; for example, in our modern world, this could be instincts that protect life and limb, such as someone driving a car very skillfully to avoid an accident or the mother who lifts the car to save her child. Instincts, seeded by fear, save lives by enabling quick, mindless actions. Fear is built into our very important survival mechanisms.

However, fear can be mistaken, misaligned, and misused. Thomas McCurdy stated, "We are all of us, not merely liable to fear, we are also prone to be afraid of being afraid."[6] Fear is an energy, just like any other thought, emotion, or action. Fear's energy can be described using words packed with profound meaning. Let me say fear hurts, judges, holds close, attacks, clings, grasps, hoards, separates, shuts down, runs, hides, holds, fights, argues, and contracts. One big lesson for me from Dr. Jampolsky's book was that there are two basic emotions: love and fear. All other emotions stem from these two. With my prison treatment counselors, I've had to argue this point. They believe and are taught that there are many, many emotions, not just two. Which is true. They've jokingly stated, "Men use the eight basic Crayola crayon colors when it comes to emotions, but that we need to use the sixty-four set." When I'd state there were only two *basic emotions*, they'd balk, saying I was being too simplistic. However, as I stated to them and I'm stating to you, the reader, the way to find one's basic emotion on any matter is to play the "why game."

The "why game" may be unfamiliar to you, yet we've all played it with a child or as a child; for example, the child asks, "Why is the sky blue?" You give an answer, and the child again asks why. After multiple explanations and multiple "whys," they are still asking why. You finally have to state "because God made it that way," or "I really don't know why." If you do the same with your emotions, you'll end up either with fear or love as the base emotion (i.e., anger boils down to fear). Po Bronson stated it like this: "You want to know where your fears are hiding? Tell me what you know about yourself. Tell me what you can't live without."[7] In addition to love, this quote speaks to fear's emotional aspect, not evolutionary aspects. While we need fear, the instinctive type of fear, to stay safe and secure from physical dangers, we don't need to fear everything.

Psychologists have names for irrational fears using the suffix of "phobia." Here is just a sampling: *Pyrophobia* is fear of fire, *Claustrophobia* is fear of tight spaces, *Acrophobia* is fear of heights, *Bathmophobia* is fear of steep slopes, *Nytophobia* is fear of darkness, *Agrizoophobia* is fear of wild animals, *Omithophobia* is fear of birds, *Brontophobia* is fear of thunder and lightning, *Hylophobia* is fear of forests, *Nephophobia* is fear of clouds, *Homichlophobia* is fear of fog, *Ombrophobia* is fear of rain, *Siderophobia* is fear of stairs, and *Xenophobia* is fear of strangers. Some of the phobias I've selected, when you were skimming the list, likely generated the thought, "Well, it can be wise to be afraid of that one." That was my intent anyway. Rational fears can also have irrational fears. There are also phobias that you would've chuckled at; for instance, *Selenophobia* is fear of the moon. It's hard from our modern perspective to be afraid of the moon, but even that one can have a rational side. If the moon was to fall out of orbit and crash into the earth, all life would be destroyed, and that'd be a bad day. Why "*Selenophobia* is irrational is the likelihood of that happening is too minuscule to generate" even a tiny worry in one's lifetime.

Again, worry and fears are valuable, even emotional ones. That being said, the kind of fear that's opposite love is fear based on emotions, thoughts, and attitudes; and all these are in conjunction with relationships with other humans. The list of phobias also includes many of these relationship type. While *glossophobia*, fear of public speaking, will not kill a person, it's scary. This kind of fear is not based on one's literal safety or security though a person can be ostracized for speaking poorly or as a fool. *Glossophobia* is probably the most common irrational (and rational) phobia, but really, it's all in our heads. Yes! Fear (rational and irrational) is sold and cultivated by society through news stories, election campaigns, and gossip. These communication vehicles provide a disproportionate view of the world and its inevitable dangers. To understand more on this specific topic of fear, I recommend Daniel Gardner's book *The Science of Fear.*

My point is we're taught and constantly conditioned to be afraid all the time. My fears and *Cognitive Traps* enabled my hurtful crimes. Fear affects our relationships as we become distrustful as it did to my relationships. Fear creates a *Victim Mentality* as the default way we see the world, and we perceive our relationships as dangerous. Even great relationships can be affected because of what psychologists call *Loss Aversion*, which is defined as "being so determined to avoid any option associated with loss that one is willing to risk everything." In other words, losses loom larger than gains, and our behavior is affected. We give all the blame to conditions and circumstances. While context really does matter, so do you and I, so do our choices. Context does not control what we choose to do, or how we react, but does control what choices we have to make. Our freedom lies with what we choose given those choices . . . the conditions and circumstances. The choices are an outward sign of our character, and they also influence our character. The key to good decision-making is to have the right intent, right attitude, and right thought. In the end, it's the combination of our intent, attitude, and thought (within the context) that determines our choices and thus our character and our action's outcomes.

Dr. Jampolsky taught me, "When we get caught in the ego's thought system, our beliefs are created from fear that the past is going to predict the future and the future is going to be just like the past."[8] At the time of my criminal actions, my ego was caught in the state described by Dr. Jampolsky.

The ego here is the one that has been described for over 2,500 years by great philosophers, mostly from the Asia. One *Cognitive Trap*, saying the same thing, has been described by psychologists as *The Rule of Typical Things*, defined as "using the plausibility of some element of the scenario to judge the likelihood of the whole scenario." The ego thrives on fear, conflict, hate, revenge, and even murder. Fear gives the ego power, or at least, the ego perceives it that way temporarily. But the ego is constantly seeking more, more of everything. Eckhart Tolle put it this way: "The ego always wants something from other people or situations . . . It uses people and situations to get what it wants, and even when it succeeds, it is never satisfied for long."[9] Psychologists call this phenomenon the *Hedonic Treadmill.*, which is defined as "a person adapts and always wants more." If you earn more, then you adapt. This applies to many things, not just money. The ego is Fear-based. Being ego-focused itself creates a *Hedonic Treadmill* and will not lead to happiness.

Dr. Elisabeth Kubler Ross famously stated, "There is a little bit of Hitler in each of us."[10] No one wants to have "a little bit of Hitler in us." But when we listen to our ego and its fearful messages, we give into it, and then we're likely to act in a megalomaniac manner. I suspect Hitler was one of the most frightened people who has ever lived on this earth. His rhetoric spread like crazy through the fearful culture of Germany in the 1930s. Dr. Jampolsky stated, "Fear can be known as the most virulent and damaging virus to humankind. Most of the world's beliefs system of how we communicate with each other and ourselves is based on fear."[11] This echoes what was written earlier about politicians, the media, and gossip. Fear motivates because it is egocentric. Its power lies in the *Scarcity Mentality*, defined as a "mindset where there is only so much of a given resource." For me, I had such a mind-set when it came to love and my relationship with my wife. There was only so much love, and I was seeking love from outside myself . . . from other people. My *Scarcity Mentality* caused me to seek external validation and, in the end, commit criminal acts.

The Spiritualist Deepak Chopra has stated, "Fear best thrives in the present tense. That is why experts rely on it; in a world that is increasingly impatient with long-term process, fear is a potent short-term play."[12] The world is run by people's ego; and fear is driving everyone to make short-term plays, to jump on the *Hedonic Treadmill,* and to start running as fast as one can. Long-term plays or real strategic thinking take effort in both the conceptualizing, communicating, and understanding. Most of us humans are not willing to put forth the required effort. The outcome we see all around us is people destroying other people, their community, and the planet. It's "short-term thinking" that enables this. It's being egocentric, which is, in turn, motivated most quickly by fear. Deepak Chopra also stated, "Fear's main tactic is to make the illusion seem real . . . when: you give into fear, you are either projecting into the future or reliving the past."[13] When I did my illegal actions, I was taking the "short-term play." I was not thinking long term, and I hurt others. I needed to, and now have, put forth the required strategic thinking . . . Thus, this book is for me, and you.

As already mentioned, the ego's inferred and, many times, stated goal is to get more. In the rich Western world, this is very apparent, but it is also applicable everywhere around the world. Even poor people can get caught on the treadmill. Fear in a relationship is likely to become a self-fulfilling prophecy. I can attest to that fact with my marriage. Fear created a downward spiral into my marriage's death. Fear creates a mind-set that affects our beliefs, our thoughts, our attitudes, and our actions. Another big portion of my earlier mentioned treatment has been based on psychologist Albert Ellis's Rational Emotive Behavior Therapy (REBT)—how we think, feel, and act. Samuel Smiles stated, "Sow a thought, reap and action; sow an action, reap a habit; sow a habit, reap a character; sow a character, reap a destiny." [14] Living a Fear-based life will create a fear-filled destiny. Another quote making the same point about fear is Cus D'Amato's statement: "Fear is like fire. You can make it work for you: warm you in the winter . . . cook your food . . . give you light . . . produce energy. Let it go out of control and it can hurt you, even kill you."[15] If we think, feel, and act out of fear, then in the end, destruction is all but inevitable. Let's put fear in its place.

This can be seen in how U.S. Pres. Franklin D. Roosevelt handled WWII. He told the people, after the 1929 stock market crash, that "the only thing we have to fear is fear itself."[16] This motto created what is now called The Greatest Generation, of which my parents were active members. Now consider George W. Bush's fearmongering that created an unwinnable war on terrorism. Even though tragic, the events of 9/11 did not threaten the existence of the United States or even any other country. The fear from 9/11 was used to justify revenge that has ended up costing millions of more lives and trillions of dollars. Instead of "The Greatest Generation," we now have what I'll call The Most Scared Generation. And that's saying something compared to my baby boomer generation, which went through the constant Cold War nuclear bomb threat. The character of each generation, it seems, can be defined on how it handles fear. The same applies, individually, for me and you.

Another big lesson I learned from Dr. Jampolsky is our fears; "everybody's fears are really a cry for help." People's hurtful actions are "a cry for love." Love is the long-term objective, and even the ego's short-term play is just a misguided cry for help. The Buddha taught, "Hate (fear) will never put an end to hate (fear)—only love can. Hate (fear) wants to destroy its objective, a person seen as obstructing the hater's happiness; but love wants even the hating person to be happy, not to be any sort of obstruction—that's how love can overcome hate (fear)."[17] As you can see, I substituted fear for the word "hate," following the insight I received about the two basic emotions. Dr. Jampolsky taught, "Love is the total absence of Fear."[18] Here is where I will introduce my next insight, **my Love-based insight:** *Unconditional Love is hard to do, but it's attainable and it lasts*.

Once we realize that there are two basic emotions, the next step is to realize that we have a choice in which one we experience at each given moment. Dr. Ellis's REBT comes into play here. We have a choice. While we can't control society, or anyone else for that matter, we can control ourselves. We can control our mind-set. We can set it to the default of love. It's hard for us to see that we have a choice because the ego is so strong. It has lifelong conditioning and experiences to draw from in its effort to promote fear as the most important priority. When we go through life with a fearful mind-set, we miss out on love and the joy that love brings. We miss out on all those love-filled opportunities. Jesus had five basic messages: first, God is love; second, fear not; third, know the truth; fourth, love you neighbor as yourself; and fifth, love one another as I have loved you. *All positive emotions stem from love.* If you want to be happy, then love. Love is both a noun and a verb . . . Love is powerful enough to be both at the same time.

This is where another lesson taught by Dr. Jampolsky comes into play for me. When it comes to relationships, "you are Love." You have the power to benefit others around you. Love too is energy. Love is energy that heals, accepts expands, gathers, shares, stays, gives, values, appreciates, smooths, mends, binds, and forgives and is transparent, open, and forthright. Peace activist and Zen monk Thich Nhat Hanh stated, "Love is the capacity to take care, to protect, to nourish. If you are not capable of generating that kind of energy towards yourself, it is very difficult to take care of another person. In the Buddhist teaching, it is clear that to love oneself is the foundation of the love of other people. Love is a practice. Love is truly a practice."[19]

Another lesson I learned from Dr. Jampolsky is this: "All that I give is given to myself. To give is to receive another lesson from Jesus—this is the law of Love. Under this law, when we give our Love away to others we gain, and whatever we give we simultaneously receive. The law of Love is based on abundance; we are completely filled with Love all the time, and our supply is always full and running over. When we give our Love unconditionally to others with no expectations of return, the Love within us extends, expands, and joins. So by giving our Love away we increase the Love within us and everyone gains."[20] Wow, what a profound insight concerning us and love.

Dr. Jampolsky is a living example of what he wrote. Here is a story demonstrating his love: A few years ago, while in prison, I asked my father to buy me another copy of *Love Is Letting Go of Fear* for my Christmas present. He did, and I quickly reread it, enjoying its simple yet profound message. I turned to the back and saw it had Dr. Jampolsky's address. The copy I received in 2013 was reprinted in 2011, and so the address was only two years old. I decided to write Dr. Jampolsky to tell him my story, to tell him how his book and the tape-recorded interview really blessed my life, and to thank him. Writing from prison, one gets used to people not writing back, and I didn't expect a letter from him. However, to my surprise, he did write me back; and he sent me free copies of his later writings. From my limited information, at the time Dr. Jampolsky wrote me, I figured he was eighty-eight years old. Yet he took the time to care about me and to send me his love. I didn't know it at the time, but I would really need his books as I was about to go through another loss in my life. My Sweetheart, who had stuck with me for four and one half years of my prison experience, had decided to move on. While the loss of My Sweetheart crushed my heart into fine powder, I was still able to reach inside me to give bounteous unconditional love.

That was one of the biggest lessons I learned back in 2005 when I stopped my criminal actions and, again, a few years ago—love is abundant. Having an *Abundance Mentality* versus a *Scarcity Mentality* on love really changed my life and my mind-set. While I still lost both my wife and the woman who was "My Sweetheart," in the last decade, it was not because I did not give them my love. I'd learned that lesson, and I worked very hard to give my abundant, unconditional love to both of them. Of course, giving unconditional love makes one vulnerable, and we can still experience pain. I have. However, the suffering is better able to be dealt with when we see the love within us as abundant. Again, we see ourselves as love with the ability to expand that love outward. Love is limitless. Humble people are better able to give unconditional love because they are better able to see the value of the other person. They are better able to give and receive love, to be influenced by others, and to see the other person's "cry for love." Charles Haanel stated, "The only way to get love is by giving it . . . fill yourself with it, until you become a magnet."[21]

The Buddhist teachings, to which I've been exposed and immersed when I came to prison, fit perfectly with the lessons I learned over a decade ago—the lessons of two basic emotions of love and fear. Then, with the lesson that there's a way ahead, once we realize we have a choice . . . that we choose between fear and love. Finally, when we next understand that the long-term play is love, that love brings us natural and easy happiness and joy. Buddhist teacher Chogyum Trungpa Rinpoche stated, "If we accept that love is a combination of care, commitment, knowledge, responsibility, and trust, we can then be guided by the understanding. We can use these skillful means as a map in our daily life to determine right action."[22] I now understand that love is not scarce but is abundant. I see the power of our mind to make it so. We, with our minds, determine our experience; and we determine the truth of that experience. We're the ones to start to love within and then give that love unconditionally outward. I'm not sure who said it, but the next quote is very applicable: "People were created to be loved. Things were created to be used. The reason why the world is in chaos is because things are loved and people are being used."[23] The ego uses people; love gives. With my crimes, I used someone, thus the problem.

My last realization concerning love is this: everyone is love. While that may be very hard for us to see or experience with many people, it is true for all. Again, when we see people, even the ones who hurt us, as people who are crying out for love, our perspective changes. Our experience changes. Our truths are changed. Those people are crying out for love that they really have deeply buried or covered within themselves. It's our choice to love them anyway. Physicist turned philosopher Amit Gossami provided a very profound quote when he said, "Can you imagine loving someone from choice—not because you are in love, not because there is the possibility of ego-gratification, not because you have a reason to love? This is love from level of the Buddha. We cannot will it. We can only choose to surrender to it in a creative opening."[24] Romantic love is and can be an add-on to unconditional love. That said, if romantic love is also not unconditional, then the relationship is doomed to fail. As Gossami stated, we have to "love from a Buddha level." This can be from a Christlike, or Allah, or Yahweh level. Mind-set is key.

Love enables real compassion and forgiveness. Many times, I hear or read that forgiveness is not so much about the other person; it's more about the person forgiving as he/she is able to "let go." While that sentiment may be true, if it really is about the person forgiving and not the person being forgiven, then the person forgiving is not really letting go or forgiving. If their intent is self-serving in any way, then it really isn't unconditional love, nor is it right action. In Steven James's fiction book *The Knight,* the character named Christie stated, "Our choices decide who we are, but our loves define who we will become."[25] Being love means you forgive because that is what unconditional love does . . . It isn't self-serving. We must forgive and let go because love is in both you and me . . . It is in our Buddha or Christlike nature. Thomas Merton profoundly said, "Love is our true destiny. We do not find the meaning of life by ourselves alone—we find it with another."[26]

Realizing I am love and seeing others as love too is a basic principle in Eastern philosophy. It has helped me deal with the impermanence of this life and all the loss. It has helped me deal with the injustices and prejudices. It has helped me forgive. I've needed to forgive myself as well as others. Caroline Myss wrote, "Love is the fuel of our physical and spiritual bodies."[27] Love is what keeps us healthy and happy. Both health and happiness are so interrelated that even the many psychology and sociology studies conducted to measure happiness and healthiness separately have concluded that the solution to one is the other. Love fuels us because we are love. Put another way, Eckhart Tolle stated, "Love isn't a portal; it's what comes through the portal into this world."[28] I'll add, you and I are portals. We, each being a portal, just need to be open.

In the beginning of this chapter, I wrote about how my remorse drove me to action, to my repentance. Later on in the chapter, I wrote about a list of words that describe fear and love. I'd like to add a word to the fear list and two words to the love list. I propose that "regret" is a word that belongs on Fear's list because regret is fearful. When one feels regret, they are longing for something that was lost. However, "remorse" belongs on love's list because it suggests a prolonged and insistent self-reproach and mental anguish for past wrongs. I believe remorse is motivated by love as is "repentance," another word to add to the love list. While regret is Fear-based because of what was lost, remorse and repentance are Love-based because they rise out of concern for another. Remorse is penitence-initiated. Put another way, when penitence and sorrow for one's actions meet love and compassion, remorse and repentance are the natural occurrences.

Love has the power to change grievous mistakes and pain into something beneficial to all concerned. Love has the power to make things right again. Steven Levine stated, "When your fear touches someone's pain, it becomes pity. When your love touches someone's pain it becomes compassion."[29] When going to trial, my father's advice was to "tell the truth because the truth will set you free." I followed my father's advice as, of course, his wisdom is well above mine. Though I've been put in prison and I'm not physically free, I am free! My remorse and repentance are Loved-based, right action. The lessons I learned over a decade ago from my counselor and Dr. Jampolsky have been added upon with my prison experiences and my Buddhist mindfulness training as you will read more about in this book. I'm honored to have you along as a witness to this journey as I share very personal feelings and as I share general observations for us all.

In his book *Tuesdays with Morrie*, Mitch Albom tells of his experience with his dying college professor, Morrie Schwartz. Morrie is teaching all of us about life as he was dying. Morrie states profound wisdom when he said, "Love always wins."[30] Although it is hard to see that from inside these prison walls or my cell window, I know it to be true.

I'm love, you're love, we're love together, and you and I are to give love *always*!

BEING ALONE

In the introduction, I described my experience entering the "Incarceration Nation." One key aspect of my story was that I was completely and utterly by myself . . . I was alone. I've been solo camping, but this was different because it was not solitude by choice. Even in a prison full of people, you can still be alone. In fact, I'm never by myself, but I'm alone. While we go through life, we're connected to someone else almost all the time, starting at birth. In prison, there is always someone there. Then you may ask, can I be alone? When one is sent to prison, or dies for that matter, one goes by themselves . . . You really are alone, not connected to anyone. You cannot take people with you in any literal, practical manner for love and support. For some people, prison was the first time they were ever really alone, and being alone is the punishment. One is "separated from society," which means he or she is sent to a human warehouse, where all links to society (family and friends) are completely broken. The prisoner can work to reconnect, but at first, all connections are severed. It takes their concerted effort to reestablish connections. Those first few days I was in county jail, I was disconnected from everyone, friend or family.

I did not even have another inmate to communicate with. For many, reconnection never happens. It took a while to reconnect and rebuild my outside support structure. It took work on my part. I've observed that many people, especially those who don't like themselves, do not even try to reconnect. Maybe it's out of embarrassment, or they don't really have anyone to begin with . . . someone who could be counted on when the chips are down. And when one is in prison, the chips are really down.

In our society, forcing someone to be alone is punishment and can be considered cruel if done too long . . . solitary confinement. For example, in this prison, maximum custody and death-sentenced inmates are locked in their cell twenty-three hours a day with one hour out to exercise and shower. If you mess up in "general population" (GenPop), you are sent to the Special Housing Unit (SHU) and locked down in the same area as the maximum and death-sentenced prisoners, and you are treated just like them and/or become one of them if you are found guilty after the prison's administrative review. One person I met in my current prison had been kept in true solitary confinement for the year before his trial. He was kept separate from everyone, and even the guards would not even talk to him because of his crime. Therefore, he had no human interaction for one entire year.

Currently, I live in what many of my 2.3 million nationwide fellow prisoners would consider a luxury prison because I have my own 7' wide x 10' long x 8' tall cell, and having one's own cell is very nice. My living space is what I jokingly call a toilet with a cot, but it's my own toilet. Each cell has a desk shelf and a seat bolted to the floor and wall. It has white concrete-filled, cinder block walls; a white concrete ceiling; and a plain concrete floor.

All the "furniture" is gray, and there is a steel mirror over my sink toilet, a steel-framed 4" wide x 72" tall window at one end, a steel door with a food tray, and 6" wide x 30" window at the other end. So despite the relative "luxury" of it only holding one inmate, me, it still is Spartanus and bleak. In GenPop, everyone at this prison has their own cell and compared to other older prisons I've read about, like San Quenton, where two people are stuffed into a 6' wide x 9' long x 8' tall, it's a benefit to be able to stand up straight and use the toilet by myself. However, I do have an intimate understanding of the crowded way to live as well. Both the county jail and the special housing units I was housed in are two-person cells. (A couple of times, I lived on a portable cot called a sled in a two-person cell which now holds three people or more.) Let me tell you, it's no fun to be in the same cell, or "toilet," when one's cellmate needs to stink up the place . . . Believe me. As an example for you to have the palpability of living like stacked wood, I'll share a story of my third "cellie" that may bring the reader a smile or a wave of nausea. One evening, my cellie was on the upper bunk, and I was reading a book on my lower bunk when his feet flopped out over the edge. He then proceeded to rub and scrape his dirty, stinky, fungus-toed feet together; and millions of flaky, dried skin cells fell down on me, making me gag. Such is the fun of living in a toilet room with someone else.

This brief overview of my living conditions brings me to my first insight. This Fear-based insight was very effectively communicated to me by a wise fellow prisoner named Scott. One evening, as he and I were walking the asphalt track, I was venting about some of the silly, idiotic things that other prisoners do all the time. As an explanation, Scott said to me, "Well, the majority of the people in here don't like their cellmate." It took me a second as my first thought was "What's he talking about? We (in GenPop) each have our own cells." Then it hit me. He was saying the people I was talking about do all the juvenile things they do because they don't like themselves. The many years I've spent "inside" have only proved Scott right, and the fact that we are all "alone" both in prison and without highlights his wisdom. Thus, **my Fear-based insight** is as follows: *the majority of people in prison "don't like their cellmate," or most people don't like themselves.*

So why don't inmates like themselves, and does that insight extend to the "outside" as I've alluded to? Let's cover "inside" first. Of course, my fellow inmates, like myself, more than likely have remorse, regret, and guilt for whatever crime they committed and for the hurt they caused their victim. That may well be the reason. However, more likely, the fact they do not like themselves was the cause of why they committed the crime in the first place . . . the reason they acted out. The sooner lawmakers, politicians, judges, juries, social workers, etc., have this realization, the realization that people offend because they need help, the sooner we can reduce the number of people in prison. Eddie Cantor stated, "When I see the 'Ten Most Wanted' list . . . I always have this thought: If we'd made them feel wanted earlier, they wouldn't be wanted now."[1] Therefore, we can conclude that not liking one's self happens "inside" and "outside" of prison and is a big reason people are in prison.

To anecdotally validate this conclusion, if you, the reader, think of the people you know or even ask yourself the hard question: do they like themselves, or do you like yourself? You'll realize like I did that many, many people don't. Of course, society and the media don't help people's self-image with the many negatively reinforced beliefs, advertisements, and news stories. A person is told by the many messages that they are not good enough based on various reasonable and unreasonable standards. For the most part, what equals success is focused on possessions, prestige, and power . . . things that boost one's ego. Since not everyone can have many possessions, gain prestige, or have power, one is left feeling less. Even if they "do have it all," the *Hedonic Treadmill* effect will make them unhappy.

But we can't put the blame solely on the media as parents, family, teachers, friends, peers, and the individual themselves degrade the person in one way or another (more on others in chapter 3).

As to me, while it's true that I was very insecure about my primary intimate relationship at the time of my crime, I did not hate myself. I'm sure my self-confidence is from years and years of hard work to overcome the societal and self-imposed stigma when I was very young as I was mercilessly teased for sucking my thumb. But that's another whole book that I doubt would be of interest, nor do I have a desire to write about. To repeat from last chapter, I was, however, insecure. Though I like myself, I do have great remorse for my hurtful actions and its impact to my victims, and I was very disappointed in myself for my lack of self-control. Both my remorse and self-disappointment drove me to seek and get professional help to overcome my *Cognitive Traps* and to build up my security with my key relationships. To reiterate, remorse is a powerful, positive, Love-based motivator, while regret reinforces self-loathing. That said, my youthful experience helps me understand our normal human tendency to self-deprecate. It's a daily battle for every one of us to like ourselves as we tend to judge ourselves very harshly. It's our ego using the fearful tools at hand to maintain its control. Our internal judge's harshness can make life very lonely. As James Lane Allen stated, "We do not attract what we want, but what we are."[2]

Not that I don't struggle with my self-esteem, but I did learn when I was very young that I had to like myself because it seemed no one else did or would, certainly not my peers. For the vast majority, prison makes people revert to an earlier stage of their development, acting more like children than grown adults. As I alluded to in the introduction, I feel prison is like *Lord of the Flies*, and I'll add, to be more descriptive, it's when *Lord of the Flies* meets *Animal Farm*. Another analogy that I've shared with family and friends is "junior high school on steroids." The assaults, fights, rapes, bullying (more on bullying in chapter 5), and murder in prison are caused by people trying to regain some control of an uncontrollable situation . . . a *Coping Mechanism* or strategy. What is *Coping*? *Coping Mechanisms* are "things people do to reduce the negative emotional, psychological, and physical fallout of stressful life circumstance and daily travails." In short, *Coping Mechanisms* are for the ego's protection. We'll talk more about the ego later.

I'll share a light example of when I was bullied. One day I was working in the woodshop, using the drill press, when the 2:00 p.m. break was called.

But, I was almost done and only had a few more holes to drill. So I kept working. One of the longtime prisoners who worked in the shop came over and threatened to beat me up if I did not stop right then. Well, I did stop, but he did not need to bully me to get to do so. He could have come over and spoke rationally to me, but that was not the way prison works. He had to show his power. He felt the need to bully me even when force was not needed. Bullying is commonplace, and there are only two ways to resolve it: to fight, what is seen as standing up for yourself, or to continue to be a whipping post. Being mature and discussing the issue has very, very little effect and is viewed as being a wimp. So being incarcerated forces people to become what society does not what them to be, with the ultimate outcome of the people being released back out in society having learned or having reinforced the negative, hurtful *Coping Mechanism* or negative strategies to deal with life. The people are not given the skills or experience of how to like themselves, and so the cycle continues, and they likely reoffend and return to prison. Of note, the woodshop bully murdered another inmate within weeks of his confrontation with me. He received another life sentence and is now in another prison. However, I've heard he has since stayed out of trouble, and I wish him well.

The normal survival strategy in prison is to align one's self with those who are in power, which means coercive power or force. Most likely, these people are the most violent and manipulative, and they are the people who dislike themselves the most. Having lost everything when the government sent them to prison, all prisoners revert back to strategies that worked when they were young, for most especially where "might meant right," learned from family and/or peers. For most of us, junior high school was a time of lack of control while one struggles to find their place in their family and in society. It's an in-between state where a young person works to break free of their parents' control and grow up into adulthood. In prison, grabbing power is seen as a way to regain prestige and status, and aligning one's self with them is a way to regain a sense of control even though it is a Fear-based strategy. Although these people gain status in prison mostly through bullying, they are not really respected by anyone because people see though their self-promotion. That said, that does not stop the weak from aligning with the bullies to gain perceived safety and security . . . to establish a prison friendship based on using each other.

I've watched it time and again as a new person arrives and surveys the scene in GenPop, watching to determine who's who, where they sit for meals, who controls the TV remote, or some other measure of prison power.

Then the new person works to find a way to get in the good graces of what are called heavies in this prison. Usually, the heavy manipulates the person to get something they want, to include attacking someone else or stealing something, or worse. Thus, they are bonding themselves to each other. One person whose cell was right next mine would vent to me about the very person he was snuggling up to . . . There was no respect. He admitted it was just a way to ensure his safety and security. Benjamin Franklin once said, "Those who can give up essential liberty to obtain a little temporary safety, deserve neither liberty or safety."[3] In my cell neighbor's case, he was giving up his integrity and liberty. Obviously, I was a person he felt would not rat him out because talking to someone about powerful person (one of the heavies) is a way to get hurt, ostracized, or killed. In prison, as in the jungle, being alone can be dangerous.

This all creates an environment where people in power really don't know how little respect others have for them because they have people "befriending" them all the time. As Edith Sitwell said, "The aim of flattery is to soothe and encourage us by assuring us of the truth of an opinion we already formed about ourselves."[4] However, deep down inside, all people involved in the transaction know they really don't like themselves for doing what they are doing. They know they are either a "user" or are "being used." Neither position builds one's self-image. While gaining power gives people's ego the feeling they are successful, it still does not help them like themselves. It creates a false feedback loop. Mike Evans stated, "Your perspective of yourself will determine the possibilities you pursue."[5] As my friend Scott helped me realize for my Fear-based insight, the majority of the people I have been incarcerated with do not like themselves, and neither power nor alignment with power settles that need.

If we look in society, we see the same thing. We see rock stars, movie stars, politicians, rich people, and many others who have attained what is considered success, only to find they are not happy . . . caught in on *Hedonic Treadmill*. It's lonely not only at the top but also at the bottom. Marc Angel stated, "Being alone does not mean you are lonely, and being lonely does not mean you are alone."[6] The vast majority of the time in prison, you're not ever alone. Even as I'm surrounded by hundreds of strangers and acquaintances, I feel very alone and lonely most of the time. One of the longtime inmates here has a quote he puts on a prison event posting. It stated, "You came here alone and you'll leave here alone, but while you're here, you don't have to be alone." His statement is true in every aspect. However, being in the company of others does not always resolve loneliness, especially if the relationship or company is with fake or disingenuous people or with a relationship that is based on using each other.

In the last fifty years, many psychology and sociology studies have proven that what other people think really matters to us. We can lie to ourselves and say it doesn't, but really, it does. University of Iowa psychologists Robert Baron, Joseph Van-delle, and Bethany Brunsman[7] designed an experiment in which they told participants they were testing the accuracy of eyewitness verifications. The test involved slides that appeared briefly and then questions about what they saw on the slide. There were three people in the room to view the slides and answer the questions, but two of them were part of the experiment and would give false answers. The real test subjects were then asked to verify the answers or stick with what they saw. The subjects routinely gave a wrong answer to back up the other people (the nontest subjects) or changed their answer when the others did not validate their answer. We are social beings, and what others say matters . . . Believe it.

As Don Miguel Ruiz stated, "We make assumptions that everyone else sees life the way we do. We assume that others think the way we think, feel the way we feel, judge the way we judge, and abuse the way we abuse. And this is why we have a fear of being ourselves around others. Because we think everyone else will judge us, victimize us, abuse us, and blame us as we do ourselves. So even before others have a chance to reject us, we have already rejected ourselves."[8] I think he puts it clearly as to why the majority of people do not like themselves, and why other people's opinions mean more to us than they really should, or even need to. Naturally, we're ego-focused beings, and external feedback seems very important to us. I admit, it's been so with me.

As I stated earlier, many of the people around me committed their crime because they didn't and don't like themselves; they didn't feel safe or secure. Therefore, rather than threaten people with long prison sentences, foolishly thinking that will force them to never commit a crime, we need to help people learn to like themselves and help them feel safe and secure. Prison does not build autonomy, but incapacitation; and incapacitation hinders rehabilitation. How then do we help people, including ourselves, like themselves? The ancient Buddhist bodhisattva Tokmay Sangpo answered it this way: "If the internal enemy of hatred is not tamed, when one tries to tame external enemies, they increase. Therefore, it is the practice of the wise to tame themselves by means of the forces of love and compassion."[9] As the bodhisattva (note: a bodhisattva is a being who has attained enlightenment but chooses to stay and help other obtain enlightenment) stated, the only way to build a person's self-image is with love and compassion, not prison or loneliness. This leads me to **my second Love-based insight:** *accepting one's self for who one is, and having love and compassion for one's self leads to naturally liking one's self.*

The famous rabbi from old Prague asked us two questions that help us hone in on this insight. Rabbi Hillel asked, "If I am not for myself, who is for me? And, being for my myself, what am I?" If not now when?[10] Really, being alone is very hard on most people, including for the reason stated in the Fear-based insight . . . not liking one's self. However, in the Love-filled insight, being alone may be the way for one to really get to know who one really is. Master Lao-tzu taught, "Ordinary men hate solitude, but the master makes use of it, embracing his aloneness realizing he is one with the whole universe."[11] The way to overcome the dislike a person has is to really get to know who they are. Sure, prison is one way to be forced to take a hard look at one's self, but it surely isn't the only way, or even the best way. Prison is a toxic environment. Counseling, treatment, and mindfulness training are much better ways of really helping a person look at themselves . . . true rehabilitation.

Master Lao-tzu also stated, "Mastering others requires force; mastering the self requires enlightenment."[12] Also, Socrates stated, "Let him who would move the world, first move himself."[13] The loving and compassionate means or way of helping others to like themselves is the only way to really eliminate crime and hurtful actions, and it starts with being loving and compassionate with one's self. Prison does not do it. In fact, in most cases, prison breaks people more and incapacitates them for their future life outside prison. By the way, over 95 percent of prisoners are eventually released.[14] The person who comes out of prison stronger, more self-assured, more resilient, more loving, and compassionate, in a word, "better," is the anomaly. The vast majority come out worse than when they went in, accompanied by a broken support structure and family relationships, in a word, "bitter." Most ex-cons are destined to return to prison,[15] and their children are now more likely to go to prison, creating a terrible cycle. While in prison, the spouses are more likely to be on welfare and live in substandard housing. They're more likely to be evicted over and over. Then the children follow the parent into prison, and the cycle is renewed.

We all make mistakes, and in some cases, these mistakes are also considered a crime. We hurt other people, and we struggle through life trying to be successful and respected. We all have flaws, foibles, warts, etc. We don't measure up to others. We don't do the right things or even the things we know we want to do. Heck! How many New Year's resolutions have we broken or even failed to make for fear of failure? A lot, I'm sure. My point is it isn't really easy or natural to like one's self. Or so we think. So how do we learn to like ourselves? Let me give some examples of choices to help us in our quest for a compassionate life full of wisdom. Cornelia ten Boom, who survived Nazi atrocities and was still able to forgive one of her guards she met years later, stated the following: "Happiness isn't something that depends on our surroundings. It's something we make inside ourselves."[16] Notice that Ms. Ten Boom used the word "make" versus "happens." She experienced happiness as a choice, not a happenstance. In the nonfiction book *The Boys in the Boat* by Daniel James Brown, the main character, Joe Rantz, is told by his father at age fifteen, when he is being left behind to fend for himself during the 1929 Great Depression, "If there's one thing I've figured out about life, it's that if you want to be happy, you have to learn how to be happy on your own."[17]

My eldest brother stated when I was a teenager that "happiness is by choice, not chance." The common theme is, alone or not, we have to make the choice to be happy, or to like ourselves. Other people's opinion may validate you, but if you don't like yourself, it will not last. Self-doubt will creep back in, and soon, you will be seeking the next person to stroke your ego . . . the next person in power to align with to feel safe and secure. We have to make the choice to love and to be compassionate with ourselves as the bodhisattva stated. We first need to recognize that those flaws, foibles, crimes, and mistakes really are what make us perfect. This is the first step to liking one's self. "What?" You might ask yourself when you read that sentence. Does what you just read contradict itself? Doesn't the flaws, foibles, crimes, and mistakes make us imperfect? Well, if you have the industrialized version of the word "perfect" as your default, then that's a valid question. Western religion as well as the industrial revolution added a meaning to the word "perfect" to mean flawless. However, if we trace it back to its Greek origins, we find the word means "complete" versus "flawless."

Flaws and foibles make us human, and those flaws and foibles make us complete. Here are some steps to help us on the journey to compassion and wisdom: The first step to like one's self is to *accept ourselves* for who we are with all the mistakes, flaws, foibles, and all. We need to see that as the renowned Buddhist nun Prema Chadron reminds us, "We are perfect as we are."[18] She is using the true meaning of the word, not the bastardized industrial revolution meaning. That's a big step for many people as they've been conditioned to feel they are always lacking. Once a person accepts themselves fully, they're able to accept others for their flaws and foibles. If one does not like themselves, it's near impossible for them to accept someone else. This step requires a person to know themselves. Also, to see themselves in an accepting manner, not a judgmental, demeaning, discounting, minimizing manner.

The second step is to remember what Tokman Sangpo stated: "The wise tame themselves by means of the forces of *love* . . ."[19] Motivationalist Marc Angel stated it another way when he said, "Learn to love yourself first, instead of loving the idea of other people loving you."[20] So one first accepts one's self, and then the person can love themselves. However, for many people, loving one's self is even a bigger step than accepting one's self. That said, anyone and everyone can and should love themselves because if they can't love themselves, then they really are not able to truly love another person. Loving one's self is natural if you really do accept yourself. But if a person still struggles with liking or loving themselves, the next step is sure to help.

The third and last step is the last word that Tokman Sangpo stated: "The wise tame themselves by means of the forces of love and *compassion*."[21] Compassion is hard for many people because they are so puffed up in pride that they can't give anyone a break, least of all themselves. However, when any person goes through a humbling experience, such as financial, societal, or relational failure, having compassion is easier. As to prison, when one has nothing left but your broken self, it can be very easy to have compassion for others. That said, from my experience, most people in prison don't use the humbling experience to turn introspective. Likely, it is, in part, the toxic environment that's forcing them to regress to a more immature state. They've not given themselves a break, and they sure are not going to give someone else a break. This even when the world has taken everything from them. I believe pain and suffering serve the purpose of enabling compassion, but it still has to be a choice. Life is full of pain and suffering (in and out of prison). Most people are missing the chance to have compassion for themselves. Thus, they dislike themselves more and more as time goes on. Life is hard even when everything seems smooth. No one escapes some level of pain or suffering . . . No one! I know I've not escaped it, and none of the prisoners around me have either. I'm sure you, the reader, have experienced pain and suffering. My heart goes out to you. As Marc Angel stated, "Happiness is not determined by what's happening around you, but rather what's happening inside you. Most people depend on others to gain happiness, but the truth is it always comes from within."[22] To repeat, here are the steps to liking yourself: 1) *accepting* yourself for who you are, 2) *loving* yourself, and 3) having *compassion* for yourself. Then if you are able to give yourself a break, odds are you will give other people a break as well.

The Buddhists have a meditative practice that helps with the three abovementioned steps called Tonglen.[23] When doing Tonglen, you first start with the intention of a loving heart/mind (Bodhichitta). Then you look inside and see the pain and suffering you go through. You breathe in the pain and, with the out breath, release peace and love. After a few minutes, you shift to someone you care about deeply using the same breathing and visualization techniques. After a few minutes, you shift to an enemy or antagonist, realizing the pain and suffering they are going through that makes them become so nasty and mean. After a few minutes of that, you move to a stranger and then to larger and larger groups of people. You are actually visualizing the depth of their pain and suffering. You take it all in with your in breath and send out acceptance, love, and compassion with each out breath. This exercise or practice really helps the meditator feel acceptance, love, and compassion for themselves and others. If these steps seem beyond your capability, try Tonglen. Any Buddhist or "mindfulness trained" meditator can help you practice.

In this chapter, I shared with you my insight that most people don't really like themselves, and they depend on external circumstances and others to make them happy. However, in reality, we are really are on our own as everything can be taken from us in the blink of an eye; and all that is left is you. It does not take being locked up to validate that truth. There are examples all around us. Underneath it all, you are naked and alone. Therefore, recognize that you're perfect as you are and that you can accept yourself as a complete being *because* all the mistakes, flaws, and foibles (as well as the shiny parts of life) make you complete. You would not be you without all the pretty and messy stuff that makes you up and surrounds your life. You are you *because* of the life you've lived. You're perfectly you! Be satisfied with yourself and recognize all your life's challenges, struggles, and beauty that you've faced. If you can do better, then choose to do so, but don't dwell in the past. Focus on the choices you need to make right now.

I likened us to a rock we find on the shore of a fast river or stream. It's round and smooth and kind of polished. How did it get that way? It did not start out that way, but as it was washed downstream over time, it hit other rocks, and all the rough edges were knocked off. Now after the corners and sharp edges have been smoothed, it is something that a person, especially a small child, would pick and put in their pocket. It has value because of its journey. We are weathered and smoothed like the polished rock . . . We are complete. Life and other people are constantly knocking off our sharp corners. We have value, and we should therefore love ourselves and have compassion for all the bumps and bruises we encountered along the way . . . We should have compassion for ourselves and "give ourselves a break." Like yourself for no other reason than you're the person who knows yourself the best; you're the one who really knows what you have gone through, and you know what your intentions really are and how much effort you really gave. Liking, loving, and being compassionate to one's self is the first step to true happiness. To me, the answers to Rabbi Hillel's questions ("If I am not for myself, who am I? If I am only for myself, what am I?") are to love myself for who I am and then be compassionate to myself. This mind-set will help me focus my life to be a positive, compassionate force for everyone else around. This, in my view, answers Rabbi Hillel's second question by stating, "I'm for everyone."

I'll close with a quote from the Dalai Lama who said, "Love and compassion are most important, most precious, most powerful, and most sacred. Practicing them is useful not only in terms of true religion, but also in worldly life for both mental and physical health. They are basic elements supporting our life and happiness. With practice, they become an effective and beneficial driving force for life."[24]

PEOPLE'S REACTIONS

In the last chapter, we've discussed my insight that most people don't like themselves and that the way to be able to like one's self is to accept ourselves for who we are. Then we're able to love ourselves. The last step to really be secure in who we are is to have compassion for ourselves, recognizing that life is difficult. By realizing life is hard and if we are genuinely doing the best we can, we can have peace of mind even in the face of very difficult times. With that quick review, let's go to the next couple of profound insights that were both learned, or confirmed, when I came to prison. Having realized that most people, in and out of prison, have a hard time liking themselves, let's look at why we must look for validation internally versus externally.

One interesting thing quickly became very apparent to me when the "switch," so to speak, "was turned" (as I was being investigated, and it was clearly apparent I would go to trial), was people's reactions. People backed away . . . some very far away. It was as if I had leprosy, and they were going to get infected by even associating with me. I was a contagion of something very bad. This happened on both a professional and personal level. They didn't even know why I was being investigated, just that I was, and that was enough for such a harsh reaction, enough to start the normal human chain reactions of judging and then alienating me. Let me acknowledge not everyone did this as I've had many people stand by my side, and I'm very thankful to those people who've stuck by me from then until now. However, many others were very quick to push me away, which really surprised me because many of these people were dear friends with whom I'd lived, worked, and played with for many years. These were people considered to be my close friends and my dear family. Many of these people were very dear to my heart and hold a place still today.

One example is my former friend Lydia. One day I received an e-mail from her, and she asked to have lunch with me, to which I agreed. She proceeded to tell me what was going on in her life, dancing around the real reason why she really asked me to lunch. She knew, as it was common knowledge among my coworkers, that I was being investigated, but they'd no idea why. Finally, after a summary of events in her life, she asked me what was going on with me. Being under investigation, I was counseled not to tell people anything about the investigation. So I talked about everything but what she really wanted to hear. Finally, she came out and asked why I was being investigated. I told her I couldn't speak about it to anyone for legal reasons, to which she replied she understood. She added that she was the kind of friend who would come and visit me in prison, if it went that far, and I could turn to her for support, or if I just "needed to talk." Though she and I stayed in touch before the trial, as soon as the trial was over, she faded away. She's never come to visit me as she promised she would. Once I was inside, she stopped communications with me very quickly after my effort to reconnect. This is but one example of many people's reaction.

Once I was convicted, friends started dropping like flies because that proverbial switch was thrown, and I was now a convict. I was the same person I was before my conviction . . . the same person who'd been to football games with them, helped them move, and much more. I was the same person who worked by their side day in and day out, the same person who'd worked by their side at the soup kitchen, and the same person who'd listened to their concerns and dreams. But the investigation and conviction gave them the excuse to judge and condemn . . . to react with their gut, ignoring all the clues to my true character. While a conviction does say I made a criminal mistake, it doesn't change who I am. However, to others, it does define my character. I've become what I'm convicted of. Let me define the word "character." Character is who I am . . . how I think, feel, and act (react) the vast majority of the time. A serious mistake doesn't define my character, but that's exactly what happened to me with many people.

Friends were not the only people who backed away. Like society as a whole, I've even had family members, immediate and distant, who've judged and condemned me and will not communicate with me even though we are blood. They too, even though they've known me all my life, or all their life, have discounted me. This has really surprised me, as my family was very close, and love seemed to abound naturally. However, unconditional love isn't natural, just because people are related by blood; it's a conscious choice as we've discussed in chapter 1. Even though my family members know I'm not a career criminal and my offenses were the first and only time I made such grievous mistakes, some are willing to judge and condemn me. Like Don Miguel Ruiz stated, "We make assumptions that everyone sees life the way we do."[1] I'd made the assumption that my family members weren't judgmental and that they'd have my back for the rest of my life because that's what family does, because they're people who knew me, and "that's what I'd do." I've said all these point to myself over the years. I saw my family and friends through the lens of what I feel I'd do if the roles were reversed. Even though I've been blessed to have many people sticking with me through this crucible, I've realized that I'm the only person who really knows me and my character . . . how I think, feel, and act. We can associate with someone our whole life and still not know them, only how they've acted. I now feel it's impossible to really know someone else.

My trial was another eye-opener. As already stated, I'd admitted my grievous errors years earlier to key people in my life, and I'd gone through a yearlong professional treatment to prevent any reoccurrence. So when I was turned over for investigation, many years after my confession and treatment, it was as if I was unrepentant, and I'd never gone through "rehab." That and all my other amelioration efforts were not given any weight. Needless to say, I was baffled that everything I'd done was so quickly forgotten by the many people who knew . . . I'm still baffled today.

Despite people's selective amnesia, I stood up at trial and pled guilty to the things I could, the things I knew to be true, the same things to which I'd confessed to years earlier. However, the prosecution was even to minimize that honorable action. The judge and jury were quick to ignore the context surrounding the trial, as the factor why the trial was happening years after my confession. Also ignored was why the attitude of the witnesses was hostile and severe versus supportive of a person who'd made the necessary changes to prevent reoccurrence. I'll say the prosecution did a good job, calling me a liar, painting me as a man who was and is completely irredeemable. They were very successful in inflaming the passions and prejudices of the jury. Not only that, the judge verbally gave the jury permission to ignore their doubts. I was convicted despite no physical evidence and plenty of reasonable doubt concerning the charge to which I pled "not guilty." Despite the fact that many years had passed since my criminal offenses, the fact that my confession was self-initiated, and that I'd completed serious amelioration efforts, I was sentenced as if all my honorable efforts never happened. To this day, society considers my trial objective and fair and my sentence just.

For the readers' edification, be aware. The military justice system is less fair as military members voluntarily give up many constitutional rights to "support and defend" that very document—the U.S. Constitution— meaning, the military justice system is allowed to bend rules to suit their needs. The U.S. Supreme Court has allowed Congress to enact "statutes regulating military life, and has established a comprehensive internal system of justice to regulate military life, taking into account the special patterns that define the military structure."[2] Having its own systems allows the military to pick and choose what rules it will follow. I'll affirm that any U.S. justice system is probably better than many in the wider world, but just like people, errors are bound to happen. All justice systems are a man-made construct and are going to follow the societal thinking and perceptions; they reflect "People's Reactions." Currently in the United States (military or civilian), accusations equal proof . . . There are many current examples where the person is tried and found guilty in the media first (i.e., Bill Cosby). Then even at trial, accusations are taken as fact. Thus, the person is "guilty until proven guilty."

What has also been telling to my next insight is how the inmates treat one another. The type of crime is how one is judged in prison. The circumstances and any other factor do not matter. Who you were before your crime only counts if you were a thug, and you are bringing that "thugness" into prison with you as "street credit." What your crime is determines who you are and where you belong in the inmate hierarchy. The more violent the crime, the higher you are up in the prison hierarchy. How inmates treat one another is almost solely based on the category to which you've been adjudged by the courts. My current prison may be less so, but in other places I've been and read about, people with higher violent crimes are not even allowed to talk to someone with a less culturally acceptable crime. Judgment and stereotypes are used like currency in prison.

Also, the label of convict allows the guards and prison staff to minimize and discount who a person is, or as psychologist Martin Buber[3] taught, we each have two types of interactions with other people—as a "you" or as an "it." Just like in the famous psychology study at Stanford[4] in the early seventies (The Stanford Prison Study), all the guards and prison staff change how they treated the inmates from a "you" to an "it." Becoming an "it" allows the guards and staff to lump everyone together and minimize their humanity. What Martin Buber taught applies to all the other labels we use in outside life, to do the same thing. Race, color, religion, political affiliation, sex, sexual preference, country of origin, and many, many more are all ways for us to shorthand how we treat people . . . to make discounting and minimizing people easier. These observations associated with my investigation, trial, and incarceration lead to **my next Fear- based insight:** *people are very quick to judge, minimize, discount, condemn, and are slow to seek to understand the whole story.*

Prison is a microcosm of society as a whole. You see people from all walks of life, and every category of people is represented. When a person comes to prison, one walks into uncertainty on everybody's part—inmates, guards, and staff. You don't know them, and they don't know you. We humans don't like uncertainty and work hard consciously and subconsciously to resolve any conflict any way possible as quickly as possible. Psychologists tell us why. We are quick to rid ourselves of any *Cognitive Dissonance* because this mind-set is uncomfortable for us. *Cognitive Dissonance* is defined as "a disconnect between our thoughts and feelings . . . put another way; from what we tell ourselves and how we really feel." However, by being quick to resolve our inner conflict, usually through rationalization or justification, we drastically increase the odds of making a mistake or not understanding the rest of the story. It's been demonstrated over and over that if we let our passions and prejudices guide us, we'll make mistakes, some seriously very harmful.

One big difference between prison and a party or bar, where people are being annoying or belligerent, is you'll see the same annoying, belligerent people around you day after day, week after week, year after year when you are in prison. Also, in prison, they never really sober up. You really can't get away from them, and they can't get away from you. You're stuck together. As mentioned, normal human nature when faced with uncertainty is to stereotype, discriminate, and judge or condemn; and while this shortcut may have less impact in the wider world, in prison, it's highly concentrated . . . Prison is a cobweb of gossip, rumor, and mind games. The whispers when you first arrive are constant. Whether it's about you, gossip remains throughout one's entire prison experience. I've had to get used to people constantly talking about me or someone else.

I couldn't count how many times I've seen people gather together in small groups to whisper about and listen to hear the latest gossip or rumor. Prison is redundant and monotonous, so anything new is big news. Most inmates have nothing better to do than talk about you or someone else. The "viral" infection of the rumor or news is very fast. The other day, there was a fight at one of the work details. People went to work at 6:50 a.m., the fight took place at 7:00 a.m., and I heard about it in another completely separate work detail, well, away from the location of the fight, by 7:05 a.m. That's pretty quick for an environment that has no technology to transmit the communication but word of mouth. It's affectionately termed Inmate News Network (INN), and we have news anchors.

In my current location, the prison staff has longtime inmates brief the new guys who've just arrived at the facility. New guys are held in a separate area until they are ready to join GenPop. In the briefing by the longtime inmates, the new guys are told what to expect when they are introduced into GenPop, and it's helpful to the new people. However, for the people already in GenPop, this briefing serves another purpose. The other nefarious purpose is intelligence gathering on the new guys. The longtimers come back with news about the new people, and before a person even enters GenPop, he's already judged and categorized, and he has to work hard to change people's opinion. The longtime inmate who briefs the new people is measuring them according to their own internal narrative and past experiences. Really getting to know a person takes suspending judgment and recognition that there is no way to know all the facts and circumstances in such a short exposure time, if ever. However, that takes humility, and the people who are selected to brief are far from humble. Though the prison staff controls who's selected, who's offered or allowed to volunteer is determined by the heavies. If an inmate is unpopular, they will be relegated to obscurity.

Psychologists have a few explanations for the effects so far discussed in this chapter whether it takes place in prison or outside in normal life. The first explanation, or *Cognitive Trap*, of how our minds work is titled *Generalization*, which is to say we stereotype based on general categories. The next trap is titled *Availability Bias*, which is to say we use the most recent or most available (easiest to obtain) information to make our judgment and decision about something or someone. While these two explanations make sense as a way to resolve mental conflicts, they really don't speak well of normal human nature; and in fact, most of the conflicts in human history are caused because people are inherently cognitively lazy. I say this because once a person really gets to know a person, including their circumstances, feelings, perspective, and dreams and desires for the future, it's hard not to see that the person is really not too different from us . . . from our own self.

However, I feel the biggest mistake we make when we judge anyone (how people react) is titled by psychologists as *Fundamental Attribution Error*, which is to say that by making quick, uninformed, arbitrary judgments, we have a tendency to fixate on supposedly stable character traits and overlook the influence of context. As the psychologist Richard Nisbett stated, "The basis of the illusion is that we are somehow confident that we are getting what is there, that we are able to read off a person's disposition."[5] Yet there is no way for us to really know someone, to know their genetic predisposition, to know their environmental conditioning, to know the intent of their heart, or to know how they are thinking at any given moment in time. Thus, we're more likely to error than not. Therefore, we need to be suspect of how we react. My family and friends whom I thought really knew me didn't, nor do I really know them. It takes a real concerted effort on both parts to find out the rest of the story. This is true for convicts as normally, they are considered disposable.

You, the reader, may be saying to yourself, "Well, I can't go through life getting to know everybody. I just don't have that kind of time." That's true, but does judging and reacting without all the facts really help or cause more misjudgments? There are many examples of hurtful, dangerous, and damaging events of human history that we now in hindsight condemn—the Inquisition; the Salem witch trials; the annihilation of Natives in Africa, North and South America, and Australia; worldwide slavery, the Nazi Germany's death camps; the Russian pogroms; the Khmer Rouge's purge in Cambodia; or even the current radical Islamic terrorist actions. Labeling people allows us to minimize and discount them . . . to make them an "it" as Martin Buber explained. People and societies do this naturally, and it takes real effort to do otherwise . . . to beat our default setting.

The default setting creates the following: If someone commits a crime, they're now labeled after their crime, most likely for the rest of their lives. One who steals is a "thief," one who commits a sex act is now a "sex offender," or one who kills someone is now a "murderer." We treat people like a wild animal who, after attacking a human, now has lost all fear of humans and now is a constant threat, never to change or learn. However, remember what *Fundamental Attribution Error's* definition stated. The context is ignored, causing one to fall into a serious *Cognitive Trap*.

Yet as we've discussed, context matters. The context surrounding the why the person did what they did is critical, as are their genes, culture, conditioning, etc. As Charles Perrow stated, "Making a judgment means we create a 'mental model' of an expected universe. You are actually creating a world that is congruent with your interpretation, even though it may be the wrong world."[6] This is stating that when we label and judge others, we're not really basing our thinking on facts but on how we see the world. A person who commits a crime shouldn't be defined by the crime. That's not "who" they are! You would not want to be defined by one or any of your mistakes, would you?

I know that's contrary to what may be common thinking, but it's in line with what's real and true. It lines up with what psychologists tell us about how we function. The *Fundamental Attribution Error* thinking applies to how we view all characteristics of all people, negative and positive. We know by rational thinking that a person who is honest can lie, a person who is peaceful can be violent, a strong person can be weak, etc. However, this cognitive recognition can cause us serious conflict with how our lower-level life form "gut reaction" is telling us to respond. The biggest conflict for each of us is it's hard to admit to ourselves that we could be "that person." No one wants to be "that person" or even admit that we have the capability to be "that person." It hurts one's ego to come to terms with that obvious fact. Gandhi put it best when he said, "It is only when one sees one's own mistakes with a convex lens, and does the reverse in the case of others, that one is able to arrive as a just relative estimate of the two."[7] This leads me to **my Love-based insight:** ***we all make mistakes but everyone's core nature is good.***

Confucius put it this way: "Men's natures are alike; it is their habits that carry them apart."[8] Using mistakes, inmates and non-inmates alike, *Generalize* people, making it easier to take away another person's humanity. When one is thinking in shorthand, we ignore or don't seek to understand what is real and factual . . . the whole story. We think and feel the context does not matter. If we make a mistake or commit a crime, our natural inclination is to blame the environment and not ourselves. Then the contexts, conditions, and circumstances matter to us as the integral part of why the mistakes or crime happened in the first place. I'll submit why . . . We're able to see the context when it's us making the mistakes. We're able to better see more things affecting us much more clearly because we lived it and saw it firsthand. I'm not saying we see everything or even know how our past conditioning and life experiences influenced our actions, as many of those things are completely obscured to us. However, we likely see more of the environment than another observer sees. Therefore, we want others to give us the benefit of the doubt. Likely, they're doing the opposite . . . blaming you, the person, and ignoring the context.

That said, when we look at others and we see someone else's mistakes, foibles and follies, or find out about crimes they've committed, we're quick to blame them, alone. We see only their flaws and tend to ignore, discount, or minimize the contexts, conditions, and circumstances surrounding the events. In a word, we "blame their character." We don't blame our character if things are bad or we make mistakes. We blame the conditions or circumstances. As stated, we want people to give us the benefit of the doubt and take into account the conditions and circumstances. If that same flaw or mistake we saw in someone else was ours, we'd give ourselves the benefit of the doubt . . . the same benefit of the doubt that we're very quickly, unwilling to give everyone else. It's happened in all the examples I've used in the beginning of this chapter. To the jury at my trial, it was not just an anomaly that I committed my crime; it was my character, and therefore, I was not likely to change unless forced.

As told, the judge did not stress the importance of giving me the benefit of any reasonable doubt. Therefore, it followed that punishment and separation from society was the only option. Other proofs of my character and my amelioration efforts were quickly discounted and minimized, and the contexts and those circumstances were quickly ignored as was any factor to "why I committed the crime." Errors were made concerning my fundamental nature or attributes. I know I'm susceptible of such *Cognitive Traps*; and I'm very sure you, the reader, agree that you are too.

Marilyn Ferguson stated, "Your past is not your potential. In any hour you can choose to liberate the future . . . Ultimately we know deeply that the other side of every fear is freedom."[9] What Ms. Ferguson is saying is we all can change. Western culture, what historically used to be called Occidental culture, mostly falls under what psychologist call *Theory X* thinking. *Theory X*-type people believe all people are inherently evil, and they need to be forced to be good. Western laws are written with this mind-set. Yet Western culture, as a whole, does believe change is possible. It's "just" societal institutions, rules, laws, and religion are seen as the required tools to make the change possible. Coming to prison revealed and immersed me into another way of thinking . . . *Theory Y* thinking. According to psychologists, *Theory Y*-types of people believe everyone's core nature is inherently good, but mistakes happen. Even with mistakes, people are still good and valuable. Predominantly, Asian cultures, what is historically called Oriental culture, have this mind-set; and my exposure to Asian religions in prison has introduced me to Eastern philosophy. I've immersed myself into that kind of thinking. Buddhism and Taoism are the major schools of *Theory Y* thought; but Hinduism, Sufisism, Janism, Sikhism, and others also are more *Theory* Y than *Theory X*.

When the Age of Exploration happened, the Occidentals found the Orient[10] and saw an uncivilized or weaker people, mostly based on religion and Oriental *Theory Y* thinking. The colonizers push their agenda on the civilizations they came upon, using their *Theory X* mind-set as justification to conquer and make the people subservient. Centuries later, the industrial revolution even made it worse because many Asian countries voluntarily gave up their historical cultural thinking to become a world player. Think of the movie *The Last Samurai* as a good example of what happened in Japan during the Meiji Restoration. History shows there are many others that responded to the fear of colonization like Japan. Luckily, Asian civilization was able to preserve their writings and some autonomy throughout the generations of colonization, and now the West has started to embrace Eastern philosophy, including psychologist Carl Jung. *Theory Y* has found its way to the West.

This holistic *Theory Y* thinking reiterates that giving people the benefit of the doubt is best course of action in the long run. When we judge, discount, minimize, or think of another person as an "it," we lose the opportunity to learn from that person. We lose potential friendships, and we harm the other person's ability for growth and learning opportunities by denying them what we can offer. We also lose our own growth and learning opportunities for the same reason. The ancient wise man Master Lao-tzu stated, "Show me a man of violence that came to a good end and I will take him for my teacher."[11] This flexible attitude toward people who've errored is not the norm in many Western cultures, as things are seen as more black and white. People's attributions are considered fixed. The famous Zen Buddhist teacher Shunryo Suzuki put it this way: "The cause of conflict is some fixed idea or one-sided idea. You can find meaning in various practices without being caught in them."[12] Having a flexible mind-set (a beginner's mind) is now recognized by psychologists and sociologists as healthy as it does not harden one's thinking. It is even said to help reduce the chances for Alzheimer's. So although we stereotype or generalize about other people, it is recognized as a limiting way of thinking. "It doesn't work to generalize about a relationship, between a category, and a trait when the relationship isn't stable, or when the act of generalizing may itself change the basis of the generalization,"[13] writes worldwide best-selling author Malcolm Gladwell. We limit our growth and learning when we generalize. We hurt the other person, especially when it becomes a societal norm to judge a person in a certain manner, which is commonly referred to as discrimination. Publicly and politically, discrimination is considered bad, but society still encourages such action.

Now it should be obvious to the reader that a change in mind-set is necessary, but how can we change our mind-set in the face of uncertainty about someone else? How can we react better? The first step of many steps is to recognize that we are the same more than we are different, even prisoner, homeless, mentally ill, etc. This may be difficult as years of conditioning may have taught a person otherwise. However, studies of religion, cultures, psychology, physiology, genetics, etc., show time and again that there is much more in common than differences. We all make mistakes; we are capable of making any kind of mistakes, given the right circumstances and conditioning. Back in the early sixties, there was a classic psychology experiment carried out by psychologist, S. Milgram,[14] to figure out why people will carry out great harm when ordered to do so (i.e., the Germans blindly followed the Nazis as they killed millions). Participants were asked to administer electric shocks to someone in another room (who was in on the Milgram experiment) if they gave wrong answers to a set of questions. This well-known psychology experiment demonstrated that many people kept giving shocks even when the victim (who was an experiment collaborator) was perceived to be unconscious and thus unable to speak to even answer the question. What would you do? We all think we'd be the one to not unreasonably punish the test subject, but unless you're in that exact situation, you don't know. Recognizing our sameness eliminates the willingness to punish or hurt. That recognition opens us up to loving feelings and compassion toward our fellow humans and their plight in this ever-changing life. This softens our reactions . . . people's reactions.

There is a popular TV show now titled *What Would You Do?* The show has actors play the parts of people doing things that should make people pause and eventually intervene to prevent something unethical or illegal from happening. Some people do step in but most don't. Recently, a few of the people who did "the right thing" have stated it is because of the fact that they have seen the *What Would You Do?* TV show, and it has steeled their resolve to do the right thing, even when no one else is thought to be looking. I submit this TV show helps the viewer see that people are more like themselves and that context could affect their thinking. They see that they could be the one sitting by as something unethical or illegal happens around them. They see that they are like others more than they thought. They are more aware of their prejudices, thinking errors, and emotions. The *What Would You Do?* effect (WWYDE), I submit, is where we each would make better decisions if we asked ourselves that question when faced with a situation where it seems automatic to judge, discount, and minimize. By mindfully and preemptively asking what we'd do given a generally envisioned ethical or moral dilemma, we'd likely be less inclined to take away someone's humanity. Everyone and anyone can utilize WWYDE to improve one's reactions.

The second step is to recognize that our worldview is not as factual as we think it is. Alan Wallace states, "When we observe fault, an intelligent response is to immediately check the extent to which we are projecting our own faults and past conditioning onto the other person."[15] This is how we need to respond and react in all situations. We need to not only have an open mind, but we must also be familiar with our own mind, thinking processes, attitudes, and emotions. Humans have a very special ability that scientists call *Metacognition*, literally Greek for "after"—"meditation." While it does come naturally to a certain extent, rarely are we taught how to effectively think or reflect on our own thinking and emotions. This was certainly true with me before treatment and imprisonment. Because of our *Metacognitive* capabilities (the ability to observe our thoughts, attitudes, emotions, and sense of self), we can decide how to think and feel. However, the ability to self-reflect, scrutinize our mind, and modify behaviors takes a lot of mindfulness training and practice. Alan Wallace goes on to say that we must constantly "think: My own experience largely determines how I interpret others actions . . ."[16] This may seem to contradict that we are more alike than different. However, that is not what he is saying. What he is saying is we can't project our thinking on the other person because it causes all the thinking errors we've discussed thus far and others we'll discuss later. Lastly, Alan Wallace goes on by paraphrasing the ancient Buddhist sage Sechibuwa by next stating, "Sechibuwa suggest we first check whether this might be the fault of our own mind."[17] Here we learn the best way to give others the benefit of the doubt is by realizing that our mind needs to be trained well before we worry about other people's thinking, emotions, and actions.

The last step we'll discuss in this chapter is to give everyone the benefit of the doubt and, if they have made a mistake or committed a crime, realize that labeling them or generalizing and stereotyping undermines their potential to be a human being . . . It dehumanizes them or turns them into an "it." Human beings have the innate capability to change, improve, grow, and learn from the past . . . They are not wild animals. They don't need to "be put down" like a wild animal that has attacked a human. Humans have the innate ability to change, to learn from their mistakes, and to grow. I know I am capable of learning, changing, and growing; so everyone else is too. All this is based on our core nature that is good and works, in the vast majority of the cases, to remain good . . . to think *Theory Y*. As a fellow inmate, Steve has stated to me, "We cannot dehumanize others without dehumanizing ourselves in the process." Taking these steps, using our very special *Metacognitive* capabilities, we'll soften our reactions and reduce our natural inclinations to fall into the many *Cognitive Traps*.

I'll close this chapter with a quote that tells us not to judge, minimize, discount, and stereotype because we are each facing life's challenges as best we can. Other people, even those close to us, don't really know what we are going through or the intent in our heart; and we don't know the same about them . . . what they think or feel. Former U.S. president Teddy Roosevelt stated the following:

It is not the critic who counts; not the man who points out how the strong man stumbles, or where the doer of deeds could have done them better. The credit belongs to the man who is actually in the arena, whose face is marred by dust and sweat and blood; who strives valiantly; who errs, and comes up short again and again; because there is not effort without error and shortcoming; but who does actually strive to do the deeds; who knows the great enthusiasms, the great devotions; who spends himself in a worthy cause, who at the best knows in the end the triumphs of high achievement and who at the worst, if he fails, at least fails while daring greatness, so that his place shall never be with those cold and timid souls who know neither victory nor defeat.[18]

You and I are the "man in the arena." We each are. You and I have a penchant to be good and do good . . . Believe it. You and I will fail and make mistakes, but that does not discount or minimize your humanity. In fact, it makes you and me perfect as previously discussed in the last chapter. Keep going and keep fighting, and only by quitting do we lose. Don't let other people's opinion or actions keep you and me from mindfully knowing who we are and our worth. People will judge, minimize, and discount you and me; but our fundamental attribution is good and valuable. Recognize that all other have that same penchant and inherent value too. Many times a day, under various conditions, people react poorly; but you and I don't have to. Let's use mindfulness, seeding our own WWYDE, to react with love as the basis of our decision to every ethical and moral situation and dilemma. I, myself, am working toward this utopian state of being. Please join me.

SECTION TWO:

MY INSIGHTS OBTAINED WITH MORE

OBSERVATION AND STUDY

CAUSE AND EFFECT OF SEPARATION

The first section of this book discussed the insights that became clear to me in early part of my trial and prison experience. I learned very quickly how most people don't like themselves, which causes a great deal of insecurity on their part. Immediately after the start of the investigation and, especially, after my trial, I experienced that people are quick to judge and minimize others. Prisoners are especially susceptible as they live in a highly toxic environment. Inmates do so to make them feel better about themselves. Putting someone else down is a quick way to gain a temporary boost to one's ego. As we've discussed, others judge, label, minimize, and discount others in an attempt to dissuade themselves that they're not capable of such flaws or foibles. We also established that there are ways to overcome these natural *Cognitive Traps.*

This next chapter and section discuss insights I've gained with more time and study. First up, where do many of our natural, habitual tendencies originate? Our natural, habitual tendencies, including fear, are an evolutionary survival mechanism that's been around for millions of years.[1] Neurologists tell us we have reptilian and. mammalian portions of our brain that have remained unchanged throughout the ages. They know this because they still exist in reptiles and mammals today. These brain areas drive our instincts and are known to process incoming stimuli very, very quickly . . . most of the time before we're even aware of what's happening. They're habitual. The "older," evolutionary speaking, portions of our brains work on a subconscious level. Our archaic hominid progenitors also had the same brain regions found in reptiles and mammals; however, they'd also developed more brain areas that enabled higher-order thinking. These forebrain areas (larger in humans than any other creature) enable complex problem-solving but process at a much slower rate, relatively. Neanderthal and Denisovan man lived for millions of years in small hunter-gatherer tribes, where every member was known by sight, and problem-solving was what we'd consider very simple by today's standards. Back then, if someone violated the tribe's peace and order, causing a problem, the person was cast out, very much like behavior we see today in other pack and herd animals . . . Ostracizing is the archaic, lower life form's way of problem-solving.

Since hominids were not the most ferocious member of the food chain, being cast out was basically a death sentence because by themselves, the lone hominid was bound to be eaten by a larger, faster, more lethal predator. Armed with just reptilian, mammalian, and a simpler version of our current higher-functioning forebrain, the archaic hominid's tribe, like the pack and herd, enabled greater odds of living and passing on genes to the next generations . . . Safety in numbers is a known evolutionary advantage. Early humans (Cro-Magnon man) also lived in hunter-gatherer tribes for tens of thousands of years but with an even higher order of thinking capability, which enabled higher-level communication and interaction and more complex social structures. This, in turn, enabled larger societies with a greater degree of problem-solving and cooperation.

The name we call our direct progenitors, Cro-Magnon man is Homo sapiens, which means "wise man." The current, dominant theory states the higher level of problem-solving and cooperation is the reason the other hominids and much of the megafauna were wiped out. Also, Cro-Magnon's more complex, higher-order thinking ability enabled better protection and survival through better communication and cooperation. Very recent genetics (having mapped DNA in both Homo sapiens and many of our archaic ancestors) has revealed that Cro-Magnon interbreed with the Neanderthals and Denisovan man. Then only Cro-Magnon man survived into the present. Neanderthal and Denisovan man were likely wiped out by the Cro-Magnon man after millions of years of roaming the Earth. The DNA of most people with European heritage shows that they have 2 to 4 percent Neanderthal DNA.[2] Denisovan man lived in Asia, and their DNA makers show up mostly in modern Asian's DNA. However, with hundreds of thousands of years of interbreeding, the DNA lines are mixed between the various cultures. It's now big business to map one's DNA, to establish our genetic history. There are companies like "23&Me" or "Ancestry.com" that'll map one's DNA.

Homo sapiens' ever-increasing sophisticated levels of communication, compared with any other forms of fauna, enabled Cro-Magnon to draw intricate cave drawings as old as 35,500 years ago, develop agriculture about 13,000 years ago, develop large civilizations about 8,000 years ago, and develop megalithic architecture about 6,000 years ago.[3] Their communication and problem-solving abilities elevated Homo sapiens to modern man with multimillion man cities, advanced technologies, and an over seven billion people. Yet, we still also have our reptilian and mammalian brains telling us to ostracize problem people . . . to cast them out of the tribe and, in many cases, send them off to their death, figuratively or literally. Although we've created complicated reasons to abandon, judge, minimize, and discount, using power, religion, and law to rationalize our base justification, our evolutionary instincts are the basis of many archaic, lower life form thinking's actions. Yes, doctrine, rules, and laws are better than lawlessness; but the consequences of these doctrines, rules, and laws are, in many cases, still archaic and barbaric and don't fit the moniker that "wise man" connotes. After 200,000 years of evolution, we still, many times, default to abandonment and alienation as the solution to perceived threats, listening more to our archaic brain than to the more reasonable, thoughtful, compassionate, logical, and slower forebrain portions.

In prison, natural order is spontaneously archaic and barbaric as tribes are formed, and an "us-and-them mentality" is persuasive. Prisons are places where we, as a society, are forcing people to revert to use their lower-order brain functions to survive. Even people who mostly used higher-order thinking have had to revert back when faced with prison's survival environment. There is a rock song by Guns N' Roses titled *"Welcome to the Jungle."* It fits prison and any other place where reverting back to our barbaric roots is persuasive . . . where it's bad every day, where it can get worse in an instant instead of getting better, and where survival is the greatest need. "The Jungle" is code for a lawless, free-for-all place where anything and everything of lower life form thinking and reacting can and does happen. Prison just reinforces the *Scarcity Mentality* and creates people who are learning or reinforcing conditioning, which ends up creating more problems than it solves (more on that in the third section of this book). Here's an insight supporting story:

One day when I was first incarcerated, I was sitting at a table in the middle of the pod (a building that houses seventy inmates), playing a card game.

Sitting there, I looked up and watched as one person went into another person's cell and walked out with a bag of the other person's belongings. I was new to prison, and I didn't know either person. So I asked the guys I was playing cards with, "Who's cell is that?" I was told it was a person who had been cast out of a section (prison for "tribe"), and so there was no one in the pod there to protect him . . . He was fair game for anyone who wanted to do anything to him. I went and talked to another person to see if we, together, could help this person get his stuff back. With the backing of our section's heavies, we confronted the thief. However, by the time we got to talk to him, the person's belongings had been spread around the pod, and there was no chance of getting any of it back. That was not my first or my only time where I saw inmates hurt each other, nor would it be my last. Why was he cast out to be left on his own where bigger "predators" could attack him? The answer: archaic, barbaric, natural tendencies.

The other day, I was talking to a person, and he was telling me about a new person who'd been in reception and had a surgery and could not walk upstairs. After the operation, he was moved from the infirmary to GenPop with the medical direction that he couldn't go up and downstairs. As is with tradition, new people (called fish) are assigned the less desirable cells in the pod on the second level. This person came to his pod during the day when everyone else was out working and talked to the guard, letting him know the medical guidance not to live on the second floor. He was given a cell on the first floor, which upset the heavies, and he was cast out of his new section. He was now "factionless" with no one looking out for him. That same day, he went to dinner meal, only to find he'd no place he was allowed to sit to eat in the dining facility. The person I spoke with had to advocate for "the fish" to resolve the situation, but though he is back in the section, he still is a black sheep. For all of us, it takes a very concerted effort to use our higher-order thinking.

My last prison example is about a new person who in his last prison became a member of the Aryan Brotherhood (AB) for protection. He even went so far as to get a tattoo to show his allegiance, though he'd no real desire to be an AB member. He was young and felt he needed protection at that prison, which probably worked for him at his previous prison. He arrived at the prison I'm at, and although there is segregation (more on that in chapter 6), there is no Aryan Brotherhood. Seeing the AB tattoos, however, the black inmates were very angry; and he was in danger of being assaulted or worse. So to get protection, this individual felt compelled to become a Muslim because he knew they'd protect him based on a conversation he had with a senior inmate, who visited him in the reception block . . . and that strategy worked for him. He was protected by becoming a Muslim, mostly because the senior Muslim inmate, to whom he talked to in reception, was black; and he told the other black men to leave this new guy alone. The black Muslim heavy was a man who had a very high level of prison creditability. Because of his crime and prison status, his wishes were respected without question. Years later, now that the threat is over, interestingly, this person with the offending AB tattoos is now Catholic. By the way, he wasn't the only one who'd felt compelled to become Muslim for protection in this prison. The reader may have wondered why prison gangs exist and how people are radicalized in prison, as I did before coming to prison. Well, the alienated and disenfranchised, the separation effected, gather together for protection, just like our archaic ancestors have done for millennia . . . just like animals and birds have done for millions of years. People are ripe for radicalization when they're in a survival mind-set.

A psychologist, Philip Jackson, stated, "No matter what the demand or personal resources of the person facing it, there is at least one strategy open to all. This is the strategy of psychological withdrawal, of gradually reducing personal concern and involvement to a point where neither the demand nor one's success or failure in coping with it is sharply felt."[4] We can always stop having care and compassion for one another, but this strategy has consequences too. We humans have a saying to describe the effect of abandoning or alienating another person. We say they're "out-of-sight and out-of-mind." Just like casting out an offensive tribe member did for our archaic ancestors, we've many ways to abandon the undesirable and offensive people in society, to include prison, elder care centers, mental institutions, or any other facility and institution our society has devised to separate a person from society. We, out of fear, are putting those people out of sight so they no longer have to be part of our mind. We, as societies all over the world, have done it in recent history to people who likely just had autism by calling them "idiots" and institutionalizing them for life. Not only society, but individuals respond to someone or something that offends us or causes us anxiety by casting them off. Psychologists call this type of behavior *Aversion Reaction*, and it applies to societies and individuals. **My Fear-based insight is this: *the out-of-sight, out of mind" reaction is very common. Abandonment still seems to be the norm.***

Prison's stated objective is to separate offenders from society, while some people's actions are dangerous, and the fear of them being violent or repeating another offensive action is highly justified based on their past actions. These few individuals are put in prison to protect society. However, most offenders are just people who've made a mistake and did so because of thoughtlessness, neglect, or trying to better their perceived hopeless situation. This describes the majority of first-time offenders, which is the bulk of the U.S. prison population and likely the same all over the world. It describes me and my fellow inmates. Again, using archaic, lower level life form thinking, justified in laws and doctrine, we send first-time offenders away because we feel they're like dangerous animals who, after one serious mistake, are unable to learn, grow, and change . . . They're irredeemable. Again, we treat people like a grizzly bear who's attacked and eaten a human. Now the "animal has to be put down because it has tasted human flesh, is no longer afraid of humans, and will attack again." When we lump people together and treat them like bears, we're ignoring the context and circumstances. When we abandon, judge, discount, and minimize, sending the person off to prison, or some other institution, we're not really solving the problem but pushing the problem down the road. We're using our fears to dehumanize them. In the vast majority of the cases, we're causing more problems, as families are destroyed, and many times, the person's support structure fades away as time goes on, which is statistically shown to increase recidivism. We're kicking the proverbial can down the road, making the situation worse when the person is released. A quick reminder: over 95 percent of inmates are eventually released to society.

This abandonment applies not only to prison but also to life's various relationships. I've a friend whose parents divorced when she was very young, and the children were divided up between the parents, and they moved a great distance apart. Because of the alienation of each parent to the other, the siblings were raised apart without any contact until they became adults. As she went with her mother, she felt abandoned by her father. There was always this nagging question in the back of her mind: "Why did he not choose to take me?" The father had taken the other two older children, and though she was with her mother, the anxiety of the separation with her father affected her life and the way she approaches romantic relationships. If things get difficult, her default solution, past separation based, is to push people away and forget them . . . to abandon them to protect herself.

Another example is a person I know who'd been offended by her father, so now she pushed her father away and will no longer communicate with him. Over time, the alienation now has expanded to all her siblings and their families. She included her children in this aggression, whether they understood, in the rejection of her father and her extended family. Her reptilian and mammalian portions of her brain tell her that it's better to ostracize what has offended her to protect herself and, ostensibly, her family (her tribe). By her reaction to protect herself from hurtful emotions and feelings, she's now has created a wave of pain and suffering, rippling out like on the surface of a pond for herself and generations to come. Treating someone as if they were dead to you only keeps all concerned from having closure, or having past wounds healed.

Though it's a natural tendency, abandoning people really hurts not only them but the person rejecting as well. Let's talk about the pain caused to the person being rejected, experiencing the loss. It likely triggers a rational fear that metastasizes to an irrational fear of abandonment *(Athazagoraphobia)*, which can cause great suffering. We've all also felt *Separation Anxiety* at one time or another in our lives, and being shunned retriggers those anxieties from early childhood even if one had a relatively secure childhood. Everyone has experienced the effects of separation at one time or another. The reaction to both fear and anxiety is also obviously deeply embedded into our genetics from our archaic progenitors. These natural tendencies generate more fear and anxiety, many times irrationally. A destructive abandonment cycle is passed on generation to generation. Despite our natural inclination to shun, our true safety and security is still dependent on cooperation of the group, as shown by our current human condition. Even with billions of people, we've got our core relationships, providing us, likely since childhood, with safety and security. If those needs are interrupted in any way, it can cause us pain and suffering that, in turn, causes us to habitually react with our gut versus our head. Each person experiencing loss goes through the grief cycle, including shock and anger, sometimes getting stuck in those stages.

As to pain and suffering caused to the alienator, this person may gain short-term peace; but just like prison, they are only kicking the proverbial can down the road for the pain and suffering to be resolved later, if ever. They also miss out on the learning and growth we each get from interacting with each other, especially close relationships and especially if there are problems. It takes being able to love yourself first to be able to love a person who's hurt you . . . to break the fear cycle. As the current Dalai Lama stated, "This, in turn, is essential if we are to survive in this ever shrinking world we live in. For if we each selfishly pursue only what we believe to be in our own interest, without caring about the needs of others, we may end up harming not only others, but also ourselves."[5] This brings me to **my Love-based insight:** *it isn't about you, but it all starts with you.*

The reason why scientist think Cro-Magnon man was able to have the explosive intelligence, what is called the "Great Leap Forward," about 50,000 years ago is most likely the increased level of communication, which leads to a higher level of cooperation.[6] The mental leap has progressed to this day with what I'd term "a giant bound" in the last 150 years. The higher-order thinking first started with hunting and gathering strategies and tactics, enabling a mammal with no sharp claws or teeth, which isn't the fastest or strongest or the biggest or the most fierce, to rise to the top of the food chain. Then the higher-order thinking started the agricultural revolution, which gave rise to civilizations. We're a successful species because we take better care of one another, as a whole, than any other species. Obviously, modern man owes this present powerful position in the world to the fact that, Homo sapiens sacrificed some of their own individual needs and desires for the greater good for the whole. Psychologists call this *Social Utility*, which is defined as a general urge to take care of others even when doing so uses up one's own resources.[7]

Joseph Campbell stated it this way: "When we quit thinking primarily about ourselves and our own self-preservation, we undergo a truly heroic transformation of consciousness."[8] His statement applies to both societies and to each of us. We've effectively used our higher-order thinking based on love, care, and compassion to ensure survival. Looking at the history of our consciousness, in the terms of communication and cooperation, we know things are much, much better than in generations past. We live in the safest time in history. Interestingly, that communication is a double-edged sword. Politicians and the news media make things seem much worse than they really are. As counterproof, our life span keeps getting older and older, and we're statistically much safer. This fact is one testament to how we, as societies and individuals, are taking better care of one another than in the past. For example, I brought up autism earlier. Now we know that many, many people have autism as a mental condition. The incident rate seems to be increasing, yet experts believe it's more likely that we're doing a better job of recognizing what autism is (with all its variant symptoms) and who has it. Now instead of casting them aside for life, like we used to do, we've found a way to live side-by-side . . . We're more wise, compassionate, and tolerant of them and their condition. We've also found ways to help them live more successfully within society. Criminals are not that much different. With wisdom, compassion, and tolerance, their behavior can be changed. Really, criminals and noncriminals alike can change.

Another recent example is how we treat people who look different than we do. Dr. Martin Luther King stated, "The world is dangerous not because of those who do harm, but because of those who looked at it without doing anything."[9] Dr. King was expressing that people should no longer sit idly by watching the mistreatment of other human beings. The *Xenophobia*, fear of strangers and foreigners, has been the norm for generations based on race and color and has greatly declined in just the last 100 years. The majority of people now, thanks, in part, to better science, have realized that despite differences in skin color, culture, religion, sex, sexual orientation, etc., we're really more alike than different. Science testifies of this fact more and more each day. We still have a long way to go, as this chapter's first insight shows, to overcome the archaic and barbaric habitual tendencies that are part of our genetic makeup. Our higher-order thinking has enabled this slow and gradual change. When we look at Homo sapiens' history, we see that the higher-order thinking is pretty recent. Relatively speaking, in 200,000 years, our compassion and toleration for others of our and other species is very, very recent. There are many examples in the last 5,000 years of history both of good and bad human thinking or "not thinking" ...listening only with our gut. To quote one of the early enlightened beings, the Buddha stated 2,600 years ago to "think beyond yourself and your own suffering."[10] Notice Buddha says "think." Please, again, reflect to Rabbi Hillel's profound questions in chapter 1. The answer is to think beyond ourselves for the greater good. Our lives aren't really about "us" but those whose lives we touch.

As my insight states, we're "alone," but we're all part of something bigger. I like the way the father of psychology, William James, put it when he said, "We are like islands in the sea, separate on the surface, but connected in the deep."[11] Psychology teaches us that the four basis fears are 1) dying, 2) having to choose, 3) that the world is intrinsically meaningless, and 4) that we'll end up dying alone. Focusing on the last one, I've read that dying alone is a prisoner's greatest fear. Yet even in prison, we aren't really alone. For the most part, there is someone close by whether a guard or another prisoner. Prison sections, tribe mentality, and "us and them" thinking enable protection; however, at what cost? We'll be discussing that question more in chapter 10.

Speaking of dying alone in prison, a fellow inmate, named Chris, died last year. He'd a serious pain in his head and was finally taken to the hospital, where he was told of his brain tumor. He'd a tumor years before, and it'd been removed. However, the new tumor came back with a vengeance, and he was told that his condition was terminal. His family was told, but there was no way for them to come to see him because of lack of funds and the distance from home to his prison location. Of course, being a prisoner, his prison friends weren't allowed to be with him at the hospital; and he died there without any close relationship by his side. He was a very popular prisoner, but even with all his prison friends, he was basically alone. I'm grateful to the hospital nurses and the guard who were with him. I'm sure they showed him great care and compassion. Yet even when a person is surrounded by loved ones, they still die alone. It's a journey that no one can go with us. People may have comforting supernatural beliefs on this fearful subject, but we all die alone.

Getting back to the point about one's life not really being about oneself, a philosopher by the name of Thomas Malthus predicted that the world would soon become too populated with people; and mass starvation would occur, killing millions. While poverty and starvation do still exist today, we do have over seven billion people alive today. For the vast majority, there is food, shelter, and medical care for them; and the worldwide standard of living is the highest it's ever been. There is no question that we can do much better, as the problems aren't with the capability to grow enough food, or provide enough shelter and health care, but is with distribution. That said, overpopulation is still a potent problem for the finite resource of Earth . . . We do need to take better care of Earth.

My point in bringing up the Malthusian prediction is that the reason mass starvation hasn't occurred thus far is we, as a whole society, take care of one another. Our survival is based on higher-order thinking and cooperation . . .

our *Social Utility.* Whether it's science increasing technology to produce more disease-resistant food, finding more ways distribute more food, or a person like the late Mother Theresa who'd spent her life with the poor and needy; it's people taking care of people. Small acts of kindness done by individuals do make a big difference to the whole.

I'll admit it's hard to see how kindness can make a difference when the media is constantly bombarding *us* with the news, slanted to the fearmongering, sensational, and rare. Sadly, if it didn't fit into one of those three categories, it wouldn't be "newsworthy." With fear being touted, every day all day, it's hard to feel safe and secure. Bad news seems to generate more bad news. Cruelty still happens, and there are many, many examples of man's inhumanity to man. However, as previously mentioned, when we look historically, we'll see that we're much safer and more secure than ever before. Societies, civilizations, cities, and towns buffer us from the historical dangers found in caves, forest, and plains. While we're really alone, as is very apparent when one is incarcerated, we each buffer the effects of life's dangers . . . our evolutionary advantage. The problem with prison is it's a dangerous environment. One reason it can be so shocking to be alone, really alone like I described in my introduction, is we are rarely ever all alone. Though Chris was alone when he died, in the sense that he didn't have his loved ones surrounding him or to have closure and a final farewell with his family and friends, he was not literally all alone as the nurses were there, buffering the effect of his lonely death. They did this through acts of kindness and compassion and through doing their job. They used their higher-order thinking.

Science has brought us several understandings. As already mentioned, for example, it's been revealed that a brain condition causes autism; that genetically, all races are the exact same and have the same basic capabilities; and that the majority of people's harmful thinking, attitudes, and actions are based on lack of true understanding of the person, context, and circumstances, etc. With higher-order thinking, why still abandon, shun, or ostracize as the first response? Why not continue to take advantage of our evolutionary advantage of kindness and compassion to continue to seek understanding of our brothers and sisters? Charles Darwin stated, "It is not the strongest of the species that survives, nor the most intelligent, but the ones most responsive to change."[12] Wisdom, compassion, and understanding enable humans to be very responsive. There are well-known historical examples: Lao-tzu, Buddha, Confucius, Jesus, John, Mani, Muhammad, etc.

We've already shown we can rise above the "leper colony" days past, locking away autistic people (and other mental and physical health disorders). We've worldwide "interbeing" among different races and cultures. Yet we still do send criminals and "offenders" off to human warehouses, sometimes to die either naturally or by society's hand, ignoring their intrinsic worth as human beings. Convicts are called offenders because they've offended us individually and collectively with their behavior or actions. Like a bad-smelling plate of food that offends our sense of smell, we push people away when they offend us. However, that action minimizes the convict's humanity by discounting their ability to learn, grow, and change for the better. (This subject will be covered more in chapters 11 and 12.)

As mentioned earlier, the majority of convicts committed their offense as a cry for help. Rather than punishing them, as the default option, let's find them help. Finding ways to help takes efforts and costs money. The· United States has the largest per capita prison population. In fact, with only a population less than 5 percent of the world's population, the United States has over 25 percent of the world's prison population. The prison industry in the United States is a $7 billion business; it costs the taxpayer over $40,000 per year per inmate, and the majority of the prisoners come from the poorer portions of society.[13] The money could be spent more wisely. Many of the prisoners have mental or social health issues or were in such a financial predicament that crime seemed to be their only choice. The people I've just described, the people with whom I currently live, just needed help. Why not continue to use our evolutionary advantage of cooperation, compassion, and understanding to help the majority and not damage them and society more by incarcerating them when other options are available? We need to recognize our habitual, default gut reactions as shortsighted and harmful.

There are more examples, than just prisoners, of ways we could help people rather than shun, abandon, and ostracize them. As stated, science is helping us understand people's behavior more every day. We as individuals can seek to understand, learn, and grow for the better in our individual relationships. The last resort should be to abandon, not the first choice. We should seek to help if no other reason than it'll help prevent people from reverting to an earlier stage of human development. By doing so, we're able to break lower level life form reaction cycles . . . natural cycles that have been evolutionary embedded through the survival process. They've become habits. When we use our higher-order thinking and problem-solving abilities, we're being "responsive," and we'll enable others to be "responsive" too. We all will adapt better to handle the conditions and circumstances better, to handle people's problems and problematic ways of thinking better, and to handle human interactions better. Being compassionate and kind, focusing on helping others, solves the problems abandonment, ostracization, and separation would cause...the "can" being kicked down the road to be solved later, if ever. Finding ways to help people be productive and find fulfilling work and suitable housing helps them like themselves, and that's passed on. We're, as a society, nation, community, family, and couple, only as strong as our weakest link.

While pushing problems and problem people "out-of-sight, out-of-mind" is normal, habitual, and natural, it only hurts us individually and collectively. While abandonment and ostracization seems like the solution, both as a society and on an individual basis, it's really archaic, barbaric, and problematic. And while the simplest solution is to shun people who offend us, it's our baser instinct that is directing us . . . It's our reptilian and mammalian brains. We've all done and can do much better. Both history and current societies have many examples of both effective and ineffective ways of handling things and people who've offended us. Rather than add to the list of ineffective methodologies that are now considered dated, archaic, and barbaric, let's find ways that are effective. We do revere people who've risen above the masses and that baser thinking, who've shown that they understand that their life is not really about them. In many cases, we've sainted them and elevated them to the title of "master"; and many of the world's religions, cultures, and societies were established by their followers. We've slowly, especially looking at the entire history of mankind, made progress in better ways of treating people. We each have examples that we can and should follow . . . masters and other people who have transcended the baser human instincts. There are many examples that demonstrate the answer to Rabbi Hillel's questions; each one knew "it isn't about you, but it all starts with you." We each can live by that simple realization.

An example of both change capability in a person who has offended and the master who was able to rise above human's baser instincts is the legendary story of Angulimala and the Buddha. The name Angulimala means "garland (necklace) of fingers." Angulimala had killed 999 people and was seeking to kill his thousandth. His necklace was made of the fingers from people he'd killed, which was pretty heavy by the time of this story. The news spread far and wide that Angulimala was seeking his thousandth kill, and no one wanted to be that victim. Upon seeing Angulimala come into town, wearing his massive, grisly necklace, everyone ran in fear. Children were quickly scooped up, and even pets and livestock were dragged along with the mass exodus. Angulimala's normal way to murder was as a roadside bandit. He'd killed groups of ten, twenty, thirty, and even forty by this method. Knowing of Angulimala's reputation and intent, one day the Buddha purposefully walked down the road toward Angulimala. Angulimala was shocked that he'd come down "his road" by himself, no less. So he walked up to Buddha and asked if Buddha was ready to die, to which the Buddha calmly answered, "Yes." Serenely, the Buddha continued walking. Angulimala told him to stop. The Buddha replied, "Angulimala, I have stopped forever, I abstain from violence towards living beings, but you have no restraint towards things that live . . ."

Immediately, Angulimala realized the powerfully profound, deeper meaning of all his previous harmful actions. He realized he'd no power to restore life, and then and there, he asked the Buddha to be his teacher, to which the Buddha agreed; and Angulimala discarded his gruesome necklace, his sword, and his bow and became Buddha's disciple for the rest of his life. Buddha knew each person is inherently good, even a person who had killed 999 people. Buddha knew Angulimala, like all of us, was capable of understanding, learning, and growing for the better. He knew the baser instincts could be transcended and that Angulimala was redeemable. He skillfully helped a mass murderer to become a high-order being. Interestingly, Angulimala is said to have reached Nirvana by living a transcendent, selfless life all the rest of his days.[14]

We've seen the cause and effect of separation, and we can see that unless we keep finding better ways to take care of people, we as humanity will be held back by our weakest links. We are alone, "a lone individual," making his or her way through the world, but we can't do it alone, nor can anyone else. Having compassion and wisdom raises us out of selfishness. Buckminster Fuller called on us to do better . . . He called us to each take on the challenge of living at a higher evolutionary level when he said, "We are facing our final evolutionary exam: is the human species fit to survive?"[15]

INFLUENCING AND RELATING TO OTHERS

Abandonment may be the norm, but I believe most people don't do it with malicious intent. The majority of the people put others "out-of-sight, out-of-mind" to protect themselves from anticipated pain or to protect their own "tribe's" safety and security. All people, including me, rationalize and justify their actions using their gut (their archaic, barbaric brain) or lower life form thinking. I've witnessed it. However, there are others, thankfully a small minority, who are malicious in their intents and actions. We've all met at least one person in our life whom we'd describe as a "bully," maybe quite a few. History is chock-full of bullies, and so are prisons, with some being truly malicious. These people who bully, hopefully, you're not one, manipulate and take advantage of others, just to be mean . . . or at least to be mean to a particular person or group. Bullying is a way to influence and relate to others. It's a *Coping Mechanism* available to all . . . Some witness it very early in life.

School bullying has been in the news for many decades, with movies being made about the subject. For example, there is a popular movie titled *Mean Girls* about these girls, "The Plastics," who are mean and bully, through humiliation, anyone not in their group. The plot centers around this new girl who joins in the meanness to be accepted into their group, but then she realizes how hurtful her actions are, and she wants to make things right. But by then, it is too late . . . She has done damage to her fellow students. However, in the end, she does make things right by getting back at the bullies, knocking them off their high horse, giving them a taste of their own medicine.

While truly malicious bullies are people who, deep down inside, don't like themselves and show how insecure they really are by their mean words and actions, they really intend to be mean because it gives them a sense of power over others. Leo Ruskin stated, "It is the weak who are cruel. Gentleness can only be expected from the strong."[1] Put another way, bullies are the weak ones. Dr. Jampolsky asked, "Is not a terrorist someone who causes another person to feel terrified? And what about bullies in school who create terror in kids who are smaller than them? Isn't bullying another form of terrorism? Another form of fear?"[2] The answer to his questions is yes!

Although bullying has been around for millions of years in various forms and is ruled by the lower level life form thinking that we've discussed in chapters 3 and 4, in the last few decades, a new phenomenon has arisen titled "cyberbullying." Now people can be mean without even seeing the person face-to-face. Online, people can be very vicious, masked in anonymity. Cyberbullying happens mostly to the young people, though not exclusively, who are still trying to find their place in the world. Young people's brains are not fully developed; and thus, the archaic, barbaric portions are very strong. Bullies use technology to influence and spread meanness.

Recently, we prisoners viewed a video where the entire movie was of computer screenshots of young people sitting in their own homes using computers, webcams, and chat and social media applications. The plot was these kids had bullied a young girl to commit suicide a year prior. Sadly, suicide is an all-too-common outcome of bullying, and it causes people to feel depressed, hopeless, and helpless. In the movie, it's a year later, on the anniversary of the bullied girl's suicide; and the ghost of the bullied, dead girl sought and got revenge, using social media as her weapon. In the end, they're all dead . . . The message: to beat bullies, bully back!

Physiologists tell us there are two types of aggression: *Physical* and *Relational*. Studies have shown men are more prone to use *Physical aggression*. Society has made violence illegal, and thus, there are more men in prison because *Physical Aggression* has been deemed hurtful. However, it is finally becoming recognized that *Relational Aggression* is also very damaging. While studies show women are more prone to use *Relational Aggression*, everyone uses it at one time or another. Many times, *Physical*

Aggression follows *Relational Aggression* actions, or they are used in concert with each other. In prison, both types are used on a constant basis by inmates and staff.

Although it is not against the law in the vast majority of instances, *Relational Aggression* also uses lower life form thinking. I submit that *Relational Aggression*, which includes withholding or breaking off communication, speaking ill of someone behind their back, and abandoning them or any time the "relationship" is used to hurt or punish the other person, is also a form of bullying. I submit that *Relational Aggression* is actually more damaging in the long run. The two movies I've mentioned are examples where relational bullying was represented, and the harm done was effectively communicated. Mahatma Mohandas Gandhi stated, "By using violence to subjugate one another, we are using violence against our own souls."[3] Gandhi, of course, never knew about social media, or may not have experienced the various other types of relational bullying, but I'm sure he'd agree that using *Relational Aggression* is also damaging "our own souls." Recently, *Relational Aggression* is now being recognized for its hurtfulness through laws against all bullying.

As stated, it's not just young people who use *Relational Aggression*. Adults do too . . . some as weapon to maliciously hurt someone in response to a perceived slight. Some do it to hurt their spouse as part of Parental Alienation Syndrome discussed in chapter 15. There is one woman who acts very innocent and sanctimonious, and she's fooled many people for many years. Her many victims are not fooled as she lashes out at them using e-mails, blogs, slanderous words, gossips, and alienation to malign anyone who does not agree with her thoughts or actions. However, over time, her maliciousness has been revealed for what it is—bullying. Many of her former friends and extended family members are very afraid to even speak their mind for fear of her vicious, public attacks and bullying. She has even used her own children as weapons, adding them to her team of slanders. She still fools some people, but her true nature has been revealed, and it's only a matter of time before more find out that she's the epitome of *Relational Aggression*.

I'm sure it is no surprise to anyone that in prison, all types of bullying are all too common, both *Physical* and *Relational Aggression*, as mentioned already. There are TV shows and movies that testify to this, to include, the *Scared Straight! Orange Is the New Black*, and *60 Days Inside* series. I've already given many examples, in the past chapters, of my prison bullying experiences, and more will be sprinkled throughout the rest of this book. In societies all over the world, bullying is used to control and manipulate others; and in prison, it is no different. If bullying others worked for the person when they were young, or they saw its effectiveness from many of the other examples, they're more likely to use it as adults. For example, if one's parents yelled to control and manipulate, then that person is likely to raise their voice to belittle someone else. Also, of any environment I know of or have experienced, bullies feel the most natural in prison. Not only *Physical Aggression*, prison bullies use being very loud and yelling to humiliate and demean someone. *Relational Aggression* works very well with people who are just trying to survive.

Some guards also do the same thing. When I first arrived at my current prison, the senior guard raised his voice, yelling at me that I was to face the wall. I complied, and he stood behind me and berated me, topping it off with the question, "Am I going to have any problems from you?" My calm reply was "No." He was using loudness to intimidate, manipulate, and control, to ensure I knew he was in charge. Why he felt a need to be mean is a matter of his past experience. Was he really mean, or was that his learned response, conditioning from the example of whoever trained him to be a guard? Did he see it as effective? Was he really malicious? Not all bullies are really malicious. Is everyone capable of bullying at one time or another? Let's investigate that further.

As briefly mentioned in chapter 3, there is a famous study from the 1970s where students from Stanford University were part of a psychology study called The Stanford Prison Study conducted by Phillip Zimbardo.[4] The volunteers were randomly divided up into two groups. One group became guards, and the other became prisoners. The basement of the psychology department became the prison. The experiment was supposed to last two weeks but had to be called off after only one week, as the "guards" became too mean and violent, and the "prisoners" were in danger. Interestingly, the *Lucifer Effect*, as it was named by Zimbardo, happened to randomly selected people, teaching us that *anyone and everyone of us is capable of cruelty*. As we've discussed in chapter 3, we don't want to admit to ourselves that we could be "that person." We don't admit to ourselves there's a "little Hitler" in all of us. Even though everyone of us can become "mean girls or boys," it frightens us to admit it to ourselves. Yet we are all capable of bullying. The prison guard experiment reminds me of the capos of the Nazi prison camps. These were prisoners themselves, but for special favors, they became as cruel, sometimes more cruel, as the Nazi guards. Capo-type responses very likely happen in all prisons to a certain degree . . . I've seen it happen in my limited experience. I've already mentioned the "heavies." The Lucifer Effect affects prisoners to bully one another, though the majority of us don't bully all the time; and when we do bully, most of us are not necessarily trying to be malicious. To paraphrase this chapter's opening paragraph, the majority of us don't bully, and some who do bully are not doing so to be malicious, though any of us can bully and be malicious.

From my observations here in prison, people who are mean-spirited (i.e., seem to be naturally malicious) are the ones who are the main bullies or heavies. Then there are "follower bullies," who are bullying because they see power in the main bully, and they are aligning themselves with the main bully for protection, or some other egocentric reason. The main character in *Mean Girls* was a follower bully, just trying to be accepted by the group of mean girls. People who are follower bullies change according to the situation, but the truly mean bullies don't seem capable of change. That said, everyone is capable of change, of course; but for malicious bullies, it is very hard to change. The malicious bullies gain not only power, prestige, and influence over others, but also a sense of satisfaction to their ego that they are better than others. It gives them a high to be mean . . . It is an addiction like any other addiction. However, their bullying heavily masks their real insecurities. The Dalai Lama stated the following: "If you can, help others; if you can't do that, at least do not harm them."[5] Bullying, extortion, alienation, and manipulation are always harmful and lead to self-loathing . . . even when it is just validating the ego. Bullying also boils down to fear.

One day I was sitting, eating, and the people around me started to speak ill of a person I knew well . . . a person who had attempted suicide the week before and was now in the infirmary, recovering. The first person, the mean, malicious bully, started the conversation, berating the person down in the infirmary; and others around me, the follower bullies, joined in. As I stated, I knew the person they were speaking about very well, and so I started to defend him and asked them not to speak ill of him around me. The main, malicious bully did not like the fact I was going against him, and he threatened me. He made a loud scene in hopes I would cower (using *Relational Aggression* with the threat of *Physical Aggression*). I'd stated my peace, and I sat there calmly, continuing to eat my meal. This just infuriated him more, and he got right in my face and was trying to get me to react and fight him . . . His *Relational Aggression* did not work, so he raised the stakes to *Physical Aggression*. Now the guards were looking as was the entire prison population in the dining facility. Luckily for both of us, another prisoner stopped him from attacking me, and order was restored. We would have both been thrown in solitary confinement, even though I'd sat quite Gandhi-ish, meaning calmly and quietly standing my ground.

Speaking of Mahatma Mohandas Gandhi, I read a book concerning Gandhi and India during that period of history. I felt like I was reading a current newspaper with the many terrorist stories we read or hear about today. Terrorism and bullying have been used for many, many generations throughout history to bully and manipulate using psychological fear. It was used by many disgruntled, disenfranchised Indians . . . both Hindu, Sheik, and Muslim. There are so many recent historical examples of bullying and terrorism—the Nazi brown shirts, the gestapo, the KGB, other Communist or Fascist secret police, Mafia, Yakuza, Bloods and Crypts street gangs, and even the police themselves, just to name a few. Bullying, manipulating, intimidating, etc., all seem to be the norm. To quote a participant from the prison TV show *60 Days In*, "Jail is full of bullies, preying on the weak ones." In prison, *bullying is the main way* people influence and relate to one another. **My Fear-based insight:** *bullying works because fear is such a powerful emotion.*

As another example of bullying, my current prison has had a Tibetan High Lama, whom I mentioned in my introduction called a *Rinpoche*, come to visit us a few times. Phakyab was asked to go back to Tibet by the Dalai Lama to check on the many Tibetan Buddhists still living in Chinese-occupied Tibet. He was able to minister to many Tibetan Buddhists. However, once the Chinese found out that he was there and what he was doing, they imprisoned him and tortured him, including breaking his legs. (He still limps to this day.) The Chinese guards and soldiers were malicious and cruel to him. As he told his story, I could feel his pain and suffering. Each time he has visited us and told his story, his English has gotten better, but the emotion of his experience was palpable even when he spoke only Tibetan with a translator. He has experienced true bullying and a very harsh prison environment. On a larger scale, after World War II, China bullied defenseless Tibetans and the Dalai Lama to flee, and the Tibetans who have remained are still under Chinese oppression. Although history shows that we as civilizations and societies have come a long way, *man is still inhumane to man*, both on the country level and right down to the individual. It feels like there is nothing we can do to stop the various types and kinds of bullying. Is that feeling true?

A personal story, unrelated to prison or general history, happened many years ago. My wife and I had taken a cruise out of Los Angeles. My children were with their grandparents up in Santa Barbara, and· at the end of the cruise, we were to meet in the high California desert. My parents had a cell phone at this time, which was a rarity back in the mid-nineties. My wife and I were to call them once the ship had docked so they knew when to leave Santa Barbara. We came out of the sea terminal to see the phone banks packed with people and long lines waiting. I decided we'd drive out of the Long Beach terminal to find another pay phone without a crazy long line. After many blocks, but still in Long Beach, we spotted a pay phone; and I pulled over, leaving my wife in the car. There was no one using the phone, and no one was close by, but there was a group of guys about twenty-five yards away. I did not pay much attention to them. As soon as I picked up the public pay phone to put in my quarter, one of the "gang" came over and said to me, "That's my phone, and you can't use it." The danger of the situation became very apparent very quickly. Obviously, I was outnumbered and likely outgunned. Although I thought to reason with the thug, that thought quickly passed. I looked over to see the menacing looks of his fellow gang members, and seeing my wife in the car only a few feet away, I quickly hung up the phone and walked away. There are times when we must give in to bullies, but that does not mean it is always right to give in to them. I've had to give into bullies here in prison to survive . . . for my safety and security.

In the short run, giving into bullying supersedes reason, but focuses on safety and security. However, giving in to bullies also plays right into the bullies' hands, giving up voluntarily freedoms and rights whether it's at school, work, or in prison. Again, the point of the Milgram studies mentioned previously, where people were asked to shock someone for getting questions wrong, was intended to understand why the German people allowed the Nazis to control their lives and take the lives of their neighbors. The outcome showed *we are all capable of bullying.* We are also capable of being follower bullies. In a follow-up study to the Milgram study, Philip Zimbardo conducted a similar study but added a person who was seen as an authority figure seated next to the test subject. When the test subject started to doubt whether he or she should continue to administer the shock to the screaming person in the next room, the authority figure would tell the test subject to proceed. Very, very rarely did the test subject refuse to go on after being told by the authority figure to proceed. The majority of the people, who are just like *us*, administered another shock at a higher and higher level. Some continued even when the person was no longer making any noise, as if unconscious, or dead. We all want to believe we'd be the one to stop the shocks.

Again, what would you do to combat the *Cognitive Trap* psychologists call the *Principle of Legitimacy*? This is defined as "when the people in authority want the rest to behave as if it matters that they are in charge." Malicious bullies, in their various forms, act as the legitimate authority. They want us to continue to bully along with them, which validates their need for legitimacy and power. It worked for Hitler and many others. Historian Ian Buruma stated, "Those who do well in tyrannies are often the least savory and most easily corrupted people."[6] Malicious bullies need follower bullies to remain in power. We allow bullies to exist, especially if we are a follower bully ourselves. Are you ever or have you ever been a bully or follower bully? How did it make you feel? Agnostic Buddhist Stephen Batchelor addresses the natural tendencies when he wrote, "Instead of a natural and noncoercive authority, we impose our will on others either through manipulation and intimidation or by appealing to the opinions of those more powerful than ourselves. Authority becomes a question of force rather than of integrity."[7] This describes my prison experience. Politicians and prison heavies use manipulation and fear versus integrity.

I had a conversation the other day with a fellow inmate who told me prison politics (code for "heavies" taking power to control and manipulate others) was necessary, or the prisoners would all go around causing mayhem. With his *Theory X* mind-set (that people are inherently bad and must be forced to be good), nothing I could say was going to change his mind. He was justifying bullying to maintain order. Does that sound familiar? That's what Hitler and others have done throughout history. It's what current politics and the media espouse today. It's the *Principle of Legitimacy*. Like the Nazis, other tyrannical governments, and the death camp capos, the prison heavies sell the story, that without them, disorder would rule; and therefore, inmates, as individuals, must sacrifice their freedoms and rights so that the heavies can protect GenPop. That was basically this fellow prisoner's argument. That is why bullies have power. Most of the time, we, as a society or an individual, give our power to them voluntarily.

You may think you'd act differently if you had been part of the Milgram or Zimbardo studies. You may think you'd resisted the Nazis or the Red Army. You may even ask yourself, "Why would people be attracted to a powerful bully?" I don't wonder; I see it every day. Prison is a daily example of what happens when lower life forms rule. Many, many of us humans are so scared by life that we welcome harsh, unjust, illegitimate authority. It's easier to be told what to do, when to do it, and what to think. Many people change their thinking to become follower bullies for self-security and safety. Mahatma Mohandas Gandhi stated, "Manliness consists not in bluff, bravado, of loneliness. It consists in daring to do the right thing and facing consequences; whether it is in matters social, political, or other. It consists of deeds, riot words."[8] Fighting bullies is not safe.

Speaking again of Gandhi, I'm reminded of one of his favorite poems, "Hellas,"[9] by P. B. Shelly, according to a biography I read about him. It goes as follows:

Stand ye calm and resolute, like a forest close and mute,

With folded arms and looks which are weapons of un-vanquished war. And if then the tyrants dare, let them ride among you there, Slash, and stab, and main, and hew—what they like to, that let them do.

With folded arms and steady eyes, and little fear, and less surprise, Look upon them as they slay, till their rage has died away.

Although many lives were lost in the independence of India, Bangladesh, and Pakistan, Gandhi brought the British Empire to its knees through peaceful means. We celebrate Martin Luther King for following Gandhi's example, and there have been examples of peaceful protest for thousands of years. People like the Buddha, who was providing an alternative to the highly restrictive Hindu caste system; Jesus, who was working to change the conditions around the Roman occupation; Ashoka, the peaceful Buddhist king who gave up war making; and Marcus Antoninus Aurelius, who ruled Rome in a great time of peace. All these people faced mean and malicious people, and for some of them, it cost them their lives. I know there are so many more examples, but history is written by the victor, and many of those inspiring stories have been lost and forgotten. Just like the current news narratives, broadcast every day, twenty-four hours a day, fear rules. In fact, reading history is mostly reading about wars, conflicts, revolutions, and all sorts of physical aggression. Exceptionally, looking back at British-Indian history, Gandhi corralled the more Indian militant factions; and while he was alive (he was eventually killed by a militant, radical faction of Hinduism), his nonviolent protests were more successful than the terrorist tactics. While historically, bullies have done damage, it seems the only way to combat a bully is with force . . . to bully back. Gandhi and others have shown that is not the case. There are ways to nonrelationally and nonphysically relate and influence. *Physical* and *Relational Aggression* are Fear-based *Coping Mechanisms*.

As an example, one day I was walking down the stairs; and a very malicious, mean, nasty, rude inmate was on the phone next to the stairs, and I could hear a bit of his conversation. I'd witnessed this person using his lower level life form thinking all the time as he bullied and manipulated other prisoners, bending them to his will. I, for one, stayed far away from him, as he was very unpredictable and dangerous. I know many of the terrible things he did to people. I knew him by his actions. However, hearing a snippet of his conversation, I knew he was talking to his mother; and he was being very courteous and loving to her, as one would expect from anyone. However, this was from a hardened, mean person . . . a person who, it seemed, reveled in hurting people around him. He closed his conversation by saying, "I love you too, Mom." It hit me hard that even the worst prisoner, a person who had murdered people, is loved and does love others. It hit me even harder that love, even with him, was more powerful than hate and fear. This confirmed **my next Love-based insight: *kindness,*** *compassion, and love are more powerful and effective in relating to and influencing bullies.*

Returning to Phakyab Rinpoche, the times he told us his story about being imprisoned by the Chinese, their torture and maiming of him, the horrible prison conditions in Tibet, and his eventual release, the most important portion of his story had yet to be revealed. While it's true, his story confirms my previously mentioned insights: about people not liking themselves (in this case, the Chinese guards); people being prone to judge, minimize, and discount others; and people abandoning others (either mentally, emotionally, or physically) to dehumanize them; the fact that we are on our own (especially when a person is placed in an institution) and that bullies rule in environments that are conducive to lower level life form thinking. The Rinpoche told us about his feelings and mind-set during this hurtful, traumatic experience. With tears in his eyes, speaking in broken English, he stated that he felt love and compassion for his jailer torturers. I'd mistaken this as his post-traumatic stress. He explained that his heart broke because he knew they were doing much more damage and harm to themselves than to him. In a word, he *loved* them despite how they were treating him. The palpable feeling was of his love and compassion. I felt his empathy and compassion, his forgiveness and peace of mind. The Rinpoche is a living example of manliness as defined by Mahatma Gandhi. Feeling compassion under torture is astounding and courageous.

It starts with us. If we learn to love ourselves, we're less likely to judge, discount, and minimize others. We are less likely to treat others as an "it." With knowledge of our own self-worth, we're able to accept people for who they are; and with internal validation, we're able to have compassion and love . . . even for bullies. We'll see that we can stand up to bullies calmly and courageously. We can still stand on our principles, not backing down even when the things are at their lowest. We'll know when to seek help and see who needs our help. Even the worst person we know has something that they can teach us. We can see the other person suffering (even if it is only their own delusions of grandeur or fight for external validation and legitimacy) and see a way to help them. The key is again to start with ourselves and expand love outward. The Buddha once said, "You could search the whole world over and not find anyone more deserving of your love and compassion than yourself."[10] As we've discussed in section one of this book, unconditional love is the key to accepting one's self and having love and compassion for one's self . . . then comes others. Once you know love and feel compassion for yourself, you are better able to see what another person needs, even a bully. During my time committing my crime, I was insecure and was really crying out for help. I was seeking external validation. I was seeking love outside myself, and I was wrong to do so. Everyone is going to cry out for help sometime in their life . . . Some people cry out all their lives. To hear anyone's cry, we just have to be open and accepting. Bishop Desmond Tutu stated, "My humanity is bound up in yours, for we can only be human together."[11]

Returning to the "mean prisoner" who was on the phone with his mother, he did not seem to like me at all and could feel it whenever we were around each other. One day I found out he was taking a college class, and I was impressed that he was trying to improve himself, even with a life-without-parole sentence. So one day a few weeks later, I went up to him and offered to help him write his papers, clarifying I would edit what he had already written. He was surprised that I would approach him with an offer to help. Although he was taken aback, he accepted my offer. His attitude toward me changed afterward, and he did ask me to review a few of his papers. He's been transferred to another prison, but I predict he is still trying to improve himself, and he may be less judgmental about a person who is of another race or whatever it was that made him initially dislike me. He may even be less malicious. Maybe my kindness has made a difference somehow.

I'm reminded of a quote I read in a biography by Lily Casey. The author was quoting her mother, who had stated, "Anyone who thinks he's too small to make a difference has never been bit by a mosquito."[12] We each can make a difference even if it is a long way off, and we'll never live to really see the outcome, or something or someone we can see changes right before our eyes. Mother Theresa stated a good rule to live by when she said, "If I look at the mass, I'll never act. If I look at the one, I will."[13] Seeing the vicious inmate in a new light enabled me to break the prison boundaries to offer my help. I was looking at the one. I saw him as a "you," not an "it." I saw him as a human, not a bully. That is what I believe Mother Theresa was saying. She was just agreeing with Martin Buber without ever knowing it or his teaching. She was following her heart to do what was right. She, like so many others, was using higher-order thinking to make a real, long-lasting difference. She was being kind to one person at a time. She saw "the one."

The story I told about the malicious inmate on the phone with his mother has an iconic, archetype parallel to a parable we were taught as children. We're all familiar with the story of the lion who had a thorn in his paw. For our fellow humans, the thorn could be a metaphor for anything . . . a cry for help or love. As we've discussed, many people don't like themselves for many reasons, and they are in such circumstances that their cry for help or love can take many different forms. People just want the thorn taken out. Even a malicious bully, a lion, needs the thorn taken out. The many masters have shown us various ways to take out the thorn in ourselves and others. We can be the thorn-pulling mouse, making a difference through kindness, compassion, and love.

Sure, we see historical bullying cycles and conditions repeat themselves, and we can't help but feel if we could just stop the cycles somehow, all would be well. However, we can't change the masses. We have to focus on the one. Our role is more simple—we just need to be kind to one another . . . to everyone. We all need to remember our life is not really about us. All our lower level life form thinking, *Cognitive Traps*, and archaic, automatic actions just get in the way. While we see bullying all around us, in one form or another, whether it is China, North Korea, Islamic terrorist, or a neighbor, coworker, boss, ex-spouse, police, guards, prison bullies, etc., it is our kindness and compassion that really make the difference in the long run. Our actions ripple outward. We look at history so that we don't repeat it, but really, it is not that helpful. History, whether of an empire, nation, society, religion, city, or individual, does not really help because it usually overlooks the real difference maker: "the small acts of kindness." The Dalai Lama has stated, "Providing services is a form of kindness, of nurturing, no matter what the motive."[14]

Recalling the story about the lion with the thorn, it was a story of a small act of kindness, on the part of the mouse, in the face of a perceived danger. Sometimes it takes courage to be kind. Mother Theresa served others even though she was in constant danger of contracting some disease or becoming a victim of some act of terrorism. When we pull out the thorn, the lion (or bully) may be able to see that they were just very upset because of the pain. However, now they look favorably on the person who pulled the thorn out, and a friendship may ensue. Bullies don't create order . . . That is just "safety in numbers" or "herd mentality" run amuck. Its people looking out for one another that create order and peace. If a person has to pay someone for protection, then that is just a strong person (a bully) taking advantage of the weaker person . . . a transaction. In prison, it does not really create a friendship or any real concern, compassion, or even empathy. Small acts of kindness are the first step to real and substantial change for humanity.

Interestingly, in my prison experience, the examples of the small acts of kindness grow as one goes up in custody . . . conditions that enable higher-order thinking. One kind, prison tradition is people holding open the door for the next person coming out or going in. With "higher custody level" pods (when an inmate serves time with good conduct, he or she is moved up in custody and is given more freedom), it happens all the time; and in fact, if it does not happen, then it is considered rude and disrespectful. I see people who don't even like each other and would never talk to each other still holding the door for each other. Another, which is not generally applied in lower custody, is distribution of laundry. Usually, when the laundry returns in big carts, people take care of their "friends," distributing it to their cell. However, in one pod I lived in, everyone's laundry was distributed to their door while they were at work. I don't know who started the tradition, but it was very kind, and it continues even though the person may be gone. Now when inmates came back from work, they just have to walk up to cell, and the laundry has already been sorted. Now I've started the tradition in my current pod, and others are helping the tradition grow. Treating one another kindly is the key to continuing to build up humanity to survive and to thrive.

An excerpt from Naomi Shihab Nye's poem "Kindness" reflects what happens to a person when they come to prison and how important kindness becomes:

> *Before you know what kindness really is you must lose things,*
> *Feel the future dissolve in a moment like salt in a weakened broth.*
> *What you held in your hand, what you counted and carefully saved,*
> *All this must go so you know how desolate the landscape can be,*
> *Between the regions of kindness.*
>
> *Before you know kindness as the deepest thing inside,*
> *You must know sorrow as the other deepest thing.*
> *You must wake up with sorrow.*

You must speak to it till your voice catches the thread of all sorrows
And you see the size of the cloth.

Then it is only kindness that makes sense anymore,
Only kindness that ties your shoes and sends you out into the day
To mail letters and purchase bread, only kindness that raises its head
From the crowd of the world to say: It is I you have been looking for,
And then goes with you everywhere like a shadow or a friend.

This poem's excerpt reflects that true kindness can be all around us as everyone can and does suffer at one time or another. Our humanity is intricately interwoven with everyone around us. Yes, we are alone (meaning "a lone individual") navigating through life; but our thoughts, attitudes, and actions are intertwined with everyone else. As previously mentioned, our lives are not really about us. This poem is an echo of wisdom learned by a life full of experiencing pain and suffering. Suffering or envisioning suffering, ours or others, engenders compassion, which leads to wisdom.

Separated by hundreds of years and cultures apart, these next five quotes confirm the fact we are (to use the word of Zen Buddhist monk, Nobel Peace Prize winner, and antiwar activist Thich Nhat Hanh) "interbeing" with one another.

Sir Thomas Moore stated it thusly, "We are all in the same cart, going to execution; how can I hate anyone or wish anyone harm?"[15]

The Dalai Lama said it this way: "Consider a group of prisoner who are about to be executed. During their stay together in prison, all of them will meet their end. There is no sense in quarreling out the remaining days. All of us are bound by the same nature of suffering and impermanence. Under such circumstances, there is absolutely no reason to fight with each other."[16]

Daisaku Ikeda put it this way: "A great revolution in just one single individual will help achieve a change of a society, and further will enable a change in destiny of human kind."[17]

Dr. Martin Luther King stated, "We are caught in an inescapable network of mutuality, tied in a single garment of destiny. Whatever affects one affects all indirectly."[18]

Margaret Mead said the same by saying, "Never doubt that a small group of thoughtful, committed citizens can change the world. Indeed, it is the only thing that ever has."[19]

Kindness is the action that greases the wheels of human interaction; bullies and bullying are the friction that stops us all . . . They are another weak link to our human progression. Bullies will continue to play their negative part in society, slowing human progress down, but we each can make a difference in the long run through small acts of kindness. George Bernard Shaw talks about how bullies stop human progress when he said, "The reasonable man adapts himself to the world; the unreasonable one persist in trying to adapt the world to himself. Therefore, all progress depends on the unreasonable man."[20] As time goes on, the kindness will affect and effect the bully or unreasonable man like the fabled lion. Through kindness, one person at a time, each bully or unreasonable man will be converted to humanity . . . Through kindness, we humanize them.

Bullying, including terrorism and war, is still part of humanity's daily life, but so is service, compassion, love, kindness, care, and concern. Even in prison, where the rules of the institution and prison politics prevent people from really helping one another because the institution knows the bullies will and do extort the weak, kindness sneaks in. Living with bullies on a daily basis makes things hard, but one-on-one, people are helping each other and making a difference. Yes, prison causes people to revert to an earlier stage on the individual's development and inhibits society's progress. That said, there still is kindness within the walls and fences. Treating bullies with kindness, care, and compassion is the only way the bully will see the need to change whether he or she is a malicious bully, or just a bully follower, or whether they are using *Physical Aggression* or *Relational Aggression* as a cry for help or love. Johann Wolfgang von Goethe said, "Treat a man as he is and he will remain as he is. Treat a man as he can and should be and he will become as he can and should be."[21] Kindness is the tool that will help people be as they should be, including ourselves. We have the power to humanize through love. I truly believe compassion and wisdom naturally generate kindness and vice versa. Kindness generates compassion and wisdom.

UNDERSTANDING OTHERS

I served in the military for over twenty years, and the military is truly integrated. I know the military had its racial problems back in the seventies, but in all my years, I never saw any segregation. That is until I came to the military prison. I knew other prisons had gangs and segregation, which I experienced firsthand in the county jail where I was before being moved to my current military prison. However, I was very sad and surprised to see it in a military prison. To clarify, the institution administration itself does not segregate. It's the inmates who segregate themselves with the institution condoning it by taking no action to prevent or eliminate it. Of all the things I've experienced in prison, this was the most surprising because of my experience during my military service. We were brothers and sisters in arms, willing to die for one another, for your freedom and liberty, and for our great country. Yet come to prison and it reverts back to lower level life form thinking—"we have to look out for our tribe," where tribe is defined by race, color, and culture.

Our pods are built in a triangle shape with three TVs mounted to the stairs that lead to the second tier at the middle of each side. Under the TVs are a pair of phone stands with a total of six phones per pod. The institution distributes people as evenly as they can to the pods so that each pod is balanced by race, color, and culture, which in of itself is telling. However, what happens after that is up to the prison population. The TV becomes the focal point for the segregation as one TV is for the black people also referred to as the brother section. Then there is a Hispanic or Latino TV, but this section is a mixture of race and cultures. The "Latino section" includes Indian, Native American, Asian, as well as all Spanish-speaking heritage country members. Last is the "white section," which has people of European heritage. When people come to GenPop, the first division imposed by the heavies is among these three sections. As mentioned in chapter 4, it affects where one sits in the pod and dining facility. It also designates who the heavy ones are.

Each wall of the triangle-shaped pod is made up of twenty or thirty cells (it is a right triangle), and each wall is divided up among the three sections. The phones under the TVs belong to the same group as the TV. In medium pods, the use of phones and even looking at another section's TV is strictly restricted and reason for censure . . . for *Relational* and *Physical Aggression*. For cell assignment and phones, this division relaxes as one goes up in custody, but racial ownership of the TV remains. Why people move up in custody is not based on race, color, or culture but on sentence length and staying out of trouble. So the higher the custody level, the more imbalanced the sections become. For example, as I write, I'm in a minimum pod; and the "brother section" has eight people, the "white section" has thirty-two people, and the "Latino section" has one person. Recently, I put in a written proposal to the heavies in my minimum custody level pod to eliminate the race, color, and cultural division in the pod. My idea was to make the sections equal in number and intra-racially organized. My plan was rejected and ridiculed. One longtime inmate heavy told me, "This is a great idea. I can tell you care, but it will never work because this is prison." That was what he said to my face, but behind my back, he laughed with the other heavies. They all thought it was hilarious that I'd even suggested it. I witnessed them gathering in groups with my proposal in hand, laughing. Even with that reaction, I know it's doable even in prison. I know segregation shouldn't happen, but it does.

While the military prison doesn't have a gang problem per se, the segregation serves the same purpose. The section (gang) becomes the inmates' protector. For most, it's just a matter of being a member of that race, color, or culture. However, there are some who pay protection fees; and if they don't, then people will steal their stuff, and the chance they'll be beat up or worse is greater. For the weaker or peaceful inmates, they can be taken advantage of by this system. I've already told the story about the guy who had someone steal his stuff, which he never got back. Being alone, especially in prison, makes one vulnerable to bullies. The bullies are interested in power and control. They get it from their victims and their acolytes (what I titled in the last chapter as the follower bullies). There are some people who fall somewhere in between a bully and a victim, mostly because they do the minimum to validate the *Cognitive Trap* titled *Principle of Legitimacy* to keep the bullies at bay. Whether you want or believe in segregation in prison, you are forced to comply or pay the price. While not as overt, this happens in general society too.

Most people naturally vacillate toward their race, color, and culture group and would feel uncomfortable being with another even outside prison. I myself have no problem being with any of the groups. This prison has "culture organizations" that have an overt charter of educating all prisoners about their specific culture. Membership is open to all as are the positions of leadership, which are annually voted on by the membership. However, in practice, only people from the specific race, color, or culture are ever nominated or elected. I've been a member of all three organizations my entire time here, and I was elected into a leadership position for two years on one of the councils. There are people who get along with all three sections and others who will only ever associate with their own perceived organization or group. In my opinion, the culture groups both help and hurt the inmates' segregation propensity, creating an "us and them."

Sharon Salzberg observed, "We have a strong urge to dichotomize human beings, to separate them into opposing categories. Stereotyping is an evolutionary mechanism designed to enhance survival form of shorthand for getting by in a dangerous world. We try to manage the messiness of life by creating an orderly zone of recognizable types characterized by certain traits that are associated, however loosely. Then we generalize our preconceived typologies to all member of a class or group or nation."[1] As we've already observed, the *Cognitive Traps* of *Generalization* and *Stereotyping* create an "us and them" mentality. We naturally see the world in which we have to compete for resources, and being alone puts us at risk. Prison is no different. If one isn't the malicious bully type, who is just seeking to save his or her addiction to the thrill of being mean or causing someone else physical or mental pain, then people are just seeking safety and security. I don't believe it has to be that way, but I'm in the minority . . . In here, I may be a minority of one. This brings me to **my Fear-based insight:** *our primitive instincts and fear-based thinking are what drive us to segregate and discriminate.*

I really like a quote from Immanuel Kant that, in my mind, sheds light on this subject. He stated, "When it comes to making ethical decisions, human rationality isn't a scientist, it's a lawyer. This inner attorney gathers bits of evidence, post hoc justifications, and pithy rhetoric in order to make the automatic reaction seem reasonable."[2] We segregate and discriminate naturally, spontaneously using lower life form thinking (our gut instinct), and then we use what we perceive as reason to justify the why. This applies to prison and to life outside. It applies to you and to me.

Interestingly, there are many places in my prison that are not segregated. For example, our prison work centers are mixed with all races, colors, and cultures . . . and custody levels. The self segregation seems to happen in places where there is the *Cognitive Trap* called *Scarcity Mentality*, and these segregated places become barrier to understanding of one another. If there is a situation where anyone feels that they'll not be treated fairly, segregation becomes their default reaction . . . all from a primitive instinct. However, that division creates more and more segregation and more and more misunderstandings. Sharon Salzberg went on to observe "The problem is that once we have organized everyone into tidy categories, we may be unwilling to look beyond those labels. We commonly designate our own group as the norm, the Ins, while everyone else is the Other. Designating our own family or group as the standard, while assigning everyone else to categories that are somehow inferior, boosts our feeling of self-worth. But it also locks us into the us-versus them mindset virtually assuring us an unending supply of enemies."[3] While there was a time when the survival of our group rested on ensuring our group had enough to eat, a safe place to sleep, etc., those days are mostly gone. Our species will survive even the most dire disasters, save a very large asteroid. In our world today, the segregation is more of a liability, as previously mentioned, to validate the few's legitimacy to rule . . . whether it's a government, a heavy, or a gang.

A book I read years ago provided a unique insight to the topic of segregation. The author wrote of what the earth's population would look like if it was shrunk down to 100 people using the 2002 data.[4] The breakdown is as follows: 57 would be from the Asian continent, 21 from the European continent, 14 from both North and South American continents, and 8 from the African continent; 52 would be female and 48 male; 89 would be heterosexual and 11 homosexual; 59 percent of the world's wealth would be in the hands of 6 people, and all 6 would be Americans; 80 would live in substandard housing; 70 would be able to read; 50 would be suffering from malnutrition; 30 have no access to clean water; 1 of the 100 would be nearly dead, and 1 would be near giving birth; only 1 person would have a college education; and only 1 would own a computer. The author then stated that "When one considers our world from such a compressed perspective, the need for both acceptance and compassion becomes glaringly apparent."[4] Obviously, the author was trying to help our minds, which have a really hard time conceptualizing very large numbers, see that the world is small and that thinking and being separate is inhumane. Another statistic that helps prove this point is (per National Human Genome Research Institute) we are 99.999 percent the same when we look at our DNA.[5] Breaking it down like above categorizes in general enough terms for one to realize that smaller categories based on race, color, or culture are no longer helpful. We need to see ourselves as "humans" who are responsible to humanity as our tribe. We need to look at the individual no matter where they are from, what they look like, what they believe, or what their cultural heritage is and no matter any other common form of dichotomization as one of "us" as "our tribe."

I, for one, see myself as a human responsible to help all other humans . . . and any other sentient being for that matter. I do recall a time when I was accused of discrimination. I had a subordinate who was performing very poorly. I knew it, others knew it, and my boss knew it. I sat him down and counseled him on how to do better, giving specific suggestions. I coached him for a number of months, and then it was time for a formal feedback session for his performance report. Again, I sat him down, but this time I had a rating to explain how he was doing, which still was not well. To my shock, he stated that I was rating him poorly because of his race. I explained that it was based on his performance, not his race, color, or culture. He threatened me, saying he was going to raise it up as a complaint with the leadership. I said, "Okay, let's do it now." I called the boss on the phone and put him on speaker. I explained the situation and told him that my subordinate wanted to file a grievance. My boss stated he would meet with my subordinate and asked that I deliver documentation backing my rating, which I did. In the end, I was found not to be basing my decision on anything but performance. I say that, still in shock to this day that I was seen to think, believe, or act otherwise, even realizing my subordinate was just trying to justify his self-image.

While I don't want to discount my former subordinate's feelings, he was seeing me as an enemy based on my race. That was his first thought. But why was it his first thought? To further refine the point, Dr. Stephen R. Covey stated, "We see the world, not as it is, but as we are conditioned to see it."[6] It's through conditioning that segregation seems normal. It's through conditioning that we feel more comfortable when we are with certain types of people. Like abandonment and bullying, segregation is a lower life form way of thinking. It's conditioned by our society, culture, parents, other family, and friends. It's conditioned by our experiences, our *Availability Biases*, our *Generalizations*, our *Fundamental Attribution Error*, and other *Cognitive Trap* tendencies.

We think and feel that how we see the world is "real" and "fact-based." We don't think and feel that it's just our paradigm or set of "glasses" that makes the world look the way our conditioning has led us. We feel and think we are right, and many times, our arrogance leads us to be set and firm in our ways, so set and firm sometimes we (with good intentions but with fear in our hearts) hurt other people through alienation, abandonment, discrimination, exclusion, and segregation. We in the United States throw first-time offenders in prison with long sentences. We use *Physical* and *Relational Aggression* to bully others to submit to our will because our way is the right way, or the only way. It's about force, not integrity. We become *xenophobic* and are willing to go to battle with "the other." We see scarcity of resources, which drive us to hoard, steal, cheat, and lie . . . Mostly, our lies are to ourselves. Our inflexibility and closed-mindedness leads to more errors and more pain and suffering to those around us. We create "an unending supply of enemies!" Who wants that?

In the news around the time frame of this writing, people are up in arms about the Oscar Award nominees, all being white. There have been riots because police have been abusing their power and injuring or killing black people unjustly. This has created a movement called Black Lives Matter and a counter movement called Blue Lives Matter, as cops are being targeted and killed. A woman who is genetically white passed herself off for years as of black heritage and even became a leader in the national headquarters of the National Association of African Colored People (NAACP). We have a black president of the United States, and it seems (according to the media) that most of the nation believes he can't do anything right. Although it's been 150 years since the end of slavery and 50 years since the civil rights movement made significant change possible, unjust discrimination is still on front-page news. Segregation, whether purposeful or spontaneously occurring, creates "an unending supply of enemies." How do you and I ameliorate all this? How do we build each other's humanness? It seems too big for us to make an impact.

Like I started out this chapter saying, in the military, there is no segregation based on race, color, heritage, and religion. Brothers and sisters in arms look out for one another with a "leave no man (or woman) behind" attitude. Also, as I mentioned, here in my prison, there is segregation; but there are many places and conditions where we are mixed. Though segregation does exist here in our military prison, it's likely much better than other prisons, where gangs are the norm. Likely, that's because every military prisoner has been in the integrated military. Yes, I feel this prison could do much better, and I've tried to make a difference by eliminating segregation in my pod, but I also know it could be much, much worse. History again shows us worse. All we have to do is look at the wars to see how "patriotism," *Scarcity Mentality*, and *Xenophobia* have hurt society.

Just using WWII as an example, we all hear about the 6 million Jews who were exterminated. However, that does not tell the whole story. In WWII, there were approximately 55 million total people killed, to include the soldiers. Of the 55 million, approximately 11 to 12 million civilians were killed in "death camps," including Jews and non-Jews from Europe and Russia. Outside the "death camps," approximately 8 million Russian servicemen and 16 million civilians; 10 million Chinese civilians; 3.6 million German servicemen and 600,000 civilians; 1 million Japanese servicemen and 650,000 civilians; 1 million Yugoslavia civilians and soldiers; 600,000 French civilian and soldiers; 500,000 British civilians, soldiers, and merchant seaman; 300,000 Italian civilians and soldiers; and 300,000 U.S. servicemen died.[7] This is but one example of how segregation can devastate societies. This is how *Scarcity Mentality* and *Xenophobia* can devastate and destroy.

We've already discussed how kindness is the antidote to bullying. What is the antidote to segregation, discrimination, *Xenophobia*, and patriotism gone wrong? The person considered to be the most intelligent person who may have ever lived, Albert Einstein, put it this way when he said, "A human being is part of the whole, called by us the 'Universe,' a part limited in time and space. He experiences himself, his thoughts and feelings, as something separate from the rest—a kind of optical delusion of his consciousness. This delusion is a kind of prison for us, restricting us to our personal desires and to affection for a few persons nearest to us. Our task must be to free ourselves from this prison by widening our circle of compassion, to embrace all living creatures and the whole of nature in its beauty."[8] Summing up what Einstein stated and bringing it into words is **my Love-based insight:** *familiarity with others and an open mind breeds understanding and compassion.* Psychologists call this the *Extended Contact Effect*, or put more simply, let each of us just get to know each other. Everyone is a person who's interbeing with us.

A personal story to better explain my insight happened years ago. I was deployed to South Korea during a very tense time with North Korea. My unit was posted to a combined forces base with both American and South Korean forces. I was in command of my unit and was responsible for their productivity as well as morale. On one of the days off, we were headed to the city for rest and relaxation (R & R). After breakfast, we loaded up in the van and started to drive to the largest town nearby an American base. I was riding shotgun. After driving for an hour on small rural roads, there was a stoplight in the middle of nowhere between the farm fields where two rural roads crossed. We stopped at the light. The light had changed to green, but the car in front had not moved. Javier, our driver, felt they had moved; and he let off the brake, causing a minor fender bender. The van, being a big American-made van, was undamaged by the little Korean car. But the little Korean car was damaged. We had no one in our crew who spoke Korean, but we had little cards we carried in our wallets with statements written in English and Korean of key phrases. One statement was "Please call the police." We showed it to the driver, and a few of the other people gathered. Very quickly, strangely quick in fact, we saw and heard the police coming from a small village in the middle of some farm fields off to our right. The policeman pulled up and motioned for us to follow him. We were taken to the small village's police station . . . the biggest building in the town. The police spoke no English, and we could not speak Korean, so we did a lot of motioning. We motioned for the policeman to read the card that had both Korean and English phrases. One sentence listed the phone numbers for the base to which we were posted. He understood, and they tried calling the numbers; but for some reason, I think because it was a Saturday, the numbers did not bring help. The police were getting frustrated, and so were we.

The group of ten of us all sat around this table in a lobby as hours passed. We were still there, trying to have the police call the numbers for help, when lunchtime came. It was a small village, and there seemed to be only three policemen with no police work to do but deal with us. The wives brought in the policemen's lunch, and they motioned us aside and sat at a table to eat. So we went out by the van, which was parked in the front of the station. Lucky for us, a Korean college student walked by and, in English, asked what we were doing there as the village only had Koreans. He then offered his help. Quickly, he found out that the driver, Javier, was under arrest; but the rest of us were free to leave. So I sent everyone else back in the undamaged van to our base for help, and I remained behind to make sure Javier was treated well.

Although Javier was "under arrest," we were allowed to sit on the steps of the police building to wait. Javier and I were on the steps, and we were sharing a bottle of water between us. One policeman came out and stood by us as he smoked. Again, he spoke no English; but he watched Javier and I speak, observing how we spoke to each other. He watched us pass the water bottle to each other, and he could see the camaraderie between us. I had just sat the bottle down on my right when the policeman sat next to me and reached for the water bottle and took a swig. Both Javier and I were surprised by his action for two reasons. First, we had not offered him our water, and second, it was the first friendly act any of the policemen made toward us. He tried to talk to us, though none of his words were understood. There was awkward silence, and then he noticed my wallet photos. I'd pulled out my translation card out of my wallet in hopes it would help us communicate. He saw and motioned to the photos of my family stored in my wallet. So I showed him my wife and children. Then he pulled out his wallet and showed us photos of his family. There were big smiles and laughing as we each spoke about our families. The other two policemen came out and joined in. They pulled out photos of their respective families, and though no one understood the words spoken, we understood one another. There were more smiles and more laughs. I motioned for one of the policemen to take a photo of the rest of us with my camera. The photograph shows us all with big smiles, standing next to one another in brotherhood. We could not understand one another using language, but we were able to communicate using our shared of love of our children. It hit me then that we were all alike even though we were from different countries and cultures. We still had communality. Familiarity brought understanding. There is more to the story, but I'll close, stating all worked out well. Javier was free to return to duty.

Why my prison is likely better than many prisons nationwide, although there is segregation and discrimination, is because of our past exposure to people who look, act, and feel different from us . . . our *Extended Contact*. Our various military experiences, seeing other parts of the world and experiencing other cultures before being locked away, give us a broader perspective. We also work, play, exercise, and worship beside one another. This has all bred and cultivated familiarity . . . a brother and sisterhood of humanity. The story about the bully on the phone to his mother is also a story of familiarity. However, familiarity with a closed mind will not help. An old saying that clarifies this point is this: "A man or woman convinced against his or her will is of the same opinion still."[9] It takes an open mind and familiarity to push us to relook at our paradigms and prejudices and willingly cast them away. It takes effort to recognize our interbeing.

When I grew up, I was taught in school that there were three races: Caucasoid, Negroid, and Mongoloid. I was taught that these three races were from the offspring of the three sons of Noah. The three sons—Ham, Shem, and Japheth—took their three families and spread out from Mount Ararat, which is in Turkey, with Ham going south to Africa, Shem going northwest to Turkey and Europe, and Japheth going east to Asia. I was also taught that Ham's wife was black because she was a descendent of Cain, and she carried Cain's curse, which was black skin. Science has determined all what I was taught to be a myth. We are genetically all the same as stated earlier. Our human ancestors all likely originated in Africa over one hundred thousand years ago. There was no "Curse of Cain." Black skin and dark curly hair are genetic traits that helped people survive in the sun and heat of Africa, and the differences are mutations from the people who migrated out of Africa, who needed other traits to survive. Lighter skin generates more vitamin D needed in places where the sun shines less. Hair that lies flat is more helpful in keeping the warmth trapped against the body. Genetics has shown we are not descendants of Noah and his three sons and their wives. Yet that myth still exists and influences people's prejudices, beliefs, and close-mindedness.

Genetics has shown we are not descendants of Noah and his three sons and their wives. Yet that myth still exists and influences people's prejudices, beliefs, and close-mindedness.

Science has learned a lot in the last 150 years. Some of it is still rejected by people with closed minds—minds that have been conditioned by generations of culture, family, and friends, minds that don't use the Scientific Method, empirical data, or the peer-review process. Yes, science doesn't have everything right as there's continual learning. As a whole, scientists admit that there are still more to learn, and most scientists have an open mind to other possibilities based on evidence and data. However, the fear of the new *(Neophobia)*, *Confirmation Biases*, other traps and thinking errors, and prejudices also exist with scientist; and it takes effort to overcome this resistance to the uncertain. Still, as a whole, science has brought about great understanding. We understand that no one is all black, white, or yellow. Genetics shows us that no one has only African DNA markers as millennia of migrations and interbreeding have us all mixed together. While I recognize President Obama's black heritage, he's of mixed races and cultures, just like you and me. There's no such thing as a pure race or culture. Nature is constantly mixing things up.

I, too, am an African-American. That being said, the majority of my genetics are from ancestors who migrated out of Africa over fifty thousand to one hundred thousand years ago. I've joked with members of the "brother's section" that I'm also an African-American (though it's not really a joke). At first, they are taken aback and become defensive, thinking, "What's this white cracker saying?" When I explain what I'm saying, we both laugh, and understanding and familiarity take place. We're more alike (a lot more) than we are different. A former inmate, who's now out of prison, made a great statement one day. Brian stated, "Interact with people as if they are you and you'll find you will treat everyone better." Of course, you likely recognize his statement as the Golden Rule stated in a different manner. It's common knowledge that every religion has its own version of the Golden Rule. This is because it's a principle of life. While every religion has its own version of the rule, the cultures based on the religion, the societies, and numerous governments have many times ignored the rule and its principle with dire results. "Us and them" mentality generates segregation.

One of the *Cognitive Traps*, distortions, or thinking errors that comes to play in everything we've discussed so far is *Availability Bias*, which is defined as thinking that causes us to base our decisions on information that's more easily and readily available from our memories rather than the data we really needed to make the best decisions. Our conditioning is also "availability" generated. The availability of data provided by culture, family, and friends leads us to make decisions based on that data. Opening our minds, seeking other data, questioning any data we receive, and becoming familiar through experiences are the ways to overcome unfounded discrimination. There are not three races; there is really only one race . . . human. We may be from different continents and from different cultures and societies and with different traits and with different ways of thinking and believing, but we are still all human. Any extended contact proves it to us, as my anecdotal Korean story demonstrates.

Our world, again, is becoming one big virtual continent, one big Pangaea. With worldwide migration, travel, and communication, we're becoming closer and closer. Interbreeding between peoples of different countries and cultures is now commonplace. My children, for example, have heritage from many different European countries, from Native Americans, and from East Asians. Some of my children are married and have mixed things up even further. We need to stop looking at the differences and see how much alike we really are. We need to see how our capabilities are similar, both physically and intellectually. We all have amazing capabilities. It's just a matter of our focus. For example, historically, women have been considered the weaker gender. Yet the *Crossfit Games* on the TV's sports channels demonstrates otherwise. These "Amazonian" women are able to do amazing things that I'd be hard-pressed to do in my current state of conditioning. We're genetically alike, and all have great potential. Henry David Thoreau stated something, testifying to the fact of human capabilities, when he said, "I know of no more encouraging fact than the unquestionable ability of man to elevate his life by conscious endeavor."[10] To me, his words can be taken as our endeavor to overcome *Cognitive Traps*.

Seeing that we're more alike than we're different is the first step to ridding societies of discrimination and segregation . . . Familiarity stops the cycle. As mentioned, psychologists title "familiarity" as *Extended Contact Effect*, and recent studies show that mutual trust can spread between different racial groups as quickly as mistrust and suspicion. This mutual trust applies to any group and tribe, self-segregating or not. As Jonathan Haidt puts it, we can build trust and see things more clearly beyond ourselves by "turning off the Me and turning on the We."[11]

My wife and I came up with a family motto that said something similar. It said, "Think of We, not Me." Sadly, I violated my own family motto when I made my grievous mistakes. My thoughtless, selfish actions hurt my family . . . the very people I deeply love and was supposed to protect. My word and deeds didn't match, and they had caused great pain with my children. My remorse is still very high, and I work hard every day to "Think of We, not Me" to ensure I never offend again. I'm continuously working to make sure my words and actions align. For as Ashley Montagu taught, "The only measure of what you believe is what you do. If you want to know what people believe, don't read what they write, don't ask them what they believe. Just observe what they do."[12] My remorse drove me to take action to ameliorate the damaged I cause. My actions every day are still a testament to my determination to pay lifelong, full restitution and retribution.

As has been discussed thus far, it starts with us. As M. Scott Peck stated, "The whole course of human history may depend on a change of heart in one solitary and even humble individual—for it is the solitary mind and soul of the individual that the battle between good and evil is waged and ultimately won or lost."[13] Discrimination and segregation can only be eliminated by one person at a time, starting with you and me. It does feel too big for us to make a difference, but don't discount the power of love. My wish is this book, and this chapter, transmit a message to the wider world. As with bullying, compassion and kindness to others will make a difference in breaking down barriers. Familiarity or *Extended Contact Effect* is the next step toward living our daily lives using our higher-order thinking. We need and strive to overcome our fears.

We have to become comfortable in different groups. We each need to stop being afraid and expose ourselves to people whom we perceive as different from us. We need to get to know them and, in doing so, understand them. We need to break free of the cultural and familial conditioning that causes us to build walls versus bridges. We need to see that we are a very, very large tribe of humans, and all the perceived differences are minor and truly superficial. We need to see this with our higher-order thinking. We need to realize that anything less, any dichotomization, or divisions are for people who think with their archaic mind. I see a day when even prisons will not be segregated; that may also be the day when the need for prisons is gone or greatly reduced, a day when we'll see that love, compassion, and kindness is the antidote for people crying out for help. We'll see that helping them means accepting them for who they are, to include their flaws and foibles. We'll see that we're here on Earth to help *all* our brothers and sisters. We'll see that we're *all* bother and sisters in arms against segregation, racism, discrimination, and abandonment.

I'll close with a quote from the Zen Buddhist monk who is credited with bringing Zen Buddhism to America in the 1960s. Shunryo Suzuki advised us to break free of discrimination and segregation when he said, "Little by little, with patience and endurance, we must find the way for ourselves, find out how to live with ourselves."[14]

SECTION THREE:

MY INSIGHTS MORE PERSONALLY APPLIED

HOW CAN I BE HAPPY?

I ended the last chapter by quoting Zen Buddhist Shunryo Suzuki and his last words in the quote where we need to "find out how to live with ourselves." This begs the question, what is the state of being we want to live with ourselves? Most of us would answer, "We want to be happy." And since happiness is an individually determined condition, happiness is well within our control. Happiness is obtainable no matter our conditions or circumstances. Yet for many of us, happiness is illusive and seems unattainable. I can testify, being in prison, conditions and circumstances don't automatically influence in a positive manner, certainly with my pursuit of happiness. Yes, prison is a lonely place; and there's much sadness, suffering, and pain, but being happy in prison is still a choice . . . my choice. Ben Franklin said, "The U.S. Constitution only guarantees the right 'to pursue happiness.'"[1] It's solely our own choice to obtain happiness and to experience it. We all know a person who seems happy, even with the worst of conditions and circumstances, and we wonder and are amazed at "how they can still be so happy." This chapter intends to reveal those exceptional people's secret, and it'll answer my question to myself: "How I can be happy?"

As stated, prison is a very toxic, depressing place as all your rights and freedoms are taken from you; and those factors work to suck the happiness out of any given situation. However, not all freedoms are taken away as Viktor E. Frankl stated in his book *Man's Search for Meaning*, which tells of his experiences in the Nazi death camps, "Everything can be taken from a man but one thing: the last human freedom—to choose one's attitude in any given set of circumstances, to choose one's own way."[2] Being a pessimist or an optimist affects how we handle things when we've been dealt a terrible hand of cards, or when life has given us lemons.

Psychologists have done numerous studies on the power of optimism and pessimism, and they have found a direct correlation to depression and other health-related issues.[3] They've even gone further to categorize people as either *Dispositional Optimist* or *Dispositional Pessimist* because the test subjects were so consistent in their positive or negative expectations for the future. For example, the Life Orientation Test uses questions, such as the following, to determine the person's disposition:

> In uncertain times, do you expect the best?
> Do you believe that if something can go wrong, it will?
> Do you rarely expect things to go your way?

When life is going well, it's hard to tell the difference between the optimist and the pessimist; but when life presents its inevitable difficulties and challenges, people's disposition reveals itself. Prison is a time when people have hit rock bottom, and everything has been taken away but their last human freedom to choose. How we handle things when the chips are down (another poker metaphor) comes from what we tell ourselves . . . our *Explanatory Style*. Psychologists, using one of two tools, determine people's explanatory style: (1) the Attributional Style Questionnaire (ASQ) or (2) the Content Analysis of Verbatim Explanation (CAVE) technique. The ASQ has people rate a bad event as (a) personally caused, (b) permanent, and (c) pervasive. The CAVE, developed by Dr. Christopher Peterson, rates how the person explains bad events, rating the degree which the event is viewed as personally caused, permanent, or pervasive. In both cases, the events being rated or described are based on the person's interpretation . . . how they would view the situation if it were them. How we view the world around us influences our happiness. Reading this book is helping you imagine for yourself how it would feel if you had been sent to prison. People who take the bad event personally, see it as permanent and pervasive, are more likely to be depressed and feel helpless . . . It's hard to feel happy while feeling helpless and depressed. Trust me, I know!

Prison is a place where if you weren't feeling depressed or helpless before the events that led you to prison, you're sure to feel that way after your arrival, no matter your disposition. Prison itself is not a happy place. Then as we've discussed earlier, it's hard for people to be happy when they don't already like, accept, love, and have compassion for themselves, which prison works hard to take away from all people. Prison is pretty miserable when one is constantly being judged, discounted, and minimized; and that environment generates pessimism and bitterness. Pessimism also comes through the interaction with other prisoners. Pessimism becomes a virus . . . a *Social Contagion*. The prison condition allows all the *Cognitive Traps* we've discussed to more likely affect the person into feeling depressed. It also causes the person to negatively influence the world around each of them, spreading the virus. Therefore, as we've discussed, prison germinates bullying, manipulation, segregation, prejudice, judging, minimization, discounting, and people using one another, generating a negative cycle. The self-loathing inmates feel becomes widespread.

Just last night, I was helping a person write his appeal to the clemency and parole board's parole denial. In his letter, he discussed his self-loathing before he came to prison and its effect on him committing his crime. He went on to tell how his self-loathing grew and grew because of prison. He was not happy before prison, and prison had only made it worse for him. He stated that treatment had helped him overcome his self-loathing. However, I know by just watching him that he still hates himself. It's very apparent in how he treats others . . . He still bullies, gossips about people, and is generally sad and depressed all the time. Of course, being denied parole over and over only adds to his depression. In fact, being trapped with one's effort to escape, having no success (constant rejection), brings another mind trap titled *Learned Helplessness*. This *Cognitive Trap* is pervasive with prisoners. I myself am in a constant battle to resist it. The prison environment itself generates negative emotions and attitudes, no matter your disposition.

The *Learned Helplessness* theory came from a study by Dr. Martin Seligman in the late 1960s and early 1970s.[4] The studies put animals under a lot of uncontrollable stress. The animals were given a way to escape electric shock by moving to a safe area. When the escape option was taken away, they would continue for a time to search for a way of escape; but as time passed, they gave up and would just accept the shocks. The animals stopped trying to escape altogether. Then when a way to escape the shocks was reopened, the animals still would not even try to find a way to escape . . . They had "learned helplessness." The animals had learned that their efforts would be fruitless, "so why try?" Seligman and his team found that this also applied to humans when humans were confronted with stressful, uncontrollable, and persistent conditions. The human subjects also gave up and became passive even when the conditions changed. In prison, we call this *Institutionalization*. That topic will be covered in chapter 10, so I won't talk more about it here. However, I'll state I cannot even count the number of times I've heard someone say, "Why try? Why try for parole? They're just going. to deny me." "Why try to improve myself?" With a lot of time on my hands, I've plenty of time to ruminate things over and over, and needless to say, *Learned Helplessness* doesn't engender happiness. That being said, *Learned Helplessness* isn't the only reason why prison generates unhappiness, depression, and lower level life form thinking.

Prison, above other places, has a disproportionate set of unhappy people; and as we've discussed, that is because most people in here are using the other people around them. As we've discussed, using people, no matter your dispositional outlook, doesn't engender happiness. There are "friendships." However, most friendships are built on reciprocity and not trust, or true care, or compassion. To paraphrase Stephen Batchelor, the relationship are based on force, not integrity. I watch this every day as the majority of the relationships I see are based on someone using the other person. Sure, these are the same people who are laughing, joking, teasing, smiling, and seem jovial; but underneath it all, these people are not happy. They know they use one another and would be proud to tell you so. However, they're not satisfied and don't like who they are. With a depressive *Social Contagion* and *Learned Helplessness*, there's a lot of unhappiness in prison.

Being a user most likely brought the person here in the first place, and prison only reinforces that paradigm or *Coping Mechanism*. It reinforces that to survive, a person will do anything and hurt anyone. I'll repeat the Eckhart Tolle quote from chapter one: "The ego always wants something from other people or situations . . . It uses people and situations to get what it wants, and even when it succeeds, it is never satisfied for long." As I've stated, that was the case with me. I was only thinking of "Me" and not "We" when I committed my crimes. Alternatively, I was thinking "We" when I self-reported and went through treatment years before my trial and incarceration. Paraphrasing another quote in this context is human beings are created to be loved; things are created to be used. Problems start whenever the opposite occurs. We're again speaking of the *Hedonic Treadmill*. Sechibuwa, the eleventh-century Tibetan Buddhist master, taught, "Blame everything on the one thing: self-centeredness."[5] My self-centeredness caused the problems that got me here! My ego ruled my thoughts, emotions, and actions. Having discussed the above, **my Fear-based insight** is pretty obvious by now, *people who use people are not happy!*

Let me give some more examples to validate this insight. As mentioned, some prisoners pay for protection. It's a very overt transaction. However, others pay for protection or relationships subconsciously and covertly. Almost all prison friendships are strictly transactional. One inmate, who is from Central America, was not accepted into the Hispanic section for some reason. They would constantly harass him and take his stuff. Note, these were guys from his section, and their only stated responsibility is to protect people in their section. Yet they were the ones bullying him. He finally approached a fellow inmate at work, who was also in his pod but was in a different section. He asked his coworker for protection. An agreement was made, and he moved into the "brother's section," where he remains to this day. I don't know the agreement, nor would I write it if I did as that could bring trouble. My point in bringing up his example in this action was overt and very apparent because he was a Hispanic guy now in the brother's section. I've already mentioned another very overt transaction in chapter 4, with the guy with the Aryan Brotherhood tattoos from his last prison location. Transactional relationships are all around me.

Less overt and very common transactional relationships take place every day, all day, in prison. This starts out as just communication. People gather together and *talk* about other people. If a person bad-mouths someone that the group does not like, a bond is formed, and they all pile on their venomous statements. They are creating an "us and them" environment based on mutual dislike, which, as we've discussed, is really based on fear. People have conversations, and a tentative trust is established by what is revealed. In military prison, people's "war stories" are a very common topic discussed. In some cases, it creates a bond of trust if the stories are true, or they've had a shared experience. However, there have been people who have lied about their past, trying to look tougher than they really are. Most of time they are caught in their lie because someone knows someone, or some part of their story does not match reality. When that happens, the person is rejected and ostracized . . . I've witnessed worse consequences too. These people have ended up in "protective custody" to keep them safe. Now they're more restricted and separated.

Another example of how people use people is the dining facility and section seating in the pods. Although they state they are looking out for everyone, the heavies really just take care of themselves. They ensure they're not crowded in the dining hall, or they've the best seats and cells in the pods.

In the dining hall, they make sure they've no more than four people at their table, while the rest of the dining room has people sitting six to a table (note: all tables have six seats). This is mostly with the "white section" as it's the largest section in this prison, mirroring the per capita population of the military. The Hispanic and brother's sections are not as big and are not crowded. Yet they will not give up their allotted tables to relieve the overcrowding of the white section. The Hispanic and brothers consistently have empty tables, and that's even when they sit two or three to the six-man table. The heavies of the white, brothers, and Hispanic sections state they are looking out for the population; but in practice, they only care about themselves, and their actions show it. The prison administration could stop these practices, but they don't. Letting people segregate themselves is a way to keep the prison population disunited and weak. Thus, the institution enables and condones the practice. Remember, for example, my suggestion to rid segregation in my minimum pod. A fellow inmate from my pod was told by a heavy to stay away from me because of my suggestion. The thought of such a radical change obviously upset the people in power. Interestingly, I've been banned from sitting in the Hispanic section to watch their TV . . . I'm the only person to which this applies. Currently, I'm not banned from the bother's section, but I've been moved to the very back row of mine . . . the white section. My positive initiative brought out my podmate's darker side. It threatened their *Principle of Legitimacy.*

In the pods, each section has assigned seating controlled by the heavies. Where a person sits to watch TV creates a hierarchy within the section. It states who can control what shows are watched and who gets the best cell location. How people get placed in the section is determined by who sucks up to the heavies the best. The transactions can be how the heavies get special treatment by inmates for their laundry, how the inmates who work in the dining facility hoard food to give their pod bigger shares, or who "shares foods" back in the pod. There are many ways to "do dirt" as the transactions and favors are called. The fact that an inmate is willing to "do dirt" is also a sign of loyalty as they can get in trouble for doing so. By "doing dirt," or by being willing to fight, or by bullying the weaker people, an inmate builds up their credit, or "Cred," or prison trust. The "Cred" transaction can be as simple as waiting to walk to chow time together. Now all these transactional relationships are assessed and where people fit into the hierarchy can be determined. Where one fits in the hierarchy is what builds up one's ego. Yet it doesn't make one happy.

Not all heavies are completely self-serving. There are some who work to help people and work to keep the peace. However, these people are few and far between. For the majority of the heavies and their acolytes, the ego stroking (otherwise known as prison politics) goes on constantly. The transactional "friendships" determine the pecking order, and the pecking order determines who gets privileges. Prison politics even determines who gets to "volunteer" for positions throughout the prison. Examples are the people who brief the new people, people who are on the Inmate Advisory Board, people elected to the culture organization councils, etc. "Doing dirt" is seen as a badge of courage, which enables the transactional friendships to exist. Some prisoners brag they have a bag set aside in their cell so that when they do fight, they are ready to go into solitary confinement with their small bag of possessions. They are publicly stating to the GenPop that they are followers and are willing to accomplish a transaction to be accepted.

One time, when I first got to this prison, the heavies from one section in a pod ordered some people to fight another group. Since the one group of fighters was white and the other black, the facility was concerned about racial tensions. They locked the facility down for eleven days, while they found and punished the parties concerned; and while they determined if the fight was racially motivated. Yet in the years that have followed, the prison administrators have done nothing to change the existing segregation. To this day, they've done nothing to discourage the segregation.

In prison, there's a common, well-known saying: "snitches get stitches." This statement has even made it to American society's normal vernacular. So writing with more specific details is dangerous if it got into the wrong hands. That said, sharing more of the prison politics is my way of showing that the majority of the inmates are stuck on the *Hedonic Treadmill* as we've discussed in chapter 1. It also demonstrates the *Lucifer Effect* and the *Principle of Legitimacy* we've discussed in chapters 4 and 5. Building one's ego does not bring happiness, and if there is any happiness related to prison politics (using people), it doesn't last long. Thich Nhat Hanh stated, "If you are still bound and haunted by your projects, your fear, your anxiety, and your anger, you are not a free person. You are not fully present in the here and now, so life is not really available to you."[6] I've used prison examples to make my point; however, the ego building, *Cognitive Traps* of *Hedonic Treadmill, Lucifer Effect, and Principle of Legitimacy* all exist outside prison as well. They exist in almost every society, culture, family, and relationship; and they're all based on fear, not love. For each of us, what Robert Anton Wilson stated can apply when he said, "You are precisely as big as what you love and precisely as small as what you allow to annoy you (what you fear)."[7] If fear, which manifests as ego building, rules our life, we're small and unhappy. Boxing great Muhammad Ali summarized best when he confessed, "I conquered the whole world and it did not bring me true happiness. Every day is a judgment for me."[8]

Now that we've rediscovered that using people and "being self-centered," as Sechibuwa stated, is not going to bring my happiness or, in the words of Muhammad Ali, "true happiness," we are ready to find out together what does make one truly happy. Let's start with a quote from Mahatma Mohandas Gandhi. He said, "All activity pursued with a pure heart is bound to bear fruit, whether or not such fruit is visible to us."[9] Let's make his statement have a dual meaning. First, as we, writer and reader, delve into the topic of how to be happy, we start with a pure heart, ourselves. Second, we recognize that everyone who's seeking happiness must start with a pure heart. People who use people don't have a pure heart. We then need to recall the quote that states people are created to be loved, and we're moving in the right direction. Having transactional relationships will never bring us happiness because the transactions are not about love but are really about fear and scarcity . . . force versus integrity. I'll stoutly admit my mistakes were due to self-centeredness.

As we've discussed, not loving one's self is a barrier to loving others. However, for many, loving one's self is very, very hard, mostly because people live in a transactional world. Even though all the great masters have told us to love, including loving ourselves, self -loathing or other types of fear stand in one's way. We all, at one time or another, live with transactional relationships. As a reminder, I quote again from Zen master Thich Nhat Hanh. He stated, "Self-love is the foundation for your capacity to love the other person . . . your capacity for loving another person depends entirely on your capacity for loving yourself, for taking care of yourself."[10] Yet many of us cannot find anything to love about ourselves. Well, the adage "Fake it till you make it" applies in loving oneself too. In addition to loving ourselves (or faking it until we do), we've also already discussed that being kind is the way to overcome the bullies. **The Love-based insight** builds on earlier insights. My Love-based insight is *reaching outside yourself is the key to true happiness*.

While this insight is similar to the insight about kindness defeating bullies, there's a difference. The difference is this insight is focused on one's own happiness, specifically, how I can be truly happy. The sixth-century Indian saint Shantideva in his writings said, "All those who suffer in the world do so because of a desire for their own happiness. All those happy in the world are so because of their desire for the happiness of others."[11] To clarify, true happiness comes from the "desire for others' happiness." The empirical proof for this insight comes from one's own experiences. Think back in your own life to a time when you weren't really focused on your own happiness but were focused on another's happiness. How did you feel? A big contradiction with being kind and focusing on another's happiness, is many times, people can be kind for purely self-centered reasons. People can be kind to have reciprocity in a relationship, or to look good to others . . . Both are only ego validation. While kindness is good, starting with a pure heart and a focus on others, by giving of our love to make others happy, you and I will be truly happy. Also, being focused on other people's happiness is the fuel that makes kindness powerful enough to defeat the bullies. As mentioned, compassion and wisdom (a.k.a.: pure heart) generates kindness.

If polled, the majority of people would state that their happiness is their main goal in life. Many times, the stated objective of many of the world's religions is each church member's own happiness. It may be postponed until an afterlife, but it still is ultimately about the individual obtaining their own happiness. In my opinion, focusing on one's own happiness, now or later, creates a self-centered mind-set. That mind-set, no matter how kind the action, makes it so all actions a person does are really for themselves. The reader may read the above Love-based insight and interpret it that way. The principle of the Love-based insight helps us see that true happiness is only ensued through selflessness based on compassion and wisdom. In Buddhist teachings, they say, "Don't mistake the finger pointing at the Moon as the Moon." One's own happiness is the finger, and another's happiness is the moon (the objective). Ultimately, giving for the sake of giving is most gratifying, being kind for the sake of being kind is invaluable, and serving for the sake of serving is when you've succeeded. Reaching outside yourself means not being self-centered in any way. That may be confusing since you're to love and have compassion for yourself, first, to be able to properly love and have compassion for others. Yes, that's still true, but that does not mean you are the focus. (This is directly tied to chapter 4's Love-based insight.) Again, you're the finger.

You're one of many fingers. Serving others is the moon, or sun, or stars. All humans are interbeing and are to be loved. The Buddhist have a chant or mantra (in Sanskrit, "man" means mind, and "tra" means protection) called "The Four Immeasurables"[12] that states the following:

- May all beings be endowed with happiness and the sources of happiness.
- May all beings be free from suffering and the causes of suffering.
- May all beings never be separated from happiness that is beyond all sorrow.
- And may all beings abide in equanimity free from attachment and aversion.

This chant or "mantra" is asking the skillful practitioner to reach outside themselves to focus on other people's happiness, but note, you and I are part of "all beings." We need happiness and don't need suffering, just like everyone else. So it's not wrong to be happy though it's unskillful to seek your own happiness over others. By giving with no expectation of reciprocity, by serving just to serve, and by loving for no other reason than to love, we lose our sense of self in the process. We're not doing things to feed the ego. This is the powerful focus that generates happiness for all.

We're connected and interbeing with the "Whole," the "Big Picture," to "God" or "love." Renowned psychiatrist Carl Jung introduced the world to the concept of *Self-actualization*. Dr. Jung stated the following as the definition: "The full use and exploitation of talents, capacities, potentialities . . . I think of the Self-Actualized Man, not as an ordinary man with something added, but rather as the ordinary man with nothing taken away. The average man is a full human being with dampened and inhibited powers and capabilities."[13] Being self-actualized reconnects us with the Whole. It's that simple. Being self-actualized is directly tied to selflessness.

Let's now discuss how to put thoughts, attitudes, and emotions into actions. It's fine to sit and recite the mantra above if by doing so makes a person want to act. I attest that the mantra changed my heart. Two recent studies provide academic empirical evidence that giving and serving others brings about our own happiness. In *The Journal of Social Psychology* (2014),[14] researchers in the United Kingdom had test subjects take a survey measuring life satisfaction. The subjects were assigned into three groups. One group was instructed to perform daily acts of kindness for ten days. The next group was told to do something new each day over the ten days. And the third group was the control group with no instructions. At the end of the ten days, the subjects *focused on kindness* saw the highest boost in happiness and life satisfaction, next were the people who focused on doing something new, and last were the folks given no instruction and therefore went about their day just like normal. Reaching outside oneself with a pure heart is a state of mind, and "faking it till you make it" works on this too. Through mindfulness *(Metacognition)*, we can build our heartfelt compassion.

The next study was published in the *Journal of Happiness Studies* and was conducted at Harvard Business School in conjunction with the University of British Columbia.[15] In this study, subjects were asked to recall the last time they spent $20 or $100 on themselves. Other subjects were asked about when they spent the money on others. Both groups rated themselves on a scale measuring their happiness when spending the money. The researchers then gave all the subjects money with two choices: (1) they could spend it on themselves any way they liked, or (2) they could spend it on someone else. The only instructions given were to spend the money on whatever will make them the happiest. Also, the researchers added that their choice would be anonymous, just in case they felt pressure to be altruistic. The outcome was twofold. First, they found the subjects who remembered a time when they spent money (the amount did not matter) on someone else rated themselves happier than those who spent the money on themselves. Second, the happier that subjects felt about their past giving experience increased the chances they choose to spend the money on someone else. The study's lead author, Laura Aknin of the University of British Columbia, stated, "The practical implications of this positive feedback loop could be that engaging in one kind deed would make you happier, and the happier you feel, the more likely you are to do another kind act." We not only lose our sense of self, but we've also given ourselves a reason to love ourselves. You "fake it until you make it." Soon, your Love overflowing and a person who's happy no matter the situation (an optimistic disposition). Chanting a mantra or praying for another's happiness sets the intention; and then the act of kindness or selfless service becomes a *Social Contagion*. The following recent statistics prove the point:

- 68 percent of people who volunteer feel better physically.

- 89 percent of those who volunteered said it improved their feeling of well-being.
- 73 percent said it lowered their stress levels.
- 75 percent felt better about their employer.
- The happiest people are lifelong servers . . . Many live into their nineties.

The Buddha taught, "Thousands of candles can be lighted from a single candle, and the life of the candle will not be shortened. Happiness never decreases by being shared."[16] Don Miguel Ruiz stated, "The real us is pure love, pure light . . . Love in action only produces happiness."[17] Here in my prison, there are many examples of "outside" people volunteering to give service. The chapel has a great bevy of volunteers who come by monthly or weekly to minister to the inmates. One such person is Naomi. Naomi, a Cherokee by decent, has volunteered to the prison chapel for over twenty years. During that time, she was diagnosed with a tumor on her spine. This tumor is too dangerous to remove, so she's living with it and with the pain it causes on a constant basis. Yet she comes regularly to share her vivacious personality and zest for life with the Native American Studies group. Her attitude and outlook is always positive, loving, kind, and uplifting. We know she has her bad days, but we never see them. She is giving service in many ways inside and out of the prison. She has a servant's heart that blesses those around her. She's constantly reaching outside herself to bless other people's lives. She's influenced so many with her skillful means of service.

Another set of volunteers that have really blessed my life are Bev and Kirk. Over thirty years ago, they started the Catholic Fellowship Group ministry. Bev and Kirk ensured the group fellowshipped inmates from all religious backgrounds though most attendees are Catholic. They've blessed thousands of men over the decades. They've also influenced numerous volunteers who accompany them in their ministry, exposing people to inmates who changed their opinion (paradigms) of convicts in general. There have been hundreds of "outside" volunteers who've come once a week on Sunday night for ninety minutes to fellowship about twenty to thirty inmates. Last year, Kirk died. Yet Bev carries on with her team of volunteers. Ever since I'd met Kirk, who was in his seventies, he'd been fighting cancer; but it was a stroke that finally took his life. After his initial stoke, he fought hard to be well enough to continue to come visit the inmates, and he made it for a few more visits. Even though he'd slurred speech and struggled to express himself, he came for another month's worth of visits. Then his health got worse, and soon, he was too fragile to come. A month later, he finally passed away. Kirk and Bev and their stable of volunteers are happy, truly happy. Bev and Kirk embody happiness through service. Kirk's smile and laugh was infectious, and I always felt that he loved me unconditionally. His zest for life was and still is infectiously blessing me. Bev continues to give her pure heart with love enveloping the group.

Two years ago, I lost my dear friend Bill. Bill was a volunteer with a national prison visitation service that I'd signed on with my first year inside. For five years, Bill came to visit me on the last Saturday of every month. Bill, who was in his eighties, spent hours with me listening and talking; and our friendship was quickly formed. Bill would advise if asked, and he shared details about his life, including all his other service opportunities, and they were numerous and varied. He listened about all my relationships and the many subtleties of the prison culture. He was my confidant as I would tell him things about prison that I told no one else because they'd worry. On his last visit, he had trouble standing at the end of the visit. I had to catch him to keep him from falling. The next month, he did not show up; and soon, I received a letter, stating he was in the hospital with a terminal brain tumor. I did send him a card, thanking him for his love and service, but I didn't really get to say a proper good-bye. When I remember Bill, Booker T. Washington's quote comes quickly to my mind: "The happiest people in the world are those who serve others."[18] Bill was also truly happy giving selfless service, and he exuded love and optimism.

There are prisoners who also give service, some through formal programs put on by the chapel or the treatment professionals. Some are doing it for a reward—a better chance at parole—and some are doing it just to serve. Buddhist teacher Nagarjuma very simply said, "Without hope of reward, provide help to others."[19] The "outside" volunteers and many inmate volunteers are living by these principles. The inmates who give service with hope of reward are the ones who cannot hide who they really are through service. Their character comes through to those around them. I testify when you live with people 24 hours a day, 365 days a year, you experience who people really are. While I wish everyone gets parole, I know people seeking a reward for serving are not as happy as those who are self-actualized. As my teacher Lama Dorje stated, "One of the keys to feeling happy as the result of doing something for someone else is practicing non-attachment to the outcome . . . so, practice equanimity."[20] Having equanimity (accepting everyone and everything without judgment) is quite challenging though it's truly possible if we set our minds to forgetting our ego, if we truly become selfless, and if we recognize the love each of us has within ourselves.

While it's true that giving, serving, helping, and loving others all release hormones into our brains, stimulating the pleasure centers with dopamine, if the reason we are doing it is only for the temporary high the dopamine provides, we're really just stuck on the *Hedonic Treadmill*, again. While giving statistics and result of studies provides understandable self-serving reasons to give, serve, help, and love, if we are reaching outside ourselves only to benefit ourselves, we've lost the point. We don't want to get caught in the *Cognitive Trap* of the *Happiness Hypothesis*, which states there is a transaction required to balance the negative, meaning we can only be happy if the scale has more positive experiences than negative ones. This trap may bring temporary happiness (even service to others can apply here too); however, true happiness isn't transactional but is transformational. It's an attitude, a way of thinking, and an action derived from our attitude and thinking. Viktor Frankl wrote, "Happiness cannot be pursued; it must be ensued."[21]

As both anecdotal and empirical studies have shown, giving service to others engenders happiness; and I submit to you I feel it also generates an optimistic attitude, helping one to have *Dispositional Optimism*. Being *Self-actualized* is a matter of aligning one's attitude of selflessness with kind thoughts and actions. It's releasing what you already are . . . love. It's letting go of fear and enabling love. I know I need to build my compassion and wisdom through kindness. Love breeds my self-actualization. Two quotes summarizing this principle teaching are as follows:

Leo Rosten stated, "The purpose of life is not to be happy—the purpose of life is to matter, to be productive, to make some difference that you have lived at all. Happiness in the ancient noble verse means self-fulfillment as is given to those who use, to the fullest, whatever talents God or luck, or the fates bestowed upon them."[22]

Ralph Waldo Emerson wrote, "To laugh often and love much; to win the respect of friends; to find the best in others; to give of one's self; to leave the World a bit better; to have played and laughed with enthusiasm; to know even one life has breathed easier because you have lived . . . this is to have succeeded."[23]

Rather than focusing on being happy, it's more adaptable to be optimistic. While we may have a default setting to our disposition, I believe it can be changed. A *Dispositional Pessimist* can train themselves through mindfulness training *(Metacognition)* and a focus on love rather than fear. We all can be *Dispositional Optimists* by focusing on ways to help others, to give others service, to be kind to others, and to focus on another's happiness. We can expect to have good and bad times and good and bad events happen to us and others. However, through love, kindness, and compassion, things will only get better and better. Nothing is permanent or pervasive. Our *Self-actualization* will make a difference in this world. Of course, it isn't an easy task to be *Self-actualized,* constantly reaching outside one's self. It is, however, a simple one. Many masters and teachers have done it and are doing it. We have the same capability. We each can be masters, teachers, and saints even if we start small and keep building more into every action every day. Having a pure heart, being focused on giving, and serving and helping others are a big first step. Having a wise and compassionate, altruistic mind-set, without any expectation of payback, isn't beyond the common person. In fact, it's the common person (you and me) doing what's in our core nature that makes the difference for the Whole. Do it for our families, societies, and countries to continue to exist and thrive. *We must help each other!*

I commit to you, the reader, I intend to make a difference in the world.

MY FAMILY AND FRIENDS' CHARACTER

Early in this book, we've discussed how when a person is sent off to prison, it highlights that one is really alone. Also, we've established that a prisoner is cut off and separated from his or her family, friends, and support structure. Then we covered how other people react when one is sent off to prison and why, for many, the other people's reactions are the Fear-based type of judging, minimizing, and discounting versus the Love-based type of realizing that everyone is good; and yet they'll make mistakes. Then in chapter 4, we've talked about abandonment, segregation, and ostracization all due to the *Cognitive Trap, Aversion Reaction*, among others. In this chapter, I'll bring what's been previously discussed generally, to me personally. While I've revealed these concepts and philosophies on a broader sense, I've not explained what it taught me about the people whom I've relied on for love and support . . . in many cases all my life. This chapter will discuss relations lost and gained. I'll discuss how I've been surprised by many people's reactions, while others reacted exactly as my experience with them would lead me to predict. Yet as we've discussed, neither response is fundamental to their character. As we've learned, all of us are capable of causing ourselves and others pain; and we're capable of being selfless, kind, loving, and compassionate. But first, I'll cover why having family and friends is so important on all levels.

We've already discussed how compassion, cooperation, and communication has given humans an evolutionary advantage. I'll state the obvious here for clarification. It's with small groups (family and friends) that this advantage was realized for many, many millennia right down to today. As a matter of transparency, I'll state this is very applicable to me and my family and friends. The tribe mentality is alive today in one's group of family and friends and is a healthy survival mechanism. Families and friends are a good thing. Yet paradoxically, our close relationships are also our greatest source of emotional pain. Many times, people in our tribe, family are "the one" easiest to see, using Mother Theresa's sentiment, who need our help and for whom we're quick to come to their aid. Yet they're also the ones who break our hearts and cause us the most emotional pain. Additionally, studies show close relationships influence how long and how healthy we'll live.

Dr. Lisa Berkman of Harvard has conducted numerous studies on the subject of how social networks affect life and death. In her Alameda County study,[1] she took more than four thousand participants of adults ages thirty to sixty-nine with a follow-up study seventeen years later. Questions were asked about the marital status, extent of contacts with friends, church membership, and involvement in other types of formal and informal groups. During the nine-year study and supported by the follow-up study of the same individuals seventeen years later, the results showed that people with a smaller social network were twice as likely to die than those with a larger social network. Additionally, researchers examined relationships by asking whether the person feels loved or cared for, has a confidant, is satisfied with his or her supportive social relationships, and if they feel lonely. The discrete support networks can be broken down into four categories:[2]

Emotional support: help with emotional difficulties or upsetting situations or communication of caring and concern;

Instrumental support: help with getting routine tasks accomplished, such as providing transportation, helping with chores, babysitting, or assisting in an emergency;

Financial support: help with economic needs; and

Appraisal support: help with evaluating and interpreting situations or with problem-solving.

The bottom-line finding of all the studies are that those of us who rate their social connections as relatively high have, on average, more positive emotional lives, are more physically healthy, and live longer than those who rate them low. In fact, the effect of social networks and relationships can have the same magnitude effect on our cardiovascular health as traditional risk factors, such as smoking, high cholesterol, obesity, excessive alcohol use, and lack of physical activity. If you have a trust-filled support system, you and I are likely to be happier and to live longer.

Our family and friends aren't only our support; they're the people we know best in the world. However, being human, they too can surprise us with their actions and reactions. I know my family and friends were surprised by my illicit and hurtful actions because they were so out of character for who they thought I was. Though their surprise is completely understandable because my hurtful actions were very anomalous to the vast majority of my life's actions. Yet their surprise shouldn't have surprised me. Really, it's no surprise. Everyone can and will make mistakes. The paradox mentioned above comes into play with all our human interactions. As we've discussed in chapter 3, a *Theory X* mentality leads one to think everyone is bad and has to be forced to be good. *Theory Y* mentality leads one to think everyone is good but bound to make mistakes. Therefore, if we view our support network and social structure with a *Theory X* mentality, we're more likely to be very surprised when a "good" person makes a mistake. We're more likely to judge, discount, and minimize that person, thinking they're rotten at their core. We're more likely to commit *Fundamental Attribution Error* with its "all or nothing" thinking toward our family and friends. We go through life thinking we know a person, but really, we don't. Admittedly, we barely know ourselves. Reminder: *Metacognition* (meditation) helps us learn about ourselves. Our family and friends are people we know well or best. The majority of the time we can be assured that what we've observed, thought, and felt about them is pretty accurate.

But just like how my family and friends were surprised by my actions, I was surprised by many of my family and friends' reaction, though I shouldn't have been. I, too, committed *Fundamental Attribution Error.* My surprise has been based on the fact that I thought they knew me. I thought they knew my actions were anomalous and that my honorable amelioration actions after my hurtful mistakes were the true testament of who I am. This has been the case for many. But for some of my family and friends, my hurtful actions became *who I really am*; and nothing else, past or present, could make up for my hurtful actions. I mentioned in the last chapter when I wrote about the *Happiness Hypothesis.* Using the *Happiness Hypothesis* as one's basis for determining happiness leads people to look at life as a scale. On one side is positive experiences, and on the other is negative experiences. I've read about a survey on the *Happiness Hypothesis* subject: people reported belief, using this scale mentality, that a person who murders someone must do twenty-five acts of "lifesaving heroism" to balance the scales (make up for their crime).[3] For some of my family and friends, they've viewed my actions using a scale mentality, most likely unconsciously.

Dr. Stephen Covey teaches in his book *The 7 Habits of Highly Effective People* of a concept he calls the Emotional Bank Account.[4] He likens all relationships to individual bank accounts to which our actions are making deposits and withdrawals with every interaction. The more deposits we make into the individual relations' accounts, we build a high account balance. This enables the inevitable withdrawals not to cause our "accounts" (relationships) to go bankrupt. Obviously, for some of my family and friends, I didn't have a high enough account balance to offset the major withdrawal that my hurtful actions engendered. I understand the "balance" concept in both the *Happiness Hypothesis* and the "Emotional Bank Account." Also, I understand that it's the other person who determines the value assigned to each deposits and withdrawals. I myself understand that I assign the value to their deposits and withdrawals as well. The value of anyone's Emotional Bank Account is based on the individual's thinking and feelings, which (as we've discussed) can be and are influenced by many *Cognitive Traps*. Obviously, this fact applies to me too. With all that "accounted for" (pun intended), I've still been surprised by many of my family and friends' reactions. I've felt their reactions are a revelation into their character. **My Fear-based insight** is *coming comes to prison, one finds the true character of one's family and friends.*

My intent with this chapter isn't to call anyone out but to discuss *Fundamental Attribution Error*, character, and loss. Though loss of freedom, possessions, and status are obviously losses because of incarceration, I'm speaking of relationships lost. The examples I'll give will show that prison causes significant relationship loss, lessening one's support structure. In most cases, if not all, I don't know why I've lost the relationships I have because communication with those individual has also been severed. So I'm left to wonder why. Naturally, I've come up with guesses to the motivation for their abandonment and estrangement. To put it in other words, I judge "their character or attributes." In some cases, the relationship seems to be completely lost (meaning I doubt we'll ever have communication again), seems temporarily lost (meaning communication is likely to come back sometime in the future), or partially lost (meaning communication has. been severely damaged and may or may not ever recover). I'll state, for the record, to which is one of the things this book is intended to serve. I intend to have all my relationships reinstated, and I'll always work to that end. Please note, I'll not be telling every story of relationships I've lost.

Furthermore, as already mentioned, I've been and still can be guilty of Fear-based *Cognitive Traps* myself. For example, I can fall into *Fundamental Attribution Error* trap when I report that losing them through abandonment and alienation is a reflection of their character. However, in reality, I'm aware that there are many factors, conditions, and contexts that are influencing my family and friend's reactions to my incarceration . . . most of which I'll never be aware. That being said, I do know that when one comes to prison, one finds out who their true friends are. Nelson Mandela put it bluntly when he said, "Many people will appear to befriend you when you are wealthy (successful), but precious few will do the same when you are poor (disgraced)."[5] Marc Angel wrote, "Making hundreds of friends is not a miracle. The miracle is to make a single friend who will stand by your side even when hundreds are against you."[6] He also wrote, "When you're up, your friends know who you are. When you're down, you'll know who your friends are."[7]

To frame possible context, for those of my family and friends whom I've lost, I'm thinking that they may be judging the severity of my crimes by comparing it to what they know of sentences assigned by a civilian court. However, my convictions were from a military court and are known to be triple what most likely would've been adjudged in a civilian court. I know about this sentence disparity because I've looked at the Federal Sentencing Guidelines, I've read newspapers stories on similar crimes, and I've reviewed reports from the Department of Justice. However, the majority of my family and friends don't understand the sentence disparity; and therefore, they may be basing their judgment of me to be harsher than is warranted using the *Happiness Hypothesis* as their guide. Please understand when you read this paragraph that I'm not stating my crimes were not serious or hurtful. I know they were! I'm framing people's reactions to better understand them.

Moreover, before I tell any stories about my family and friends (to frame the context of their reactions), I'll acknowledge that the majority of them have received their information concerning my crimes by word of mouth. Exceptionally, some of my family and friends have directly communicated with me to hear my side of the story and have chosen to continue to communicate with me despite my criminal conviction. Or I've some who have never asked me for any details because it doesn't matter to them . . . They'll support me no matter what. To me, my family and friend's reaction is evidence of their character . . . not proof. Really, to paraphrase Marc Angel, the miracle is that any family and friends stick by you when one is sent off to prison because the very purpose of prison is to separate. And prison is very effective in destroying good relationships.

Also, to be clear, I don't want to misrepresent my situation. I have many, many loyal people who are providing emotional, financial, and appraisal support; and they'd give instrumental support if I were not trapped in prison. I've many people (my son, father, stepmother, brother, sister, stepbrothers, stepsisters, aunts, uncles, cousins, nieces, nephews, and friends) who're "showing me they love me." To paraphrase another Marc Angel quote, "Anyone can come into your life and say how much they love you. It takes someone really special to stay in your life and show how much they love you."[8] Thankfully, I've a handful of friends who meet the definition of friend outlined in the following C. S. Lewis quote: "All of us should strive, therefore, to have some friendships that are deep and solid—so solid, for instance, that if they were interrupted, the unfinished conversation could be resumed months later almost in mid-sentence. Just as if we had never been apart."[9] Even with prison, not surprising to me, I've fiercely loyal family and friends. Every day I count my blessings. I know many of my fellow inmates who've no one on the outside.

All the people I've listed thus far have demonstrated evidence of their true character in my eyes. They've shown their high-order, *Theory Y*, thinking. They've shown me loyalty though I've flaws and foibles. They've worked to be Christlike and to fulfill their Buddha nature. Unwittingly, they're following the advice of Thich Nhat Hanh when he said, "We must learn to be one another with understanding and compassion, to hear what is being felt by the other."[10] They're also following a Mother Theresa quote that says, "We must make our homes centers of compassion and forgive endlessly."[11] Yes, with my deep heartbreak, I've considered suicide. However, my family and friends have helped me through very difficult times. For me, the people who've stood by me despite my crimes are people who are *living miracles*. They're people I seek to emulate, and they contribute to my peace and happiness. Despite my amazing level of family and friend's support, in my effort to guide us to my Love-based insight, the following are stories of my losses:

The first loss story is about a person who was a very good friend before my trial. After I'd been in prison for almost two years, my friend contacted me by e-mailing my son to arrange a date to visit me. I'd tried to contact him when I was first locked up and received no response. However, in the e-mail to my son, he told my son he wanted to visit me before he moved to his next military duty station. We arranged the date, and on the morning of his scheduled visit, I went to the visitation area and waited. After thirty minutes, the guards told me I had to go back to the pod and wait there. I went back to the pod and called my son, asking if I'd the wrong date or whether he'd e-mailed to reschedule. I did have the right date, and there had been no word as to canceling or rescheduling. Now I was worried my friend had been in an automobile accident on his way to visit me. My son sent an e-mail and did receive a reply a week later that my friend was all right, but he was no longer coming to visit me. I asked, through my son, for his new address so I could write him; and he didn't give it. I'd my son repeat the request a couple of times with no reply. What changed? I don't know. Sadly, there has been no word from my former friend, and now our relationship is lost. I intend to attempt to reconnect upon my release.

I've another friend who wrote me for three years. One summer he wrote that he was moving but didn't tell me his new address. The communication stopped. Not having his new address, I didn't know what to do other than write him a couple more letters, hoping they'd get forwarded to him. Three years later, he wrote me and apologized for breaking off communication. He explained the reason was his wife voiced her opinion that by being my friend, he was condoning my crimes. To keep peace with his wife, he just let our relationship fade away with the move. However, he'd a change of heart, and we've been communicating again for a few years now. I was very sad to lose my friend, and I'm extremely glad all isn't lost. We're reconnected, and he's still married . . . All good.

When I was first locked up, one of my many, many cousins wrote me a letter. It was a nice newsletter, and it seemed to me she wanted to have contact. I wrote a letter back, stating I was very glad to be in communication with her as we'd been close when we were younger. She'd moved recently; and her newsletter, with an accompanying family photograph, told of her family's comings and goings. In my letter, I wrote her, acknowledging her family's news and telling her I always was excited to hear about her family. I never received another letter from her. I've sent her holiday cards every year as I've done with my other numerous family members. I wrote a straightforward letter, asking her why she doesn't write me back. Yet I've never heard from her since that first newsletter. It saddens me that I may have lost our relationship. However, her newsletter has been more than I received from the majority of my cousins. Also, of my uncles and aunts, I've one uncle who'll not communicate with me. I've written him and my aunt numerous times, but other than telling my father that he's heard from me, no other effort has been made to communicate directly with me. I've written numerous times with no response. All his children are also nonresponsive. I don't know what's been said about me to my cousins, but I know one thing: I'm out-of-sight, out-of-mind for the majority of my cousins. Though most people aren't close to their uncles, aunts, and cousins, I'd always had a great relationship with mine; so it's been very sad and painful to have lost the love and support from those who've chosen to judge and abandon me. I'm working to recover all my lost relationships and will do so upon my release.

When I was growing up, my siblings and I were very close. I can even remember my cousins commenting on how close my family was compared to theirs. It struck me as strange because I did not see it from my perspective . . . We were just normal. Although now, looking back, I know I was very blessed to have such a great family. Sadly, that has changed in the last two decades. To this day, I don't understand why. Yes, the families have gotten bigger, and the siblings have shifted into focusing on their own children and grandchildren . . . This is normal. It could also be the loss of my mother to Alzheimer's over sixteen years ago as she was surely the glue that bound us together. Additionally, my coming to prison also has created a wedge among my siblings themselves, and some with me. With my younger brother, we were very close when we were growing up; but once the teenage years hit, we drifted apart. In addition, when I got married after my first year of college, our relationship really struggled. As with all my siblings, over twelve years ago and insights I had with my counseling sessions with Greg, I really tried to build and strengthen my relationships with all my siblings . . . to make more "emotional deposits." Being in the military and serving overseas, I'd let my wife communicate for me and the family, even with my siblings. I wanted to change that, so starting over twelve years ago, I made many overseas phone calls to reconnect, to include my younger brother. However, I was too late with him, and our communication has been extremely sparse during my many years in prison. I've written and called him, but the relationship is very tense. He's made it very clear that he wants nothing to do with me, telling my father that he'll never support me because of my crimes. He has basically abandoned me, which causes me much pain.

Although it does not completely surprise me with my younger brother, because of my limited deposits to his "emotional account," my eldest brother is a different story. We were always very close even as adults. He was one of my advisors (providing appraisal support), and although I, too, abdicated most of my communication to my wife, he and I were still very close. In 2005, when I was struggling with what to do about how to get help, I would call him. He was the one who helped me have the courage to confess to my wife, even though she and I were really struggling with our marriage. He enabled me to self-report and to get professional help. For a few years afterward, we were still close; but when my wife and I separated, I perceived he started to pull back and take sides. Finally, once I was convicted, he seemed to back away even more and has only really given the bare minimum support of birthday and holidays cards. It even took him almost six years to come visit me even though he flew over my location many, many times on his cross-country trips. The loss of our close relationship has been very painful for me. Without his love, wisdom, and advice that permeated our close relationship for many, many decades, I feel betrayed. I really valued his appraisal support . . . It'd be helpful now. Of note, he just recently visited me again.

One of the most painful for me is the loss of my children. All, except my eldest son, have followed their mother in her efforts to alienate, minimize, and discount me. While I understand to a great extent the embarrassment and hurt they must feel, they are also very aware of my honorable amelioration efforts that started going on twelve years ago. Yet they have chosen to listen to their mother and have abandoned me. Please know I will never give up on them! However, I only can do so much, especially from prison. Now the loss is even greater as I have grandchildren who have never met me and most likely don't even know I exist. My heart has been broken and has no sign of mending without them in my life. While I know I let my children down, I also know that I have been a strong example to them of a person, who when that person makes a mistake, admits it and works very hard to make things right. Dr. Stephen Covey stated, "It is one thing to make a mistake, and quite another thing not to admit it. People will forgive mistakes, because mistakes are usually of the mind, mistakes of judgment. But people will not easily forgive the mistakes of the heart, the ill intention, the bad motives, the prideful, justifying cover-up of the first mistake."[12] Other than my eldest son, it seems to me that somehow my ex-wife has been able to take the powerful Love-based lessons my children had learned from my example and turned into a lesson of fear. I did not know about it before my incarceration, but I have since learned about Parental Alienation Syndrome (PAS)[13] introduced by Dr. Richard A. Gardner back in the spring of 1991. (This will be covered in chapters 14 and 15.) I've learned that *my children are victims of PAS*. Although PAS is permanent in most cases, I have strong intentions that I'll be reunited with my children and grandchildren again. I'll forever work toward that end.

The last very painful loss I'll write about is the loss of My Sweetheart as I mentioned in the introduction. After my wife and I separated, I met a wonderful woman with whom I felt a real connection. I told My Sweetheart of my grievous mistakes and my honorable amelioration efforts for the years afterward, and she still accepted me for who I am. By telling her, I was able to help her see the kind of man I am, and she really loved me. I know we loved each other very much, and we became deeply committed to each other. Even after the trial, My Sweetheart stuck by my side. She promised to stay with me through the long haul, and she did stay with me for four and half years. She deserves a lot of credit for staying with me for so long, as the negative effects of prison are very strong. Once, after I had been locked up for three years, a fellow inmate shared with me that his wife, who had stayed with him for five years, was now leaving him. I felt very sad for him, and it made me fear I'd lose My Sweetheart. I shared my fellow inmate's story with My Sweetheart, asking her if she thought it could ever happen to us. She said to me, "That is not us! We are not them! We are stronger and more special than that. Our connection is very strong at every level, and our love is very deep. Don't worry, I'll never bail on you." A year and a half later, after all my legal appeals were done and she knew for sure I'd have to serve my whole sentence, it became time to bail. Somehow our "specialness, our strength, and our connection at every level" was not enough. The first signs of the weakening were the visits started to be more infrequent and letters became a once-a-month thing and soon, only four times a year, and the last sign was she was not feeling well when I'd call her on the phone. Abruptly, she called it off, stating, "It's not you or anything you've done. It's the situation. You have been great and have really tried. You've done everything you could. However, I can't do this! I don't think we can even be friends. Don't waste stamps to write me or my family." Being in prison, I was helpless to even be able to fight to save our relationship. Many years have gone by. We have written each other a couple of times, and I was allowed to send birthday cards to her, to her children, and to her mother; but our friendship is very tenuous. She has written, "I'm on another path now." For me, I've lost my best friend and another family when I lost My Sweetheart. It has been very painful . . . I lost the person whom I felt was my soul mate. There is a quote from a Steve James's crime novel titled *Opening Moves* that applies. The main character, Patrick Bower, says, "Only when you love someone enough to let her walk away and not hold it against her, have you found the truest form of love . . . but then it is too late."[14] All these stories help set the stage for **my Love-based insight: *pain happens, but suffering is a choice: both pain and loss are our teacher.***

I tell all these stories of losing many of my family and friends knowing I am a lucky one. The majority of people in prison have lost most, if not all, of their support structure . . . especially with long sentences. Here are three quick examples: (1) John has the support of his mother, but all his siblings and beyond have abandoned him; (2) Joe just left prison and had no place to go because none of his family would give him support. He found a church-sponsored transitional housing over one thousand miles from any relative; and (3) Dave's family had completely rejected him, so when it came time to get out, he moved to a major city on the opposite coast. Most states and the Federal government have contracts with transitional housing commonly known as halfway houses. Sadly, the reason there is a need for transitional housing and transitional helping agencies is because there is so much loss of support experienced by prisoners. There is a 67.8 percent reoffense rate, per the Department of Justice, and lack of support is a large factor in preventing ex-cons return to prison.[15] Famous author Richard Shelton quotes that "71% of formerly incarcerated people cited family support as a key factor in helping them avoid returning to prison."[16]

Loss is common in prison as it is everywhere. That said, it is greatly magnified in prison. We all lose relationships through death or some other means of separation. Loss causes pain, just as I demonstrated by sharing my painful stories with you, the reader. Each of us has painful experiences all throughout our lives. Around 2,600 years ago, the Buddha taught in his First Noble Truth that life is characterized by pain. The Buddha stated, "When touched with a feeling of pain, the ordinary uninstructed person sorrows, grieves, laments, beats his breast, and becomes distraught. So he feels two pains, physical and mental. Just as if they were to shoot a man with an arrow and right afterward they were to shoot him with another one, so he would feel the pain of two arrows."[17] In Buddhism, the "instructed person" is the person who's been taught that the "second arrow," the arrow of mental suffering, is optional. Put another way, "pain is unavoidable, but suffering is optional." Recent medical science has backed up this ancient teaching. Pain is experienced in two separate parts of the brain. The Posterior Insula registers the actual sensation of pain, and the Anterior Cingulate Cortex registers the pain's unpleasantness . . . It puts meaning to the pain. Morphine, for example, doesn't stop the physical pain; it affects the meaning our mind gives the pain. Also, we, with our minds, can change the meaning of the pain, but it takes changing our mind-set and a lot of practice.[18]

The "instructed person" is taught that to benefit from pain, any type of pain, one must change the meaning of the pain. In the eleventh century, the Geshe Langri Tangpa (a previous Dalai Lama) came up with "Eight Verses for Training the Mind." The one I repeated over and over when I lost My Sweetheart goes as follows: "When someone whom I have benefited or in whom I have placed great trust and hope, harms me or treats me in hurtful ways without reason, may I see that person as my precious teacher."[19] This mantra was a powerful tool for me to change "poison into medicine" using a metaphor the Buddha taught. It's amazing to recognize that medicines are really poisonous, especially if they are wrongly used. The same is true with life's inevitable pain and subsequent emotions. Deepak Chopra taught, "Pain isn't the truth, it's what you have to go through in order to find the truth."[20] I've, personally, found a lot of truth going through the pain described.

My mother's death and the loss of my children, My Sweetheart, many family members, and many friends could all be poisonous to me if I choose to cause myself mental anguish . . . to suffer. That doesn't mean I should ignore the emotions or mask them. Steve Jobs stated, "When you have feelings like sadness or anger about your cancer (he had cancer) or your plight, to mask them is to lead an artificial life."[21] Buddhist don't teach the masking of feelings. For thousands of years, they've been teaching we need to change the meaning by changing our perspective. It means what Sufi poet Rumi sang, "Grief can be the garden of compassion."[22] Changing our perspective can help us both recognize and influence our emotions. Caedmon Aisquith said, "The pain will only worsen if I permit myself to wallow in it."[23] Luckily, pain helps generate compassion for others.

Letting pain become a teacher is not normal to our archaic, reptilian, mammalian brain. It takes higher-order thinking. Our natural "fight or flight" instincts are powerfully embedded and take real effort to change. Paradoxically, it is our larger, greater societies and civilizations that increase the chances for relational pain. I have an Australian friend, living in Australia, who wrote me once while I've been in prison; but despite my numerous letters to her over the years, she has not written back. Without air travel, I'd never have met her and her husband. Without airmail, keeping in touch would not have even been an option. The telephone, Internet, and social media bring with them greater relationship opportunities, and greater chances for pain caused by lost relationships.

I joke with fellow inmates, my family, and my friends that prison has me stuck in the 1970s with only a pay phone and mail to be able to tend to my relationships. Nelson Mandela wrote of his prison relationship tending experience when he stated, "I saw my letters to her (Winnie Mandela) as love letters and as the only way I could give her the emotional support she needed."[24] Like Mandela, I'm working on my relationship with what I've got. I've been trying to be emotional and appraisal supportive for my family members and friends. As Eckhart Tolle wrote, speaking of the way to think, "Well, right now is how it is. I can either accept it, or make myself miserable."[25]

The same higher-order thinking that has enabled vast civilizations also creates greater challenges to maintaining relationships. However, higher-order thinking also provides the solution by the power of our thinking and imagination. We can accept our plight and then give it the meaning we need to turn the poison into medicine. We can accept our pain and then make it purposeful. One thing that helps us accept our plight is the knowledge that life is ever changing or, to use the Buddhist's word, impermanent. Having an *Optimistic Disposition* is made easier, knowing things don't last.

The Buddha's Second Noble Truth is just that. We suffer and are dissatisfied because we want things to always be good and to never change.[26] There is a Sufi story that fits Buddha's Noble Truth. It goes like this: There was a king who asked his wise men to give him a statement that would be applicable to every situation, both good and bad. The wise men were stumped for a time, and they retired to talk it over among themselves. After a day or two, they asked for an audience with the king to reveal the answer to his command. In the great hall, with all of the king's subjects listening, they revealed the king to the statement he was looking for: "And this too shall pass!" Interestingly, most of us have heard or used that statement without ever knowing of its origin. More interesting is we only apply that statement to bad situations. It is used as a statement that says, "This is bad, but it can't last forever." Yet the statement applies to everything . . . Nothing will last, pleasant or unpleasant. By accepting that fact, our mind becomes a more powerful tool.

By knowing that everything will change and is impermanent, which takes higher-order thought processes, we can become less possessive and attached to everything, which, by the way, is the Buddha's Third Noble Truth.[27] We can accept that there will be pain, but suffering is a choice. We can accept that being in prison, like being a king, will not last forever. Caroline Myss stated, "The goal of becoming a conscious person [becoming a Buddha] is not to outwit death not become immune to disease. The goal is to be able to handle any and all the changes in our lives—and in our bodies—without fear, looking only to absorb the message of truth contained in the change. The physical world and our bodies are teachers."[28] This insight helps us have more equanimity.

The uninstructed person "suffers and experiences" two arrows. All of us, including me, go through life wallowing in our pain and suffering, at least some of the time. As Don Miguel Ruiz wrote, "Humans are addicted to suffering at different levels and to different degrees, and we support each other in maintaining these addictions. Humans agree to help each other suffer."[29] Everyone's character is made up of *Cognitive Traps* like *Loss Aversion*, *Pain Avoidance*, *Availability Bias*, *Hindsight Bias*, *Fundamental Attribution Error*, and many more. Alfred Alcorn said, "People who are encouraged to see themselves as victims remain victims; and to keep opening a wound is to stay wounded."[30] Being a victim can become a person's identity. People with a "Victim mentality" keep arrows embedded to continue to feel pain and suffering. Subconsciously, they want mental anguish. Sometimes people will twist the arrow in the wound to enlarge it and to feel more pain. This too prevents healing and a scar to grow. Unless we all change to see pain as a teacher, to see loss as a teacher, to see a broken heart as a teacher, and to see by not accepting one's emotions, one is not really "living an authentic life." One, you and me, will always be a victim. As a victim, people will always be unhappy even if it is hidden deep inside.

We all hear about the "scars" people have as if scars are a bad thing. Interestingly, scars are a good thing . . . Skin is tougher and more durable as a scar. Being scarred is what makes us who we are. No one will go through life unscathed and unscarred. Seeing pain and loss as our precious teacher and our medicine applies a dressing on the wound and lets it heal to become a scar. Reopening wounds days, weeks, or years later is unproductive and is living in the past, not the now. Most of the time, people who encourage others to be victims or to keep their wounds open are doing so for their own personal agenda . . . not to be of benefit to the person being manipulated. A sign of one's family member or friend (or therapist) higher-order thinking, concern, and compassion is they encourage you to keep the wound clean, dressed, and bandaged so it can heal properly. This is done through being love-focused and by identifying one's self as a survivor, not a victim. Your loved ones encourage you to heal . . . They celebrate your scars with you.

People's character and attributes are not static and, like all things, can and will change. "And this too shall pass" applies to people's character and attributes too. Holding this statement to our hearts, we will avoid the pitfall of making *Fundamental Attribution Errors*. While it is important to think of everyone with a *Theory Y* perspective, part of the perspective is people are bound to make a mistake because everyone is subject to change. The prisons are full of good people who did bad things. But their character is also subject to change. An Irish proverb applies here that says, "Time is a fair and just teacher." To paraphrase Caroline Myss, we need to be able to handle the changes that will come in time. The Love-based insight is also one of unconditional love. Seeing everyone as our teachers allows us to accept them for who they are. It allows us to forgive major withdrawals and debts. It allows us to be humble and realize we don't have all the answers because we too are subject to all the *Cognitive Traps*.

Being "awake," "enlightened," or "a Buddha" means we see the truth in all things; and that truth is the message pain and loss will teach us if we are awake. A reminder as to what Rumi sang, "Grief can be the garden of compassion." Grief can be the medicine that saves your life and prepares you for your death. Grief happens in every moment of every day as each moment dies and is reborn.

I'll close this chapter by confessing that there are many, many days when I've gone to my cell and just cried into my pillow. The dreams of my pain and losses are so vivid and palpable that there are so many times when I wake up at 2:00 a.m. with my heart beating wildly, sweating, and I feel like screaming. I've been devastated by the lost relationships that grind my heart into fine dust. Yet seeing it all as my precious teacher has provided me with strength and courage. My grief has enabled me to unconditionally love those who've hurt me, intentionally or unintentionally. I've learned my view of people's character is very limited and shallow. At the same time, I've learned on whom I can trust and rely. My last quote's author is unknown. It says, "Throughout your life, you'll meet people you'll later forget about, and many people you'll meet also forget about you. Your friends are the ones who won't let you forget them and who in turn always remember you."[31]

I've experienced great loyalty and serious betrayal, and both have enlarged my compassion. My intent of sharing my pain described in this chapter with you, the reader, is to help you see how you too can change the poisons in your life into healing, life-giving medicine. Both of us, you and me, need to face life's challenges head-on, not making any excuses. And looking back, we pull each other along life's muddy path.

MY OWN CHARACTER

Thus far, I've shared my philosophy and my insights that have occurred because of my incarceration. While I've used prison and other experiences to assist in explaining both my philosophy and my insights, I've not explained what I've gleaned specifically about me. That's the topic of this chapter—insights into my own character. I'm sure it was obvious to the reader before reading this book, but I'll restate the obvious: coming to prison is very, very, very hard. I'll confess it's been extremely tough for me. It's been a large challenge in my already challenging life. Being in prison has affected my every thought, emotion, mood, and attitude. Being in prison has had a profound effect that's completely changed the trajectory of my former life. I've witnessed that most of the time, prison changes people for the worse, making them bitter. Some become very, very bitter.

Notwithstanding that potentiality, prison has provided me the opportunity for personal growth . . . to find out who I really am . . . I've chosen to be better. Dr. Martin Luther King explained this point by saying, "The ultimate measure of a man is not where he stands in moments of comfort and convenience, but where he stands at times of challenge."[1] As John Chatterton stated, "When things are easy a person doesn't really learn about himself. It's what a person does at the moment of his greatest struggle that shows him who he really is. Some people never get that moment. 'What I do now is what I can.'"[2] Prison has been just such an opportunity for me. Quoting a man who knew, very intimately, how prison affected him as well as millions of others, Holocaust survivor Viktor Frankl stated, "People forgot that often it is just such an exceptional difficult external situation which gives man the opportunity to grow spiritually beyond himself."[3] Now having quoted several wise people, I'll state **my Fear-based insight,** which is as follows: ***prison and other very difficult life experiences, enable a person to really find out their true character.***

The reader may ask themselves why this is a Fear-based insight as understanding one's self is a good thing. My answer to this question is that fear is what prevents people from finding out their character, and many people will miss the opportunity. Fear causes one to mask what they find or to avoid it and to endlessly carry on in ignorance. Finding out one's true character can be very scary, especially for those who don't really like themselves. We fear facing the little Hitler in us. We fear knowing we're also subject to the *Lucifer Effect*. The other aspect of why I've characterized the insight as a Fear-based is that going through the difficult time is in itself painful, over and above the added fearful aspect of finding out one's character. Difficult times generate fear. This is the side that applies to me . . . Prison is a scary experience, as was my trial. No one wants to have such challenges to find out what one may or may not like about themselves and their character. I'd rather have had a different challenge from which to learn. Nonetheless, Viktor Frankl put it best when he wrote, "An old person should think 'Instead of possibilities, I have realities in my past, not only reality of work done and love loved, but of sufferings bravely suffered. These sufferings are even the things of which I am most proud, though these are things which cannot inspire envy.'"[4] Even knowing Dr. Frankl's wise statement doesn't stop the fear.

I know my prison experience doesn't inspire envy. I closed the last chapter sharing a confession of how the loss of several relationships have deeply affected me. Losing relationships has been very hard on me. I've also shared about losing the relationships with two of my brothers. Serendipitously, just last night, I was talking to another inmate. He's a young man, the age of my second daughter. Actually, I was listening to him rap about his prison experience. In his song, he was pouring out his heart, describing the loss of his brother, who has abandoned him since he has come to prison. I told him that through his words, I could really feel his hurt and stated I could relate because of the loss of my bothers. He asked me to share with him the story behind the loss of my brothers, and I did. Having just prepared the outline of this chapter, I also had the quote from John Chatterton above fresh in my mind. So I shared it with him, and we worked together to mutually motivate each other. We helped each other continue our resolve to leave this place "Better, not Bitter."

Before we can go on to discuss my learning, I'll define the different types of learning as defined by psychology. First, there is *Explicit Learning*, which is defined as consciously learning the sequence, which is stored in our *Explicit Memory*. *Explicit Memory* stores things we can verbalize and has two subdivisions: *Semantic Memory*, which stores things we "know" but don't know when or how we came to know them, and *Autobiographical Memory*, which stores our memories of events in one's life. Then there's *Implicit Learning*, which is defined as learning that takes place outside of one's awareness (i.e., how to walk and speak), which is stored in our *Implicit Memory*, storing things we don't consciously know. So we have conscious and subconscious learning. Both, however, can be broken down further into *Experiential Learning* (learning by experience), which can be broken down further into either *Capitalization Learning* (the experience is easy and obvious, and one seems to have a talent for it) or *Compensation Learning* (the experience is really hard; and one has to encounter, struggle, adapt, and be flexible to overcome perceived limitations).

Having spent many years in prison, I've had all the above types of learning take place; and I'll share my *mostly Explicit, Experiential, Compensation Learning* with you. Some learning has been from formal classes or treatment groups, but most is from the work I've done during many years' worth of mindfulness training *(Metacognition)*, conducting introspective self-assessment. Thankfully, most things have been *Explicit, Experiential, Capitalization Learning*. They're easy to understand. Others not. Another function of this book is my attempt to capture things I've learned through experience and mindfulness techniques.

So what have I found out about myself and my character? The first thing that was reiterated to me is I'm also susceptible to all the *Cognitive Traps* that have been discussed so far and others not discussed. My susceptibility existed prior to prison, of course. To give some background of who I was before prison, I'll tell a story. I was working for a general as his protocol officer. He, his vice commander, and I were standing on a tarmac, watching as a distinguished visitor's plane departed. The general and the colonel were saying that in high military circles, the people in those circles very often defined one another by a single word or phrase. I now call this "The Attribution Game." The general explained to his vice commander, "I do this for everyone, both higher and lower in rank." They proceeded to play the game with the distinguished visitor we'd just farewelled. Boldly, I asked the general what his word or phrase was for me, and I was told that my defining phrase was "eager to please." I didn't ask for clarification as that phrase can have duplicitous meanings. However, I've chosen to take his words as a compliment. I did work very, very hard as his protocol officer. Also, I've had numerous people throughout my life tell me I'm "happy-go-lucky." I'll add that coming to prison has changed me from both of those defining phrases. I'm no longer as eager to please, nor am I as happy-go-lucky. My trial and prison experiences have made me more cautious and distrusting of people and systems, which may come across as bitter.

Notwithstanding, I do feel I'm an optimist. When I was first married, my mother-in-law had a stroke and an aneurysm. My father-in-law was very pessimistic about everything . . . I'd say he was "dispositional pessimistic," and his wife's prognosis only heightened his disposition. Everything was a battle for him, and he was constantly complaining and catastrophizing about everything. On the other hand, I was an optimist, and it drove him crazy. He'd tell me, "You're young. Just wait, life will change you to be a pessimist." While I know I'm not as happy-go-lucky as I once was, I still have my optimistic disposition. I'm still working to make a difference in· this world. I'd say that I have an outlook that agrees with Henry David Thoreau, who wrote, "Love your life, poor as it is. You may perhaps have some pleasant, thrilling, glorious hours, even in a poor house."[5]

For this book, I asked some family and friends to describe my character prior to coming to prison in one word or phrase. Some of the attributions I got were words like "loving," "organized," "fun-loving," and "adventuresome." As an example of the word "adventuresome," before my trial, I made the determination that I was going to look at prison as an adventure. I knew not very many of my family and friends had been to prison, and I was going to have a very unique experience. I knew I was going to plead guilty at trial, and therefore, I'd no doubt I was going to prison. Therefore, I shifted my upcoming situation to be a challenge rather than a crisis. This shift in mind-set has served me well. It's helped me be courageous. I was still scared, and I still am to this day. Regardless, I know my courage well. It was my courage, coupled with remorse, that almost twelve years ago inspired me to confess my grievous actions. It was my courage that motivated me to plead guilty in the spirit of honor, truth, repentance, and restitution. Thomas Stanley said, "Courage is taking positive moral action that conjured up fear."[6] My courage helped me handle some very tricky human interactions where I've been in grave danger. Nelson Mandela wrote, "The brave man is not he who does not feel afraid, but he who conquers that fear."[7] After years of prison, I've learned I'm courageous even in the face of grave personal discomfort and danger.

For example, one day a few years ago, I had three people come into my cell to attack me. There had been a misunderstanding, and to resolve it, they chose *Physical Aggression*. I didn't cower but "stood resolute" as described in the Shelly poem. I talked to them calmly and firmly, telling them I didn't intend to fight, but I was glad to talk through whatever issue they were upset about. They were not going to talk . . . Their intent was to attack! But one of them heard what I'd said, and he literally stepped back to consider my words. The other two bullies behind him stopped, following his lead. Instead of beating me up, he started to yell at me (Relational Aggression) to intimidate me. I calmly asked what was the problem. Still yelling, I was told I'd broken prison protocol, and I had to be punished. The other two people took turns yelling at me. One guy (the guy I recently wrote about helping with his parole appeal letter) weighs about 350 pounds and was so red-faced with his fists clenched that I thought he might have a heart attack. His spittle was flying out of his mouth as he spoke. My knees were shaking as I knew I couldn't win a fight if all three of them attacked, but I stayed calm and talked through the issue. After they'd calmed down too, we came up with a solution that would allow them to save face and punish me for my breach of prison protocol. I'd used my courage to bravely stand up to them, facing danger. I'd calmly defused the *Physical Aggression and Relational Aggression.*

I've learned that there are safety in numbers but that I'm also very strong by myself. I know my defaults are not hate, anger, and aggression; but are love, reason, and intelligent resolution. However, these types of characteristics aren't highly respected in prison because of lower life form thinking that results in bullying as the default among the bulk of the population. That said, sadly, I too have succumbed to lower life form thinking since my incarceration. I'd this one person who was just being annoying and harassing me, just to be funny for his friends. I was having a very tough time as I'd just lost My Sweetheart and as my clemency request was denied, yet again. So to avoid confrontation and violence, I asked another inmate to talk to this person and let him know I was not in the mood to be trifled with because of stuff I was going through.

His conversation with the perpetrator did work for a few days, but then the immature acts started back up, and it really got to me. I went to him myself and asked that he stop. His response was "You don't tell me what to do," and he threatened me. I told him if he wanted to take the threat further, then he could meet me in my cell. He came to my cell, ready to fight, and I was not calm and resolute. I stood there ready, and he could see it was not going to be an easy fight. So he backed down, and we didn't fight. Though my default is reason and peace... I too, can become angry and sometimes let fear rule my actions. I'm not proud of this story, but it did force this bully to back off. I've learned I'm vulnerable to lower life form thinking when I'm emotionally weary. John Addison taught, "You've got to win in your mind before you can win in your life."[8]

Before I came to prison, I was already working to master my mind and thinking. Though when I came to prison, I was introduced to Eastern philosophy and mindfulness practice. I learned how to meditate in its various forms. I started to "win in my mind." I've learned, through *Experiential Learning*, how to change my mind-set, which helps me better control my emotions, attitudes, and moods. I've learned how powerful of a tool my mind can be. I've watched as I've fallen into the *Cognitive Traps*, but I'm spending more time in an observer mode, enabling me to be less reactive. From my counseling and treatment years ago, I learned that my thinking errors were the reason I committed my crimes. Even back then, I'd learned some tools to help me control my attitude, thinking, and actions. However, mindfulness training has been the capstone and keystone, all in one, to my mind's protection. I do know I'm wiser. Sri Nisargadatta wrote, "When I look inside and see that I am nothing, that's wisdom. When I look outside and see that I am everything, that is love. Between these two my life turns."[9] Both before and in prison, I've learned to seek *wisdom and love*, making them central to my actions. I've shifted from love's *Scarcity* to its *Abundance*.

I've learned that "I'm Love," also that I'm naturally a *Theory Y* thinking person. I've learned that all attributions are not fixed and that though the "Attribution Game" is a nice and easy shortcut in a very busy, populated world, I'm also (when I play the game) subject to error. Additionally, prison has revealed that I don't easily become abusive or bully, nor do I easily become a follower bully. I've learned that I don't naturally or automatically use *Relational* or *Physical Aggression* when dealing with others, but being rational and peaceful is my go-to *Coping* method. That said, I'm not afraid to stand up for myself. In the immortal words of Michael Jackson, "I'm a lover, not a fighter." I've learned that being kind and considerate is very natural for me.

Serving others is my default setting. I've avoided "doing dirt" though it has detrimentally affected my prison standing . . . I'm a man of integrity. Also, I've learned that I rationally and irrationally suffer from *Athazagoraphobia* (fear of abandonment); but I've not changed my core nature of love, compassion, and forgiveness to prevent being abandoned. As an extrovert, my relationships are very important to me. I've learned that I had a *Scarcity Mentality*, especially when it came to love, which, in turn, influenced my *Loss Aversion* when it came to losing my primary relationship, my wife. I know from my *Explicit Memory* that when my criminal offenses happened, I was letting my fears rule my attitudes, my thinking, and my actions. I've learned *Explicitly* and *Compensational* by changing my mind-set, I am able to rise above my fears.

Dr. Jampolsky's book taught me years ago that "Peace of mind is our single goal."[10] While it made sense to me back then, after coming to prison and starting in earnest my mindfulness training, it has come to mean much, much more. The Buddha said, "Everyone is the master of himself, he is the oasis he can depend on; therefore, everyone should control himself above all else." The Dhammapada, Buddhist wisdom scripture, states, "There is no fire like passion, no loss like anger, no pain like the aggregates (combination of the two), and no ease other than peace."[11] In my life, I'd let my fear and self-centeredness rule my actions, which caused me to offend. I was fearful and crying for help back then, but now peace of mind is my goal and is well within my reach. I feel love deeply. I am love, and my Love-based actions have brought my peace of mind.

Through meditation, I've learned to master my mind, my thoughts, my emotions, and my actions. I'm not a master practitioner, but I am a practitioner. I've been able to face my greatest fears, my worst nightmares, and my saddest losses because of mindfulness practice. Gen. George Patton is quoted as saying, "Now, if you're going to win the battle, you have to do one thing. You have to make the mind run the body. Never let the body tell the mind what to do; the body will always give up."[12] Another quote, whose author is unknown to me, stated, "The truly free individual is free only to the extent of his own self-mastery. While those who will not govern themselves are. condemned to find masters to govern over them."[13] Why I'm in prison is because I did not master myself. Yet while in prison, I'm free because I have . . . How powerfully ironic and paradoxical. Benjamin Franklin stated it another way: "He is a governor that governs his passions and is a servant that serves them."[14] Additionally, Leo Buscagila stated, "There are two big forces at work, external and internal. We have very little control over external forces (none in reality), such as tornadoes, earthquakes, floods, disasters, illness, and pain. What really matters is internal forces. How do I respond to those disasters? Over that, I have complete control."[15] Henry David Thoreau wrote, "Direct your eye inwards and you'll find a thousand regions in your mind yet undiscovered. Travel these and be an expert in home-cosmography."[16] I have peace of mind because I know I've done all in my power to make things right, especially for my crimes. To me, having peace of mind means I could die right now and know that I have lived my life as well as possible.

For example, I was locked up in a location where there was overcrowding; and at first, I was in a two-man cell as the third man. The facility provided me with a plastic cot, which was nicknamed the sled, and I had the sled on the floor next to the fixed, steel cots in our cell. As the facility got more crowed, I was moved to a different overcrowded pod, a mini-pod that was made to house four people. There were two narrow cells that held two people each and a connecting room where the TV and table acted as the pod's activity and dining area. The room with the TV was a 12 feet by 12 feet room, enough space to bring in four more sleds. With eight people, there were only two toilets, one in each two-man cell. The people on sleds had to ask permission from the people who lived in the cell to use one of the two toilets. One day in the middle of the day, I needed to use the toilet. The one cell had its occupants still inside, sleeping, as they had worked through the night to fix breakfast for the prison. The other cell had both occupants awake and out of their bunk area. One was working in the kitchen in another part of the prison, and the other was watching TV, sitting at the only table. He was the bully of the pod, and sitting next to him were two other sled occupants who served as his follower bullies. He lorded it over the sled occupants that they had to ask his permission to use his toilet. Since the other people were sleeping in their cell, I didn't want to stink it up for them. So I asked the bully to use his toilet. He responded, "No. Use the other toilet." I told him why I didn't want to use it, but it didn't matter to him. I continued to try and reason with him, to no avail. I knew the right thing to do, so I did it. I boldly walked past him and used "his toilet," knowing there would be trouble. After I flushed and washed my hands, I walked out and sat at the table across him, looking at the TV, but ready for what was to come. Then he said, "I'm going to kill you," and he and his followers attacked. They held me down as he strangled me. Before I blacked out, I felt nothing but peace. My mind was at peace, and I was ready to die. I'd lived my life honorably. Quickly, my mind reflected on my whole life. I also remember thinking, "I'd taken honorable actions for many years to set things right for the hurtful things that my crimes had caused." While I had remorse for my crimes, I had no regrets, having lived a life well lived. In those split seconds, I reviewed and knew in my heart that all my loved ones knew I loved them. I don't know how long I was out or how close to death I really came. In spite of it all, I recovered, and a tentative peace was restored to the pod. The aggressors, having almost killed me in the twisted prison way, respected me more for standing up to them. However, the point of this story is I had peace of mind even in the face of death. I've learned both explicitly and implicitly how important peace of mind really is . . . It enables one to face death regret-free. As was discussed at the end of chapter 1, regret is a Fear-based emotion, but remorse is Lovebased. Having peace of mind requires all of us to work to improve ourselves and everything around us using remorse, courage, and repentance as our motivation, not regret. Even a *Theory Y* mind-set accepts that mistakes happen. We've all made mistakes, and we'll make more mistakes.

This is a fact of life, of being human, of being alive. While all animals make mistakes, humans, even with our higher-order thinking, sometimes can make thoughtless errors. One such event happened to me since I've started writing this chapter. In prison, we're counted over and over. For count, a person is to be in their cell or another designated location. Before this particular count, I was on the phone, having a really good conversation. Of note: The public announcement (PA) system in my pod had been intermittently effective. Sometimes it was really loud, other times not; and other times, it didn't work at all. Yet the PA is our source for the booth to give commands. Since it was intermittent, the inmates also listen for the call on the radio the floor guard carries. It isn't very loud, but if one is listening for it, one can hear what the radio is telling the booth to command over the PA system. I, being on the phone, deeply listening to the person on the other end, didn't hear any PA announcement (it didn't work), nor did I hear the guard's radio announce the "five-minute," "one-minute," and "conduct count" call. After the "conduct count," the guard came up behind me and told me to get off the phone. I immediately responded to her command and went to my cell. Though I'd quickly complied, once I'd become aware, it was too late. After count cleared, I was taken and put in solitary confinement for a few days. My point in telling this story is to point out mistakes can happen because of thoughtlessness or conditions and circumstances well beyond our control or influence. Not all mistakes, or crimes are done maliciously. With mistakes happening all the time, thoughtlessly or maliciously, we need to forgive ourselves and move on. We have to forgive ourselves on a daily basis. I'll repeat, remorse is compassion-focused, and remorseful repentance is wisdom-focused. Seeing what happened is important to be able to see where change needs to happen. However, it doesn't do us any good to beat ourselves up. One principle taught[17] by Don Miguel Ruiz is that humans are the only animals that beat themselves up a thousand times over for one mistake. This brings me to reveal **my Love-based insight:** *I need to love, to have compassion for, and to forgive myself continuously.*

So there I was, sitting in solitary confinement with just a plastic mattress and a toilet to greet me. I was upset, of course. I was frustrated that the guards didn't give me any benefit of the doubt as to why I was still on the phone when count started. I knew it was common knowledge about the pod's PA problems. My mind flooded with thoughts of how this circumstance was going to affect my future in negative ways. I had to calm down, so I sat on the mattress and meditated. For a time, my mind would not calm down, but I was able to settle down physically. Slowly, I was able to shift into "observer mode." My emotions were still very active. My fatalistic thinking was in high gear. I was experiencing but not learning. The good news was my mindfulness training enabled me to purposefully shift into an *Explicit Learning* mode. I consciously thought to myself, *What am I going to learn from this? How can I make this experience purposeful and meaningful?*

The first realization was I had to love, to have compassion for, and to forgive myself . . . and the guards. Then I was be able to settle my mind a bit better, and I was able to adjust my attitude and affect my emotions. It was not an easy process that night as the guard kept checking on me every fifteen minutes, preventing me from falling asleep. My mind finally shifted into low gear, and sleep came.

When I listen to my loved one on the phone as they tell me about the struggles in their lives, my compassion is always heightened. I'm having compassion "for the one." I love these people, and I don't want them to have pain or to suffer in any way. I give my best effort to provide them *emotional and appraisal support* as defined in chapter 8. One thing I tell them, after acknowledging their pain, is "Give yourself a break." Through this statement, I'm seeking to help them see that they're doing the best they can, given the situation they're in. As stated context and circumstances do matter, but more important is how we handle the adversity. So there I was, in solitary confinement, giving myself the same advice from the observer mode. I knew I didn't intentionally violate "count"! I knew I'd not heard the announcements though I didn't know for sure why. I had to "give myself a break." My peace of mind was at stake.

Self-forgiveness is critical to our *Self-efficacy*, how we view ourselves. As stated, before self-reporting my crimes, fear was driving my fatalistic thinking for my future as my spousal relationship was crumbling. However, shifting to love, compassion, and forgiveness back then took fear's power away for me. There's an old Japanese proverb that says, "The iron-ore in the blast furnace thinks itself senselessly punished, but the tempered steel blade looks back and knows better." Our experiences shape us and make us who we are. The old man in Ernest Hemingway's book *The Old Man and the Sea* stated, "But man is not made for defeat. A man can be destroyed but not defeated."[18] The blast furnace of life can destroy us, but it'll never defeat us unless we let it. I've learned through life's hard knocks *(Compensation Learning)* that I can't be defeated.

During my treatment over a decade ago, I was voicing my remorse to Greg, my counselor. This was about six or seven months into my counseling sessions. My family and marriage had been seriously affected by my actions, and my deep love for them was motivating me through the treatment process. Speaking of my wife's suffering because of my hurtful actions, I told Greg, "I did not want to hurt her anymore." I knew my wife was suffering, and my love for her made me want to take the suffering away. Greg could see on my face and in my voice my concern and love for my wife. He stated to me, "You are no longer hurting her. She's the one hurting herself." He was right. By ceasing my hurtful actions, by confessing, and by getting help, I'd stopped hurting others. I'd taken the honorable, right steps. The suffering she was experiencing was her choice alone. Reflecting what Don Miguel Ruiz taught, I was beating myself up a thousand times over for the same mistake. I'd also mistaken her choice to suffer as something I'd caused.

However, as we've learned, "pain happens, but suffering is a choice." Greg helped me see that I could forgive myself; I could love myself, and I could have compassion for myself because of the honorable steps I'd taken. He helped me see that I could have peace of mind, knowing that I'd done the right things. By having love, compassion, and forgiveness for myself, I was now better able to have love, compassion, and forgiveness for others. I learned that I, just like my wife, had the choice to suffer or not. When I came to prison many years later and I read Don Miguel Ruiz's *The Four Agreements*, the lesson was refreshed, helping me deal with many life challenges.

As I was sitting there in solitary confinement, I was able to forgive myself for my accidental error that'd brought me there. I did Tonglen meditation, starting with me. I breathed in my pain and suffering and breathed out love, compassion, and forgiveness. Then I expanded the meditative intentions outward. I thought of my loved ones and their challenges. I thought of my estranged loved ones, and I recognized their pain and suffering. Soon, I was not wrapped up in my own circumstance but was sending love all over this planet to billions of people. I was able to gain control of my own suffering . . . still acknowledging the pain that sitting in solitary confinement caused, knowing that the situation could impact my future in some negative way. I was also able to see that I don't really know what the outcome would be. For example, being down in solitary had many unintended consequences, many that I'll never know, as the ripples will last much longer than my short life. Writing about my solitary confinement experience will have ripples that go on for generations, even if this book is never publicly published. It may be only how I reacted to my circumstances, or how I treated others because of those circumstances that have caused the ripples.

Quoting the book *Way of the Peaceful Warrior*, Dan Millman's wise character, Socrates, stated, "It is better for you to take responsibility for your life as it is, instead of blaming others, or circumstances, for your predicament. As your eyes open, you'll see every circumstance of your life, in large part, has been advantageous to you."[19] Also, Po Bronson stated, "We're not identified by what we do—our identity is anchored in what we've had to overcome to get there."[20] These quotes teach that we really just don't know what every action and circumstance really means. Since we can't know for sure what our actions and reactions mean, they may or may not be a bad thing.

In a book titled *Thanks for the Feedback*,[21] the authors bring up a very good concept to help us navigate the complexity of life. The concept helps enable us to love, to have compassion, and to forgive ourselves. As stated, we'll all make mistakes, and we'll receive negative feedback concerning our actions or reactions. These "grades," are determined by others and by our ourselves as we see the outcome of our actions. Obviously, we need to learn from our mistakes, or we're going to repeat them. Therefore, it's important to listen to the feedback, including our own internal dialogue. It's okay to accept the score or grade we, or the other person, gives us, but for our mental health and self-efficacy, we need to give ourselves a "second score."

Our second score is based on how we handled the feedback, or how we learned from our mistakes, or what lessons we learned about ourselves because of the event or circumstances, or what steps we took after our own realization, etc. For example, my hurtful, criminal actions years ago earned me an "F" grade. No question! However, my honorable actions since have earned me an "A," to include my trial and prison time. My life isn't made up of one single grade but my grade point average (GPA). This "second score" concept gives us a second chance and enables us to better forgive ourselves. We are able to rise above our past mistakes, to live in the present moment that enables us to adjust the trajectory of our ending, whatever that may be. Stated wisely, Maria Robinson said, "Nobody can go back and start a new beginning, but anyone can start today and make a new ending."[22] We can't change past grades, but we can improve our GPA. Each day, we begin anew . . . It starts right now!

Prison has taught me a lot about myself. While I'm sure there was another less painful way to learn these lessons, I'm glad that I've used my trial and prison experience to make myself better. I'm grateful for this unenviable, challenging time of my life. I'm grateful for the many years of mindfulness training and practice. I'm grateful for the knowledge of how strong, courageous, loving, and peaceful I really am. I'm grateful to know more about my character, and I look forward to learning more with each moment's challenge. I'm grateful for my peace of mind. I've had a unique adventure that no one else has had quite like mine. It has truly been an adventure. To reflect on my analogy from chapter 2, my uniqueness, discussed in this chapter, caused by my life's various trajectories and struggles, has made me a smooth, polished, and valuable stone. I may not have "Straight A's" or a "4.0 GPA," but I'm confident I'll pass life's final.

I'll close this chapter with two quotes and an analogy: Firstly, Carl Jung taught, "The only thing that really matters now is whether man can climb up to a higher moral level, to a higher plane of consciousness, in order to be equal to the superhuman power which the fallen angels have played into his hands, but he can make no progress until he becomes very much better acquainted with his own nature."[23] Lastly, famed Western writer Louis Lamore wrote, "Up to this point, a man's life is shaped by environment, heredity, and movement and changes in the world around him. Then, there comes a time when it lies within his grasp to shape the clay of his life into the sort of things he wishes to be. Everyone has it within his power to say, 'This' I am today, 'That' I shall be tomorrow."[24]

As to the analogy, recalling the Japanese proverb stated in this chapter, we are like the blade; and life's challenges are not only like the blast furnace. Life's challenges are likened to a sharpening stone. If we're not angled right as we *pass* over the stone, we're not sharpened; in fact, we're dulled. Being angled wrong, a person in prison, or facing any other of life's challenges becomes dull (bitter). Mindfully and courageously facing prison and all the other various, difficult life's challenges, we can and will become very sharp . . . We become better. We continuously need to be mindful of our angle to keep our edge sharp. Carl Jung and Louis Lamore's statements lead me to realize, think, and feel that *I'm responsible to adjust my angle* to the sharpening stone of life.

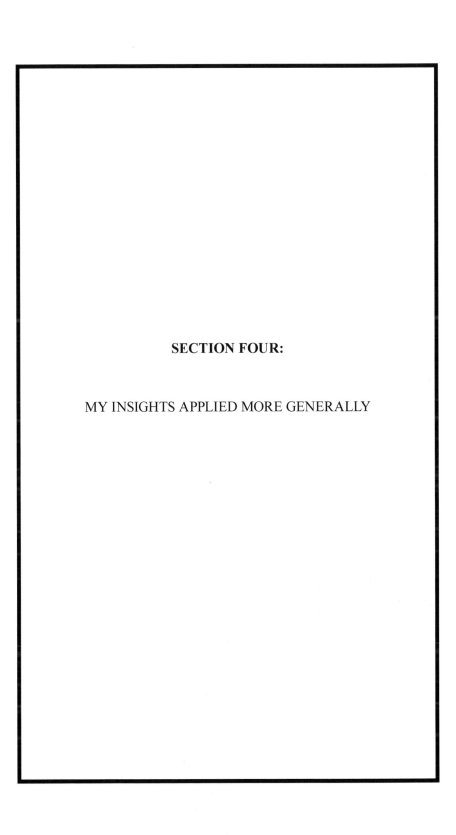

SECTION FOUR:

MY INSIGHTS APPLIED MORE GENERALLY

JUSTICE VERSUS PEACE

When I was around nine years old, my family took a trip to San Francisco. This was either 1972 or 1973, and it was a memorable trip because of the Hippie, Anti-Vietnam movement that permeated "The City by the Bay." I remember seeing "Flower children" walking around and Hare Krishna at the airport and on street comers. I remember people carrying signs, protesting the war in Vietnam, as we drove by the Haight and Ashbury city area. My family was and still is very Mountain West conservative. So, seeing this craziness firsthand, and not on the news, was very shocking, especially for me, a little kid. Among the crowds and traffic, our family vacation wound its way. Yet everything was very exciting for me as we went to various sightseeing locations. One of these sightseeing locations was the infamous Alcatraz Prison, which had recently been turned into a National Park. For me, I remember very vividly the boat ride to and from Fisherman's Wharf. I'd been in small fishing boats on the Snake River in Idaho, but I'd never been on the ocean. I remember being very excited by the giant boat. Additionally, I remember watching the colossal city become smaller and smaller as we traveled on the open-air deck of the boat out on San Francisco Bay. Conversely, I remember the ominous view of the Alcatraz Island as it loomed larger and larger as the boat approached the barren "Rock" in the bay.

When we got to Alcatraz, I remember my legs were struggling with the climb up the hill to the prison, but I was still very rambunctious and full of energy when we got to the top. I remember walking around with a tour guide as he showed us the various parts of the prison. Alcatraz was, of course, empty of prisoners, having then been closed a little over a decade earlier. However, I could still feel the presence of people who'd been there . . . I could feel their emotions. My imagination was vividly playing out the day-to-day lives of the prisoners, and I could palpably feel their loneliness and sadness. Interestingly, I can still feel it now as I write. Back then, it was as though there were ghosts walking among our tour group, sharing what it was like to live in that bleak place. I remember the laundry room and the dining hall. I remember the guard showing the group how the cell doors opened and closed by a large lever at the end of each row. Also, I remember hearing about the riots and the escape attempts. For being so young, I still remember a lot, especially my nine-year-old emotions. That being said, the feelings of loneliness and sadness I felt as a boy are now truly real for me, as I'm living in my own personal Alcatraz.

Though I'm a *Dispositional Optimist*, prison has made me very sad. I know I've joy in me, but the day-to-day grind of prison covers my joyful nature. Nelson Mandela put it best when he wrote, "Prison life is about routine; each day like the one before; each week like the one before it, so that the months and years blend into each other. Time slows down in prison. The days seem endless . . . time moved glacially."[1] While some of the readers may be saying to themselves, "Well, you broke the law, and this is the consequence . . . You needed to be punished," I'll respond with another Nelson Mandela quote. He wrote, "A man who takes away another man's freedom is a prisoner of hatred. I am not truly free if I am taking away someone else's freedom, just as surely as I am not free when freedom is taken from me."[2] With that, my topic for this chapter should be revealed. To be clear, I'll also ask the reader a question: when is taking away freedom necessary?

I've always been against locking up people unless they are *a clear and present danger to society*, and I feel even more so today. Taking away someone's freedom should be society's last choice, not its first. The reader may be saying that "there has to be punishment or crime would shoot through the roof and there would be more and more lawlessness." My response is locking people away does not solve the problems that caused the offender to offend in the first place. Prison is a manifestation of fear, not love. In fact, I submit that prison breaks the majority of people more than they were already broken before they were incarcerated, and many studies agree with that position. As already stated, in the United States, there is a 67.8 percent recidivism rate . . . Over half of the ex-cons will reoffend.[3] Why this occurs can be read about in various books. The one I'll recommend is Maya Shenwar's book *Locked Down, Locked Out: Why*

Prison Doesn't Work and How We Can Do Better. What I'll say, living it firsthand, is that I agree with Maya Shenwar and the various studies she cites in her book that show prison is only making things worse for society as a whole. Many of the statistics I've used come from Ms. Shenwar's book. One such statistic is that 95 percent of prisoners are eventually released from prison.[4] This is significant as all of us ex-cons have to reintegrate back into society, and longer and stiffer sentences only make it many times more difficult. Their difficult reintegration affects society in negative ways, causing more problems. Also, poor living conditions and poor health care further burden the social systems.

I was recently reading an article in a magazine about women on welfare and their housing issues. (I've no idea what magazine or exactly when.) These women, the vast majority are spouses or ex spouses of incarcerated men, are bouncing from home to home, being evicted over and over. Their belongings are put out on the curb and likely stolen. The landlords take these drastic measures because they are tired of waiting for rent, and many months of back rent. The courts are inundated with law suits between landlords and their renters; and many, many times, the landlord has to take the financial loss, as there is no way to recover the money from these already poor people. These families (almost all have children involved) are made homeless and struggle, many times in the middle of winter, to find a new home. With the evictions, the cycle continues. The article stated that being spouses or ex-spouses of convicts and ex-cons was the first condition, initiating this cycle that likely culminates with the children going into prison themselves.

Then the cycle starts again. Per Ms. Shenwar's book, "Between 30 and 50 percent of children placed in juvenile detention centers have at least one parent in prison."[5] Of course, many of these kids in "juvy" grow up to be offenders, again and again. Their future spouses and children become unintended victims with unintended impacts to society. Currently, the fact is 1 in 28 children has a parent in prison. This statistic is up from 1 in 125 from just 25 years ago.[6]

As we've discussed in chapter 4, it's natural, using lower level life form thinking, to just cast off people as disposable or send them off to human warehouses. Again, this is because back before civilization, the ostracized individual would likely be eaten; and the tribe would be free of the burden.

But in a vast network of human civilizations, people are still around and still influence society, especially after being incarcerated. Think of this, the courts are giving longer and longer sentences; so when the inmate is finally released, they're old and very likely poor health because of years and years of inadequate exercise, health care, nutrition, and sleeping conditions, let alone the impact to their mental health caused by lack of exposure to nature and living in a survival mode for years at a time.

I'll be getting out eventually, as an example, and I'll be reintegrating into society. It's hard for me to get a job, especially from prison, that'll utilize my education and skills. Likely, I'll be lucky to get a minimum-wage job, as the label of "ex-con" will handicap me even further. My taxable income will be one-fifth of what it could be had I not been put behind bars. So not only am I, and other prisoners, costing society big money by being in prison, but we're also not contributing taxes for the various societal needs. Additionally, because of prison, we've become a burden to society and to our various family. And remember, I'm a lucky one who has family to support me both inside and out. There are many who'll transition out to become a total burden on society because all support ties have been broken . . . They've got no one to help.

As an example, Dan leaves next month; and he's moving to Seattle, where he has no family ties. He'll be living in a transitional housing unit provided by a church group, and he's lucky he found that support. From there, he'll be searching for work and, eventually, a new place to live. Yet if he were not sent to prison as his crime was not at all likely to be repeated once caught, he could have continued to pay taxes on a higher-paying job while he got help for what caused him to commit his crime in the first place. Instead, he'll likely take a minimum-wage job, which is less taxpayer income. And this after he served seven years behind bars, where he cost the taxpayer around $300,000. Currently, the prison industry cost the taxpayer over $7 billion each year,[7] and that bill keeps growing. It's easy and naive to blame a "breakdown in the moral fabric of society" as the reason prison populations keep growing, but that's just the fearmonger's narrative. Dan, like me, was a first-time offender who just needed help to prevent reoffense. However, had Dan, or any other prisoner, only been enrolled in programs to help solve his thinking errors, it would have cost the taxpayer less than $5,000 for a year's worth of treatment, if it cost the taxpayer anything. Dan, who had a job, could have paid for the treatment himself, as I did for a full year after I self-reported. I sought and got my own treatment. Dan, I, and many others were not incarcerated to be rehabilitated; we were imprisoned to be punished. Prison, like war, is not the solution in the vast majority of the cases and, many times, makes things worse. **My Fear-based insight** is as follows: *locking someone up is really just Institutional or Societal Revenge.*

Someone told me sending someone to prison is needed to protect the innocent, but that Fear-based narrative only values the victim. Back in the seventies, a Nobel laureate, Economist Gary Becker, suggested that people commit crimes based on rational analysis of each situation. The theory goes that mankind is always, as *Theory X* thinking tells us, trying to do bad things. Not only that, each person does a cost-benefit analysis to see if it's worth the risk to commit the crime he or she is predisposed to commit. When the costs are lower than the benefit, the person *will* commit the crime. With this theory, the solution then translates to more and more police, more judges and attorneys, more prisons, and longer and harsher sentences . . . At least, that is the case in America. The theory continues to espouse that line of thinking: the cost to the potential criminal (every one of us) goes up; and because the "cost" is too high, there'll be less crime, or so the thinking goes.

However, empirical studies, a few outlined in the book *The Honest Truth About Dishonesty* by Dan Ariely, don't support this way of thinking to be correct.[8] But that doesn't matter to the politicians, or the media, because as mentioned in chapter 1, President Nixon taught fear is a great motivator. Politicians, militaries, and government officials, with the help of the media, generate more and more fear to help justify their existence. Elizabeth Samet stated, "If we live in a world of crisis, we also live in a world that romanticizes crisis—that finds fodder for an addiction to the 24-hour news cycle, multiple information streams and constant stimulation."[9] With fearmongering leaders and the moneymaking media feeding this addictive cycle, prison is touted to the fearful public to be the only answer. Consequently, Love-based solutions aren't praised, nor are they seriously pursued. Fear rules, just as Nixon taught, and it generates a self-fulfilling prophecy. Fear-based thinking is responsible for generating what's called the *Precautionary Principle*, which states we must act now if there's any chance of "this" happening again in the future. Put bluntly, it's the "cover-your-ass rule." President George W. Bush used this principle to change U.S.

Doctrine from one of self-defense to the "pre-emptive strike."[10] Then the U.S. Military invaded Iraq. We see how that's turned out. We cut off one head to now have ISIS. War was not worth it. The United States' precaution has only generated more reasons for radical Islamic people to terrorize.

The worldview of criminals is that they're evil, violent, dangerous, or unstable (or any combination thereof). The *Fundamental Attribution Errors* comes into play for societies too. With this paradigm, individuals and societies ignore context and circumstance and a person's humanness. Protecting the victim (innocent) is truly important, but they really are no more important than the perpetrator. Both are human beings, having limitless potential. Both need help.

Politicians, militaries, and government officials play upon people's emotions and fears; and the taxpayer is left holding the multibillion dollar bill. The United States has spent hundreds of trillion dollars on the recent wars from 2001 to the present. For prisons during the same time frame, that equates to hundreds of billion dollars. James Bell said the following: "We live in a country that is addicted to incarceration as a tool for social control. As it stands now, justice systems are extremely expensive, do not rehabilitate but in fact make the people that experience them worse, and have no evidence-based correlatives to reducing crime. Yet, with that track record they continue to thrive . . . Only an addict would see that as an OK result."[11] Trillions spent on war and billions spent on prison, what an ineffectual waste of human lives and money! What do we have to show for it but more war, more terrorism, more conflict, and more recidivism by recently released convicts. The issues and problems live on and on in perpetuity, not solved, causing more and more victims.

Fear (and its sub-emotions) skews individual and society's cost-benefit analysis, just like Fear-based emotions do for the person about to commit a crime. Crime is not logical! *Criminals don't do a cost-benefit analysis.* Obviously, neither do the numerous state or the Federal governments. The reader might be saying to themselves: "You can't put a price on the value of the victim . . . If we don't punish, then we are devaluing the victims." That's a regression to the Biblical Old Testament's "Eye for an Eye," and that kind of thinking is Fear-based, not Love-based. What victims need and want is peace and love, not revenge even if they don't know or understand that themselves. Revenge is lower life form thinking. Restitution can and should be Love-based.

Fear breeds the easy, quick, and very expensive solutions that have unintended negative consequences. Finding Love-based solutions takes time and effort but would be more successful and much cheaper in the long run. Love-based thinking is better when doing a long-run cost-benefit analysis. The unintended consequences of Love-based decisions would actually improve society in ways we can only imagine. However, the *culture of fear* meets the immediate misguided gratification of everyone concerned (the victim, the government official, the politician, etc.), just like committing the crime did for the individual. In the 2016 presidential election that is happening as I write, Donald Trump stated this week, words to the effect, "In the next eight years, there will be a massive recession. But if I'm elected president, there won't be." This is but one of many examples of how Trump, Clinton, and others are using fear to "show their value" to the American public, to *Legitimize* themselves, to "look presidential." Pres. John F. Kennedy stated, "The greatest enemy of truth is often not the lie— deliberate, contrived, and dishonest, but the myth—persistent, persuasive, and unrealistic."[12] One such persuasive media and politician-perpetuated myth is that criminals are not redeemable, changeable, or valuable; thus, prison is the only solution. They're using fear to *Legitimize* themselves, their job, and their pay. They're using fear to feed people's lower life form thinking. Sadly, society (maybe you too) believe their fearful message.

Robert Ingersoll wrote, "Crimes were committed to punish crimes, and crimes were committed to prevent crimes. The world has been filled with prisons and dungeons, with chains and whips, with crosses and gibbets, with thumbscrews and racks, with hangmen and headsmen—and yet these frightful means and instrumentalities and crimes have accomplished little for the preservation of property or life. It is safe to say that governments have committed far more crimes than they have prevented."[13] Ingersoll's quote has even more power when we think about all the unintended consequences that play out years and generations later. For a big-picture example, look what has happened in Iraq. The invasion has only brought about more war and has fed radical Islamic terrorists with more justification to kill innocent people. Holding prisoners at Guantanamo Bay is doing the same thing. The radical Islamic terrorists are using mistreatment of "Gitmo" prisoners and death of millions of civilians and "martyrs" as recruitment tools and justification to conduct more violence. Violence begets more violence, hate begets more hate, and fear begets more fear.

Dr. Martin Luther King echoed the statement by the Buddha (quoted in chapter 1) when he said, "Like an unchecked cancer, hate corrodes the personality and eats away its vital unity. Hate destroys a man's sense of values and his objectivity. It causes him to describe the beautiful as ugly and the ugly as beautiful, and to confuse the true with the false and the false with the true. Darkness cannot drive out darkness: only light can do that. Hate cannot drive out hate: only love can do that. Hate multiplies hate, violence multiplies violence, and toughness multiplies toughness in a descending spiral of destruction . . . The chain reaction of evil—hate begetting hate, wars producing more wars—must be broken, or we shall be plunged into the dark abyss of annihilation."[14]

Let me ask again, when is it right (or the best solution) to lock a person away? Are there people who aren't redeemable? Remembering the Buddhist story of Angulimala mentioned in chapter 4, the Buddha did not think so. Here's what thinking otherwise causes. Please picture the following: A person is cast into prison. There, he or she is reduced to nothing, and there is nothing really there to rebuild them in a positive manner. The person is seeking self-esteem, so they become a bully, or they become bullied. (The prison title is not worth repeating.) This becomes their identity for the duration of their stay behind bars. It gets reinforced daily by the prison staff and other inmates. They're labeled by their crime . . . It too becomes their identity. After only a short time, the prisoner becomes *Institutionalized*, meaning they are very comfortable in prison with no motivation to improve their status or get better. In fact, they use their perceived helplessness to justify bullying or other prison crimes. Sure, they want to get out; but really, they're acclimating to the environment where it becomes "the way it is." They *Learn Helplessness,* as prison provides the "three hots and a cot." Humans, like all organisms, seek homeostasis. *Homeostasis* (equilibrium of one's environment) enables the prisoner to adapt and survive. However, as has been quoted, 95 percent of the prisoners get out of prison and have to reintegrate. They've now *Learned Helplessness* and are *Institutionalized* . . . It's now part of who they are. In time, they're out in society, having to work and having to relate to people. They now have the extra label of "ex-con," "murderer," "thief," "sex offender," "rapist," "drug dealer," etc. Likely, they're going to struggle to get employment, housing, and health care. They'll struggle for an identity, something to build their self-esteem. Tellingly, society is still discounting and minimizing them. So they think back to the days of "three hots and a cot" when they ran the place and days when they were among peers who gave them some semblance of respect. They're emotionally ready to go back "inside." Therefore, the majority of ex-cons reoffend. Then society, looking for something to blame, says it's in their nature . . . They can't be redeemed. The conditions and circumstances that society perpetuated by taking the short view were and are never considered. The Fear-based view is the ex-con is fundamentally flawed. Thus, prison is the best place for them. The fearmongers' self fulfilling prophecy continues, and so does the cycle, again and again. So fear wins that battle.

I was telling someone the other day that I think practical jokes are fun, but I don't participate in them because I've learned a long time ago that the jokes always escalate until they're no longer fun or funny. Though not "fun," it's the same with wars and prisons. The famous American lawyer Clarence Darrow stated, "You can only protect your liberties in this world by protecting the other man's freedom. You can only be free if I am free."[15] Thich Nhat Hanh, when teaching about anger, stated, "Punishing the other is self-punishment. That is true in every circumstance. Every time the U.S.A. tries to punish Iraq, not only does Iraq suffer, but the U.S. suffers also. The same is true everywhere; between Israeli and Palestinian, between Muslims and Hindu, between you and the other person. It has always been like that. So, let us wake up; let us be aware that punishing the other is not an intelligent strategy."[16] Some of you readers, when reading those words, will say to yourself, "But people can't escape natural consequences." However, we're not talking about natural consequences, but we're discussing social or man-made consequences. Wars and prisons *aren't natural consequences;* they are man-made, fear-driven constructs and manifestations . . . They can be changed. Quoting Morrie Swartz again, it's not "fear always wins"; it's "love always wins." Wars, prisons, and punishment are Fear-based, not Love-based solutions.

Jill Fredston stated, "The past is a resource, not a destiny."[17] That sentiment applies in all situations. We can't keep looking at the past or look at people and countries' past behavior to predict the future. We'll continue to make *Fundamental Attribution Errors* if we do so. Then if history teaches us nothing, it's that *good intentions will not change a bad action into a good future.* The two *Cognitive Traps* that make that statement seem counterintuitive are *Hindsight Bias* and *Optimism Bias. Hindsight Bias* is the feeling that the past will always appear more certain than it actually was, which makes the future feel more uncertain and frightening. History is basically an illusion. Another way psychologists phrase it is as *Creeping Determinism*, which is the sense that grows on us, in retrospect, that what has happened was actually inevitable. Psychologist Baruch Fishhoff put it like this: "The occurrence of an event increases its reconstructable probability and makes it less surprising than it would have been had the original probability been remembered."[18]

Optimism Bias comes into play as we view our role in the past. Per Daniel Gardner, "People like to see themselves as being basically good, and so admitting that they are promoting fear in others in order to advance their interests sets up a nasty form of *Cognitive Dissonance* . . . .the solution is *Rationalization . . . self-interest* and sincere belief seldom part company."[19] (Emphasis mine.) Again, *good intentions cannot make bad decisions turn out a good future.* Good intentions only guarantee a good future with Love-based thinking and solutions.

An example of a good intention with a Fear-based solution is the Clinton-era crime bill that introduced the "three-strikes-you're-out rule," raising incarceration 500 percent in the last twenty years.[20] In a March 2016 *New Yorker* article by Ryan Lizza, he quoted Pres. Bill Clinton, stating, "I signed a (crime) bill that made the problem worse. And I want to admit it."[21] President Clinton, with years now passed, can see the bad, unintended consequences of his decision. Of course, we all want to protect our loved ones and others. However, the *Precautionary Principle* skews good intentions (being emotionally charged) to produce bad, unintended consequences. It's important to protect the victims, but what really will help them? What will help society in the long run? Is prison (institutional and societal revenge) the solution? If a person is actively hurting someone, then they need to be separated from that person until the aggressor's problems can be resolved. No question! Prison may be the solution to separate the perpetrator and victim, if all other methods have been tried first. Court orders, probation, and treatment may work; but if not, then prison is required. I've not said prisons should never be used. Having lived in one for years and having met many different people inside, I know prison is the solution sometimes, but it still is a short-term solution. Prison should be used sparingly. (I would say "judiciously," but the legal system is a cause of the current over incarceration.) Sadly, our society uses prison as a "closure" method for the victim. But punishment isn't going to provide meaningful and long-lasting closure for anyone. Punishment is short term, Fear-based, institutional, and societal revenge. Forgiveness is Love based and long-range problem-solving. Only forgiveness can bring true closure for any victim and meaningful help for victims and perpetrators. **My Love-based insight** is the following: ***only wisdom, compassion, and forgiveness can bring peace to victims, perpetrators, and society.***

Wisdom is another way of saying long-term thinking and meaningful, long-lasting solutions. Wars, prisons, and other forms of punishment are short-term solutions. Punishment is a short-term teaching method that works for lower-level and immature thinkers. When a child is very small, slapping their hand to keep them from touching the hot stove is a smart solution. But even then, it is explaining to the child why, appealing to their understanding, that makes the real long-term difference . . . It's the wise form of teaching. Thich Nhat Hanh said, "We think, 'I want to punish you, I want to make you suffer because you have made me suffer. And, when I see you suffer a lot, I will feel better.' Many of us are inclined to believe such childish practice. The fact is that when you make the other suffer, he will try to find relief by making you suffer more. The result is escalation of suffering on both sides. Both of you need compassion and help. Neither of you needs punishment."[22] Wisdom tells us that being spiteful is childish, but how many of us still hold spite in our hearts? It's easy for anyone to do. It's the archaic, primitive, and natural reaction. But we can be better than that. We can be wisdom- and compassion-focused. We can be Love-focused.

When I was a teenager, on the news was a story about a person about to be put to death for murdering someone. It was the first death sentence to be carried out in a long time, so it was big news. With news trucks camped outside the prison, every moment of the drama was reported. Crowds were gathered, holding signs for two opposing positions toward capital punishment. What struck me about the story is how people, especially the family of the victim, were crying out for this person to be killed . . . Their position was vengeful, hard, quick, and unforgiving. I remember the family members interview, and I was struck with the permeated sadness of their voice and expressions. They were not happy, joyful, or peaceful; they were spiteful. The many angry people standing outside the prison with signs calling for the man to be put to death weren't happy, joyful, or peaceful either. Of course, the public outcry influenced the governor not to stay the execution, and the man was put to death. The family was interviewed afterward; and they were still not happy, joyful, or peaceful . . . No one was. It made me sad that the family couldn't let go of their hate, anger, and spite for the prisoner. I thought then, *I will always work to forgive, no matter what.* The Jewish Zohar stated, "There is no true justice unless mercy is part of it."[23] Forgiveness is *the* key part of being merciful. True justice is not institutional or societal revenge.

To see where you are at on the prejudice spectrum, let me tell you a story. The other day, I was watching TV, and the channel was changed to a new show on the A&E Network. The title of this new show is *60 Days In*. This reality TV show has people volunteering to go inside prison for sixty days to see what it is like. The participants have various reasons for doing so, but none of them are there because they're sentenced to be there. One scene brought me to tears as I relived an event that has been seared into my memory. I'll share that memory with you now. In the TV show, a prisoner jumps off the second tier and lands on her head. Alarms sound, all prisoners are locked down, and the guards rush in to give medical aid. The girl is lying there, not moving, and the blood is pouring from her head. Very dramatic TV. Well, I've seen such an event in person. A man jumped from the second tier in my pod. He landed on his head, and it made such a loud bang that I thought it was a thunder clap. He lay there with blood pouring out of his head, and the guards rushed to hold him still until the paramedics arrived a very long time later. The rest of us were locked in our cells, but we could see everything that was happening. My heart went out to this person because he was so depressed that suicide felt like the only solution. Prejudice check: how do you feel about the person right now? Stop and think about it before you read on. *Pause!*

Okay, now I'll tell you why the man is in prison. He murdered someone and raped someone else. Did that change how you felt toward that person? In your mind, did he become more disposable or less of a human? I know for me, prior to coming to prison, I would have discounted him and would have written him off. Now having met all sorts of criminals (including me), I see them as human, just like me. I'd never condone what they did, nor would I condone or excuse what I'm guilty of doing wrong. Even now, knowing the details of the jumper's crime brings up serious emotions that bring on a feeling of revulsion. However, I have to admit to myself that

I don't know the conditioning any person had prior, I don't know their circumstances and context, and I don't know what conditioning, attitude, emotions, or thinking that would lead to their heinous acts. I just know they are human . . . just like me. Po Bronson wrote, "No human being is a lost cause. We don't feel that we have to put a lid on anyone or anything. We are willing to give things a chance to flower . . . even criminals."[24] Bishop Desmond Tutu taught, "My humanity is bound up in yours, for we can only be human together."[25] Bishop Tutu's words apply to all humans, the "noncon" and "con" alike. Everybody will make mistakes, some more serious than others. Alison Croggon put it nicely when she stated, "We are all mistaken sometimes; sometimes we do wrong things, things that have bad consequences. But it does not mean we are evil, or that we cannot be trusted ever afterward."[26] Everyone is worth a second or even a third chance. Just like a child, or *us* using wrongful and immature thinking, with greater understanding, higher-order thinking, and maturity, we'll have significant positive changes, preventing future offenses. Very few people are truly evil. Master Lao-tzu stated, "Treat well those who are good, also treat well those who are not good; thus is goodness attained."[27] I feel the overwhelming majority of criminals, say 99 percent, are redeemable!

I've witnessed many suicide attempts and a murder since coming to prison; and it does not matter who it was—bully, kind person, bullied, guard, etc.— my heart has gone out to that person. (Many guards have committed suicide too during my time in prison.) Prison has built up my compassion because I've also felt the loneliness, hopelessness, fear, and deep sadness that come from years and years, added upon each other, of this environment. I've felt the frustration and disappointment in the legal system as my trial included false and prejudicial testimony, and the prosecution introduced facts that were not in evidence. I've experienced the disgruntlement and anger when during my legal appeals, the government, again, introduced false evidence that prejudiced the judges against me (we'll discuss *Anchoring Effect* later on); and thus, my appeal was denied. I've been let down, again and again, as my clemency and parole requests have been denied for arbitrary and capricious reasons. I've felt the deep hurt caused by being discounted, minimized, and abandoned. Henry David Thoreau wrote, "Under a government which imprisons any unjustly, the true place for a just man is also a prison."[28] And a proverb from Madagascar says, "Justice is like fire, even if you cover it with a veil, it still burns." Yet from these very painful experiences comes my deep, profound compassion . . . my peace of mind. I'm mindful of my angle to the stone.

Being a former military leader, I came to realize that when there was a problem, the person's lack of motivation was the cause, only about 5 percent of the time. The other 95 percent was split up between poor training and the people not being given the right resources, tools, equipment, or skills to get the job done right. I think this also applies to criminals and every citizen. The vast majority just needed better training and education, or to have better tools and skills to handle the problems of life. Who then is responsible if things go wrong, when the person makes a serious mistake? Remember the teaching of Dr. Jampolsky that when someone hurts you, it's most likely that they are "crying out for love." Everyone is a victim, even the aggressor. We're all victims of conditioning, perpetual thinking errors, *Cognitive Traps*, absolute thinking, and other ego-building delusions. However, remember also what Jill Fredston stated, "The past is a resource, not a destiny." We each still are responsible for our own actions because we've the ability to choose. We just need to know how to choose wisely and compassionately and then do it. True Love-based solutions balance individual and societal responsibilities, learnings, and consequences.

Wisdom is seeing people's humanity and taking into account the unintended consequences when we act toward others (i.e., implement a solution). Compassion is seeing everyone as a person who is struggling through life, "just like me." And forgiveness is not only to let go and for yourself but also to bless everyone in the equation, people known and unknown. A reminder is in order. Self-serving forgiveness is not really letting go, nor is it forgiveness. Prisons are overflowing, wars and terrorism still are happening every day, and people hurt one another every day all because someone couldn't let go. Natalia Ginzburg wrote, "And if he (referring to a child or victim) suffers from injustice there or is misunderstood, it is necessary to let him see that there is nothing strange about this, because in life we have to expect to be constantly misunderstood and misrepresented, and to be victims of injustices; and the only thing that matters is that we do not commit injustices ourselves."[29] Having a "victim mentality" increases our chances of being unjust to others.

Agreed, dictators and tyrants need to be stopped, criminals need to be stopped, and people need to be stopped from stop hurting one another. However, force, aggression, and punishment are not the answers to really solve any of these, human ills. History keeps teaching this lesson, but it still seems to be ignored by the majority of humanity because of our innate lower level life form thinking (emotional reactions). An exceptional person, Dr. Martin Luther King Jr., stated, "Power at its best is love implementing the demands of justice. Justice at its best is love correcting everything that stands against love."[30] To build compassion, I use the mantra that you've already seen a few times in this book: "just like me." Everyone is just like me. As already quoted by wise men in chapter 5, we are all in the same cart, going to execution . . . We are all prisoners. It becomes much easier to have compassion with such thinking. It's when we have an "us and them" mentality or see people as an "it" versus a "you" (as taught by Martin Buber) that compassion fails. It's when we use lower level life form thinking that we aren't wise in our decisions; and the hurtful, negative, intended, and unintended consequences come to fruition.

For countries and governments, sanctions may temporarily work, just like prison does; but more likely, they just hurt the very people they are trying to help. In a recent book I read titled *Escape from Camp 14*,[31] the young man who escaped North Korea's labor camps told of how the sanctions were starving the people. Then when the other countries donated food, it went to corrupt government people, who then sold it on the Black Market; and the common person was still starving. Yet sanctions are better than wars. Still, the deeper question remains: why does North Korea want Nukes? Kim Jung Un is a tyrant and a dictator. He too, just like the bullies written about earlier, is seeking the *Principle of Legitimacy*. He wants power and other governments, and his own people are seen as a threat to that power. In my opinion, he and his government feel that they have no choice because they've been bullied by other countries in Korea's past history, which is a true fact of history. They now feel, I think, that if they get Nukes, then they could not be bullied around as much. They feel they were and are victimized. They feel wounded, and the wound is being kept open to justify their inhumane actions. They're using the *Precautionary Principle* in their actions to remain in power. Thus, a cycle of remaining a victim and aggression will not solve anything with North Korea but will only make things worse. Everywhere fear is being used to manipulate and control. Many times, we do it to ourselves. Where is love and forgiveness?

I told you Dr. Jampolsky sent me two other books a few years ago. One of those books, of which he is the author, is *Forgiveness: the Greatest Healer of All*; and in it, he stated, "Forgiveness is the way to a place of inner peace and happiness, the way to our soul. That place is always available to us, always ready to welcome us in. If for the moment we don't see the welcome sign, it is because it is hidden by our own attachment to anger . . . Forgiveness can free us from the imprisonment of fear and anger that have imposed on our minds."[32] I'm in a physical prison, but Dr. Jampolsky is teaching of a "mental prison" that's also very destructive to humanity. *Forgiveness is the key* to getting out of any prison. Henri J. M. Nouwen said, "We need to forgive and to be forgiven every day, every hour increasingly. That is the great work of love among the fellowship of the weak that is the human family."[33] And Doe Zantamata wrote, "However justified you may be, or however enormous the hurt, it is always possible to forgive . . . forgiving requires compassion."[34]

The first place to start forgiving and to apply the salve of compassion is to ourselves. As we've already stated, we need to remember to give ourselves a break. Then we're able to forgive others because we know they are just like us . . . no matter how serious the crime, or how scary the terrorism, or how big the past wound they inflicted was, or how much they justified mistreatment using the various *Cognitive Traps* and the *Precautionary Principle*, or how cruel the dictator's and bullies' inhumane actions. We all want peace within ourselves, within our homes, within the community, within our nation, and within the world. Revenge (disguised as justice), fear, and anger will never bring peace . . . Only love can! Peace of mind is the goal, and forgiveness is our function.

Wisdom, compassion, and forgiveness all require us (individuals, families, societies, and governments) to have *Empathy* toward one another. *Empathy* has the following four qualities[35] that everyone must implement to actuate our wisdom, compassion, and forgiveness: (1) perspective: we must be able to share the other party's perspective, (2) nonjudgment: we must have equanimity toward the other person and their feelings, (3) understanding: we must feel the other party's emotion with them, and (4) connection: we must feel with the other party. We each need to remember these four aspects of empathy if we really want to be wise, have compassion, and forgive one another. Zen master and peace activist Thich Nhat Hanh stated it best when he said, "We must all learn to be one another, with understanding and compassion, to hear what is being felt by the other."[36]

In closing, let me quote an old adage: "Revenge is sweet (which truly is debatable), but forgiveness divine." We humans each are capable of divine. We've many examples of people who were literal prisoners who've found reasons to be loving, kind, compassionate, and empathetic toward their fellow humans—Viktor Frankl, Nelson Mandela, Cornelia ten Boom, Phakyab Rinpoche, just to name a few. These examples found peace in wisdom, compassion, and forgiveness. I too have found peace. I've found the peace the Dalai Lama speaks of in his statement: "Peace can only last where human rights are respected . . . Peace, for example, starts within each one of us. When we have inner peace, we can be at peace with those around us."[37] My prayer is that we all can find peace. I pray that we all will use the key of forgiveness to get out of prison and that we all can break the cycles of fear, anger, revenge, and aggression by using wisdom, compassion, love, and forgiveness. Albert Einstein stated, "You cannot solve any problem in the same state of consciousness in which it was created."[38] Or as Dr. Jampolsky taught using different words about what type of consciousness: love is letting go of fear.[39] Let's change our consciousness to be Love-based, not Fear-based. Let's let go of our fears for peace.

RETRIBUTION AND RESTITUTION

From the last chapter, we closed discussing some very wise people and learned from these exceptional people's examples that forgiveness is the ultimate healer. Despite the wisdom of their powerful examples, it seems to me that few people believe in or practice true, selfless forgiveness. They may give forgiveness lip service but not true, selfless forgiveness. I want to make clear. Having compassion for a victim is very important. It's important to any victim that their friends and family extend care, compassion, and empathy. That said, does care, compassion, and empathy for the victim give anyone the excuse not to forgive the perpetrator? It may seem to some, even to the readers, that the focus on forgiveness minimizes the pain caused to the victim, by the perpetrator; but that's not true. Everyone's, including the reader's, care, compassion, and empathy toward any victim is truly important; and I'm not discounting those feelings or minimizing those emotions in any way. Any and *all victims* need our love, compassion, and empathy. I, for one, care very deeply for my victims; and I'm imbued with compassion and empathy for the hurt I've caused them. I've been in this state for more than twelve years now. As previously expressed, my love, compassion, and empathy generated my remorse, driving my courage and honorable actions. While it's important for *all victims* to have family and friends' love, compassion, and empathy, isn't the perpetrator's care, compassion, and empathy just as meaningful? One extremely important point of wisdom is this: having care, compassion, empathy for victims doesn't excuse aggressive (possibly violent) thoughts, emotions, and actions toward any perpetrator. That's revenge! Revenge only makes a victim's perpetrator another victim, if they weren't already. Is it beneficial to create another victim? If so, it must be done sparingly. Shakespeare's Portia from *The Merchant of Venice* stated, "The quality of mercy is not strained . . . It is twice blest: it blesseth him that gives, and him that takes."[1]

The objective of law enforcement and the legal system isn't to seek and exact revenge or retaliation but "to protect and serve." Note the statement "to protect and serve" doesn't refer only to the victims, but also to society as a whole. Logic dictates that this includes the perpetrators as well. To many readers, this may seem to be a radical concept. However, that doesn't lessen the truth of the principle that sages have been teaching about for millennia. In contrast, exacting revenge or retaliation by punishing the perpetrators and taking away their human dignity will only make things worse . . . It makes them another victim. Prussian general Karl von Clausewitz stated in his very influential seventeenth-century book, *On War*, that "War is an act of violence intended to force our opponent to do our will." He goes on to say that war is "a mere continuation of policy by other means."[2] Clausewitz is stating war is governmental use of force (revenge or retaliation), not integrity. His statement has been translated and summarized widely as "war is politics through other means." Paraphrasing Clausewitz, incarceration is politics through other means.

Integrity dictates, relating to criminal actions, a less violent, forceful, and harsh action should be the *first* attempt to help the perpetrator. For example, Maya Shenwar wrote about Transformative and Restorative Justice as better solutions to prisons. These two creative solutions should be used before prisons, along with probation. Ms. Shenwar's book does a very good job explaining that the law enforcement and the U.S. legal systems are built around incarceration, not restitution. Transformative and Restorative Justice are about rehabilitation and restitution. Emma Goldman stated, "So long as every institution of today, economic, political, social, and moral, conspires to misdirect human energy into wrong channels; so long as most people are out of place doing the things they hate to do, living life they loathe to live, crime will be inevitable, and all the laws on the statutes can only increase, but never do away with crime."[3] We can and should do better.

What is restitution? For that matter, what is retribution? Looking at *Merriam-Webster's* dictionary, we find the following definitions: *Restitution* is "*to restore*, a making good of or giving some equivalent for some injury, a legal action serving to cause restoration of a previous state." And *Retribution* is "*to pay back*, the dispensing or receiving of reward or punishment, something given or exacted in recompense." Looking at the first definition (italicized) of both words, they really basically mean the same thing: "to restore" and "to pay back." Since many injuries and crimes committed can't be "restored to a previous state," both re-tribute (to pay back) and restitution have the option of "giving some equivalent for some injury." As previously stated, our lower life form thinking's first reaction is to *exact revenge* (the biblical "eye for an eye") as the equivalent for some injury though as Jesus and other masters have taught, *forgiveness is the ultimate healer*, not some form of punishment or revenge. Additionally, think of the power of healing for the victim if something is "given" versus "exacted" in recompense. So then what's to be "re-tributed" or "restored?" What does the victim really need or want? As stated above, any victim really needs care, compassion, and empathy, especially from the person who caused their injury. A victim's higher-order thinking first desires safety and security, and then they want the perpetrator's remorse, repentance, rehabilitation, and no reoccurrence . . . All else is lower life form thinking.

From anecdotal evidence, it seems higher-order thinking is not the norm, the common reaction, or the natural tendency. Sadly, revenge is! In the news recently was a report about Leslie Van Houten. Ms. Van Houten is infamous because she was a member of the Charles Manson killers of the late 1960s. She herself committed two murders, stabbing the victims in the back multiple times. She was nineteen at the time of the killings. Now she's in her late sixties, and after decades of being incarcerated, she's been recommended for parole by the California Parole Board[4] after nineteen previous attempts with corresponding denials. Yet for only "political" reasons, the California governor denied her parole. Von Clausewitz would likely say, "Politics! I told you so!"

For this chapter, what's very interesting about the news story is the reaction of the victim's family member when interviewed on TV. It's almost fifty years after the fact, and the victim's daughter stated she doesn't want Ms. Van Houten to get out on parole. The daughter herself is in her late fifties. There's no question, she was truly a victim, having to live without her parents for all these years . . . She was robbed of a life with her parents. Also, there's no question, the way in which they died was violent and tragic. One cannot help but feel compassion for her tragedy. However, is keeping her parents' killer in prison helping her heal? Has an eye-for-an-eye thinking brought her peace in these past fifty plus years? Or is *Fundamental Attribution Error* still in play for this lifelong victim? The daughter definitely hasn't bought into the wisdom of Jesus, or the Buddha, or of Mahatma Gandhi, who said, "It is always possible by correct conduct to lesson an evil and eventually to bring good out of evil."[5] To the daughter, Ms. Van Houten is a killer and will always remain a killer. She's also blind to the wisdom of Thich Nhat Hanh who wrote, "Trying to punish the other person is only going to make the situation worse."[6] Not forgiving has bound her up in a lifelong sadness and mourning. She herself is in a mental and emotional prison. Sadly, that's her choice, not Van Houten's. Forgiveness is the daughter's choice, enabling her healing and freedom.

Though Ms. Van Houten has been a "model prisoner," as the prison officials were reported as saying, for almost five decades and she's been rehabilitated, she's done everything possible to pay restitution and retribution. Yet it's not enough for the lifelong victim, and many like her, to let go. She's still seeking revenge (justice) . . . the negative side of retribution and restitution. Likely, if asked, she'd state that Ms. Van Houten cannot be trusted. But as Kate Elliot stated, "To give trust is to gain trust. To withhold trust until there is no doubt is not trust."[7] This brings me to **my Fearbased insight,** which is as follows: *anecdotal evidence seems to say people don't believe in rehabilitation, or a criminal's ability to change for good.*

To help prove my insight, I'll offer some more anecdotal evidence closer to where I currently live. One person, in prison with me, escaped almost forty years previous to our introduction in my prison a few years ago. He'd lived for decades without getting into any trouble at all, not even a parking ticket. Then one day, through a hand scanner at an amusement park, his prints alerted the authorities; and a warrant was put out for his arrest. His family was unaware of his past crime and escape decades ago. He was seen as a pillar of society, which he was in the last almost four decades. Once arrested, he came back in prison for years to meet the societal consequences that had "been unpaid." Yet he'd proved, by his actions, that he was a law-abiding citizen for decades and a productive member of society. Yes, when he was young, he committed a crime; and yes, he escaped. I ask, is he very different from Victor Hugo's character Jean Valjean from *Les Misérables*? When one reads that story, we're cheering on Valjean. Why? Has my fellow inmate not proved the wisdom of Gandhi, who stated, "It is difficult to say for certain how a particular man would act in a particular set of circumstances."[8] He was a criminal who did good. We all have the potential to turn evil into good, as this man did. Is that not what we all really want, using our higher-order thinking? I ask, is his current punishment needed? Does the fact he lived for many decades as a law-abiding citizen not show his rehabilitation? Is his punishment now rehabilitative, or is it really societal revenge? Was living for forty years as a model citizen not restitution? Really, making someone "pay" reduces interpersonal relations down to mere transactions.

To further demonstrate my insight, I'll tell you about my parole denial. Here's the direct quote from my denial notification letter:

The Board considered and denied parole. The Board noted you have completed many facility rehabilitation programs and have the support of your family and friends. On the other hand, your crimes were very serious and despite your rehabilitation efforts you are still a risk to offend. Additionally, releasing you at this time to community supervision would deprecate the seriousness of your crimes and their impact on our society. Therefore, the Board concluded you would gain more from continued facility regimen than a period of parole supervision at this time. Finally, the Board determined you should serve more of your sentence to confinement to satisfy the legitimate retributive and deterrent aspects of punishment and to protect society.

The bottom-line message I received: you are in prison to be punished, not rehabilitated.

At the time of my first parole request, I'd finished over seven years' worth of professional rehabilitation treatment. I'd taken all available treatment options at the facility, to include crime-specific treatment groups. There were and still are no additional treatment options open to me. All formal treatment and rehabilitation opportunities have been complete for over three years now. The regulation that the board is supposed to follow states that the "Board paroles inmates when it is consistent with the ends of justice and *as soon as inmates demonstrate they can assume the responsibilities of productive, law-abiding citizens.*" (Emphasis mine.) In my case currently, I have a place to live, a standing job offer, and a follow-on aftercare treatment all lined up. So I'm good on the productive member of society and law-abiding citizen aspect (note: I'm a first-time offender). Would paroling me really violate the "ends of justice?" Not if it's about rehabilitation.

What about the validity of what the board brought up? (1) Am I still a threat to offend? (2) Would it be better for me to keep me in prison? (3) Does being released to parole lessen the seriousness of my crimes? (4) Does keeping me in prison longer prevent other people from committing crimes?

I appealed my parole denial, answering each one of these questions. I'll summarize for you my appeal request: As William Driver stated, "There is no such thing as 'zero risk.'"[9] This means anything is possible, but what about probable? The probabilities of my recidivism is officially 2.5 percent or less, this per the Department of Justice report that accounts for my specific crime, my age, and other factors.[10] Also, using the three specific recidivism potential test I've taken since my trial and incarceration, they all say I'm a very low risk to reoffend. Compounding the probabilities, my actual probability is extremely low . . . below 1.5 percent. Please note the fact I self-reported and put myself in rehabilitation years before my trial, and the fact I've completed all available rehabilitative treatment *isn't* even a factor considered or accounted for in any of the above-mentioned assessed probabilities. So the board's first point is unfounded, especially compared to the 68.7 percent recidivism chance of others as I've quoted earlier.

The board's second and third point basically state that prison or punishment is the only way to address the seriousness of crime, and prison is good for me. Is that true? As we've been discussing, no, but that's *Theory X*, lower life form thinking at its core. "A man or woman has to be forced to be good," and "punishment is the only way to force compliance." That kind of thinking has led to many of the following types of punishment: executions; solitary confinement; sensory deprivation; stockades; torture racks; castration; cutting off hands, fingers, feet, toes, ears, etc.; vicarious reprisal (punish the family for generations); exile; prison; hard labor; lobotomy; public shaming; etc. Many of the methods listed are now considered by most of humanity as inhumane. Yet the punishments listed above were the go-to method for millennia, and many of them still happen today, and not just in third-world countries. In the last chapter, we've discussed how destructive prison is; I'm hoping prison will also be considered inhumane, except in extreme cases.

What about the board's last statement? Does keeping anyone in prison make it less likely someone else will commit a crime? In David Kennedy's book *Deterrence and Crime Prevention*, he stated that "Incarceration time does not, in fact, deter. It just makes it harder as time goes on for the ex-con to reintegrate into society."[11] Also, as we've discussed in the last chapter, most humans don't do a cost-benefit analysis before they commit their crime. Studies show that the person's emotions and thinking errors are the contributors to crime, not cold logic. Stiffer sentences and ignoring rehabilitation in lieu of punishment will not reduce crime. They just add evidence for my insight that people want revenge more than they want the person to change for the better, or heal evil to good.

My point in addressing my parole denial is to show that the anecdotal evidence shows people don't seem to believe in rehabilitation. Mine isn't the only case that points to this way of thinking. I've viewed numerous other inmates' denial letters, and they say the exact same things, many word for word as mine . . . The board's actions are the epitome of "arbitrary and capricious." These are inmates who've also completed all available treatment, who've stayed out of trouble for years, and who all are first-time offenders themselves. They've been rehabilitated. As if to support my anecdotal insight, here are excerpts from my most recent parole board denial letter: "your crimes were very serious and despite your *extensive rehabilitation efforts* you are still a *low risk* to offend (italics mine)." The letter goes on to say "(The Board) notes the superb parole package you submitted and the tremendous support you have from family and friends." So after a dozen years of doing everything I possibly can to pay full and complete restitution, I've still not satisfied "the legitimate retributive and deterrent aspects of punishment . . ." Except for more incarceration time . . . in other words, rehabilitation isn't enough; only punishment will do.

As for another example, take John MacKenzie, who'd been locked up since 1975 until he committed suicide. After twenty-five years in prison, Mr. MacKenzie started receiving parole boards to determine if he was fit for parole. Per the 2016 *New York Times* editorial by Jesse Wegman,[12] in one of his ten denials, the parole board stated that it would "undermine respect for the law." Does that sound familiar? Another statement was that there was "significant community opposition . . ." (in others words, "politics"). Mr. MacKenzie had spent forty years in prison with a spotless record, had been through a Restorative Justice (mentioned by Maya Shenwar), had completed degree programs, and had supportive letters, to include guards, judges, clergy, and prosecutors, all to no avail. In an essay about his frustration, Mr. MacKenzie stated, "If society wishes to rehabilitate as well as punish wrongdoers through imprisonment . . . then society—through lawmakers—must bear the responsibility of tempering justice with mercy. Giving a man legitimate hope is a laudable goal, giving him false hope is utterly inhuman." With his quote, I'd say Mr. MacKenzie saw justice as revenge. A fellow inmate, Matthew, stated, "It is very frightening to know that forgiveness has become chaff in the wind, while the rod of correction is etched into permanent vellum, never to be changed." He also said, "If an inmate has shown he or she has taken great strides to improve his or herself, then why does the reasons of 'severity of crime' or 'not enough punitive time served' even exist? Why does parole appear to be such an arbitrary and capricious thing?"

I'm hoping my anecdotal evidence is wrong, and people do believe in rehabilitation. However, being in prison, it sure feels like the system, politicians, government representatives, prison administrators, and parole boards don't believe in rehabilitation. Their narrow focus on "justice" only being accomplished through incarceration as the go-to solution means they don't understand the cycle of destruction political vengeance engenders. Punishment isn't going to force people's *meaningful change*. Only Love-based solutions can bring about anyone's meaningful change.

History's use of the listed punishment methods and the board's statements ignore higher-order reasoning that change is really possible, without force. Retribution and restitution are really about healing all parties involved. It seems to me, and other prisoners, society misunderstands the two words to mean only inflicting punishment as payment. What higher-order thinking calls for is a catalyst for the person to change . . . This is *Theory Y*, Love-based methodology. Otherwise, as stated, punishment is really only for revenge, whether it be an individual or society as a whole, being a surrogate punisher for the victim(s). To reiterate, the Love-based view on retribution and restitution is to find a way to spark a change in the person who's offended so that they want to change themselves, to turn their evil into good, and to *restore* or *to pay back* through personal transformation. No one can be forced to change, so the goal should be to find environments conducive to helping them change their poisons into medicine, to help them transform themselves.

Let me give two examples of where that wasn't the case, where the environment was manifest vengeance, not a place of healing. One person whom I've been locked up with was held in solitary confinement for a year, as his case was being investigated. He had no outside contact, no other inmates to talk to, and the guards didn't talk to him because of his crime. He was allowed only the Bible to read, and that was it. He was sensory-deprived for an entire year. He wasn't even allowed any recreation time ever. I thought his was a unique case, but the other day, I was talking to another guy in my pod, and he told me how he'd been in pretrial confinement for a year where he too was kept completely alone and devoid of sensory input. His cell had no windows, no TV, no radio, and no other sound but his breathing. He too was only given a Bible to read, though he was allowed to get recreation out in a cage once a week. His scheduled time was always at night. So, he never saw the sun for a whole year. He experienced sensory deprivation, and it affected him greatly. Of note, this inhumane treatment was before they came to my current prison.

As written about in chapter 9, I've experienced solitary confinement, only for a few days. Many in my current prison live in solitary confinement for many years and locked down for twenty-three hours a day, only allowed out to exercise and shower. During my two days, I was allowed to have one-hour recreation time in what's nicknamed "The Bull Pen." This is a 36 foot by 24 foot enclosure with 40 foot walls on three sides and chain-link fence on the forth wall and at the top. I was in a pen. I'm thankful I was able to see blue sky and get fresh air. I didn't have gym shoes, so I tried to run in bare feet, but the asphalt was too cold and hard I couldn't continue. I ended up just walking around for an hour...like it was for me in the county jail. To me, one hour a day outside one's solitary cell is also cruel and inhumane though, in fact, U.S. Federal government regulations only require prisons and jails to provide "recreation" once *a week for one hour*. The "Rec Room" shown on the TV show *60 Days In*, which I mentioned before, is just like the Rec Room I experienced at a county jail. The concrete-enclosed room is about 24 feet wide by 24 feet long by 24 feet high. In the show, there is a high window for daylight, but there is no fresh air coming in. Thankfully, the county jail I was at had a roll-up door, revealing a heavy steel mesh screen that allowed fresh air and daylight in. Nonetheless, research states interacting with nature makes prisoners less violent. Most jails and some prisons don't allow prisoners to be outside ever! Their justification is safety and security of the facility. I feel it's laziness and shortsightedness. Interaction with nature not only makes prisoners less violent, but it also makes them healthier. Short-term thinkers will not care about prisoners' health and well-being, as for many, they see the environment as part of the punishment. The reader may be saying to themselves, "So who cares? They're out-of-sight, out-of-mind. It's not my problem. It's theirs. They committed the crime." I respectfully ask, why does the reader possibly feel that way? Many jail and prison administrators seem to only want to do the minimum as demonstrated on the TV show mentioned. The prisoners in that jail were *only allowed one hour of recreation time once a week*. I, for one, care about them. I know my compassion is higher than most because I can relate to these people, but that's not all.

Is that how we really want to treat any human being? I know I don't. Long-term thinking helps us remember 95 percent of inmates get out of prison. If society makes them live in an unhealthy mental and physical environment for years, it'll cost society additional money later on when the ex-cons' poor mental, emotional, or physical health comes into play in general society as the ex-cons age. With longer and longer sentences, the ex-cons are older and sicker when they finally get out. This is practical thinking, not compassionate thinking, but it proves my point. Sadly, people treat their household pets better than the majority of prisoners are treated. The modicum of decency any human deserves, even if they've committed a grievous crime, is to be treated better than a pet.

As we keep discussing and learning, isolation and cruelty don't help people change. Per S. Kelly Harrell, "We don't heal in isolation, but in community."[13] The prison "community" isn't a healing community. That fact I attest to you, the reader, personally. A healing community means not in prison; Aleksandr Solzhenitsyn stated, "Unlimited power in the hands of limited people 'always' leads to cruelty."[14] In many cases, taking away people's liberty and freedom is used as an excuse for being cruel, which only breeds more cruelty . . . not healing and not rehabilitation. All humans can be wise (Homo sapiens) with the right tools and training and the right environment (not prison). I've brainstormed some ideas (some already exist and are used) of environments where long-term, higher-order thinking will bring about meaningful and long-lasting change to the offenders and thus real healing for victims and perpetrators. But before I reveal my list toward the end of this chapter, let's talk about change and making evil into good or changing poison into medicine. To do so, I'll introduce the Transtheoretical Model of Health Behavior Change.[15] Per this model, there are five stages to change paraphrased as follows:

(1) The first stage is *Pre-Contemplation*: A person is thinking about changing, and/or they have a desire to change. This stage is where a person recognizes they have a problem in the first place, but they

are not yet committed to change. They have not really, seriously contemplated the change; however, the seed has been planted.

(2) The second stage is *Contemplation*: Now the person is really thinking that they need to change, and they are searching and seeking ways make the change. The person's commitment to their change has taken root, but nothing has sprouted yet.

(3) The third stage is *Preparation*: Now the person has narrowed down courses of action, and their commitment has been made . . . They will change. There is a sprout breaking through the soil.

(4) The fourth stage is *Action*: Now the selected course of action takes place. The person's commitment is almost irreversible . . . They believe in the change, and they'll make it happen. The plant is blooming.

(5) The fifth stage is *Maintenance*: The person has to maintain the actions and/or belief to keep the change vibrant. The change has already taken place, but without maintenance, it could revert back. The person's commitment must remain strong. The plant produces fruit during this stage.

Referencing the above change model, I'll introduce **my Love-based insight:** *taking "personal responsibility" is* **the best reason to** *change* for all concerned. As mentioned earlier, people need a catalyst to change, and the right environment can lead to meaningful, long-lasting change without being cruel and inhumane. People finding their personal responsibility in the world will bring about that change . . . the change that would be meaningful and helpful not only to the person but to the victims as well. Looking at the model above, nowhere is force involved. It's helping the person change their thinking, attitudes, and actions. In chapter 1, I told of my story and the many catalysts and tools that helped me change. Prison itself hasn't helped me change, though I've turned poison of prison into medicine. Dr. Jampolsky's Attitudinal Healing Therapy, Albert Ellis's Rational Emotive Behavior Therapy, along with a caring counselor are what brought about my change, preventing further offense. Only one's sense of taking personal responsibility can and will affect real and meaning change. My sense of *my* own responsibility is what brought about my changes . . . I'm continuously changing. Knowing that fact, we all need to put forth effort to find the conditions, circumstances, and environments conducive to real change.

In prison, along with helping other treatment group members see the value in taking personal responsibility for their thoughts, attitudes, and actions, I've been involved with the Franklin/Covey *The 7 Habits on the Inside* course as previously mentioned. For four years, I've been a facilitator and teacher for this groundbreaking course designed to reduce recidivism, and I've helped almost two hundred other inmates see the importance of taking personal responsibility. Also, I've been involved in mindfulness training for over seven years now, helping fellow group members learn how to properly meditate and how to practice mindfully each day, every day. I've developed and taught a mindfulness course based on Alex Lickerman's book *The Undefeated Mind*, which I'll summarize in chapter 14. These three powerful courses have positively influenced the prison to have a more peaceful environment and reduced the chances of recidivism upon my and my fellow prisoners' release. They've also helped people with the first few stages of the change model listed above. While I'm glad to have helped people (along with the prison's professional counselors, staff, and chaplains) take personal responsibility, I don't see prison being the only place that my or my fellow prisoners' meaningful learning and respective changes take place. In fact, I know it's not . . . It's a toxic environment for us, doing more damage.

In the iconic movie *The Matrix Reloaded*, *The Matrix*'s sequel, there's this great character called the Key Master. This person is imprisoned by a ruthless villain because of his skill to make keys for every lock. The heroes break out the Key Master, and he aids them on their quest. In one scene, the heroes are in a long hallway with many identical green doors. All the doors are closed and locked. The Key Master has the keys. He leads the heroes to one special door where another villain is blocking their way. My point of bringing up these iconic images is to tell of my father's wisdom. When I was young, he gave me a wonderful piece of advice. He stated I "needed to live my life in such a way where doors are open to me." In other words, take personal responsibility for my future, my thoughts, my attitude, and my actions. Paraphrasing Dr. Covey's words, be proactive. When I saw the iconic hallway of green doors, I equated myself to the Key Master, having an ability to open any door. Prevention and rehabilitation are about opening doors.

Andy Warhol is reported as saying, "They say that time changes things, but you actually have to change yourself."[16] Also, I share two quotes that I feel are imbued with great wisdom. Interestingly, two people have said the same thing using slightly different words. Charles Dubois stated, "The important thing is this: to be able at any moment to sacrifice what we are for what we could become."[17] And Max DePree said, "The greatest thing is, at any moment, to be willing to give up who we are in order to become all that we can become."[18] Also, John Pierpont Morgan voiced something similar: "The first step toward getting somewhere is to decide that you are not going to stay where you are."[19] All these quotes reinforce the principles taught in the Transtheoretical Model, *The 7 Habits on the Inside*, the Buddha's mindfulness practices, and elsewhere. Personal responsibility is how real, meaningful, long-lasting change occurs for each of us.

We've established in the last chapter and the first part of this chapter that prison or punishment is not the most effective way to help people, to change people's evil into good, to rehabilitate, or to pay restitution and retribution, which enables the victims to heal. We've established that helping people find the catalyst for change is the best way to prevent crime in the first place and to stop any future offenses from any perpetrator. While punishment and prison do serve as a "wake-up call," they certainly aren't the only such method. With prison as the last resort, let me reveal my short brainstormed list of longer-term, higher-order programs and solutions that also serve as a wake-up call and would equate to societal restitution and retribution (I'm sure there are more):

(1) Court-ordered community service

(2) Probation and mandatory treatment/counseling

(3) Mandatory career counseling and job/vocation/apprenticeship courses (shown to reduce recidivism by 47 percent)[20]

(4) Reconditioning treatment . . . specific cognitive/operant/behavioral condition courses

(5) Court-ordered monthly lie detector test with treatment provider as the guide

(6) Fines or additional taxes paid for years to the state or Federal government

(7) Court-ordered mindfulness training and *The 7 Habits for Highly Effective People* courses

(8) Other voluntary "rehabilitation" options in lieu of incarceration and punishment

(9) Curfew and/or house arrest (electronic monitoring: microchip or bracelet)

(10) Court-ordered mediation and counseling (This is the basis of Restorative Justice and Transformative Justice programs that Maya Shenwar writes about in her book.)

(11) Option to join the military. (This was normal during Vietnam but was not a formal program. My suggestion is the military have a formal program with treatment as part of the unit's objective. The military is already adept at tearing a person down and building them back up . . . In this case, it would be a treatment objective for long-term change.)

(12) Option to join an international service organization like the Peace Corps. (My suggestion is governments or the government create an organization specific to people who've committed crimes. For many, the environment they live in is causing them to have a closed mind or feeds the cycle of crime. Being in an environment, serving others as the objective, would open their worldview, enabling a major change in perspective.)

I'm sure there are other ways to create an environment that helps the person see that they need to change (the *Pre-contemplation* and *Contemplation* stages). Then that Love-based environment serves as a catalyst for positive, long-term changes *(Preparation* and *Action* stages). The point is as the old adage says, "A woman (or man) convinced against her (his) will is of the same opinion still." Blaise Pascal put it another way when he wrote, "We are usually convinced more easily by reasons we have found ourselves than by those which have occurred to others."[21] Treating people like animals (or worse than animals) is only going to make things worse, not better. *Cruel environments don't generate good outcomes.* Instead, we want environments that engender what Max Planck has stated, "When you change the way you look at things, the things you look at change."[22] Helping people change their thinking is the way positive change takes place. As I stated about a lesson I learned as a military leader in a past chapter using *Theory Y*, higher-order thinking, if there's a problem, we just need to get people the right tools and training. People are inherently good with good intentions as a primary motivator. The famous Adam Smith espoused this position when he wrote, "How selfish soever man may be supposed, there are evidently some principles in his nature, which interest him in the fortunes of others, and render their happiness necessary to him, though he derives nothing from it except the pleasure of seeing it."[23] In short, mankind is good. Therefore, let's find environments to bring out people's goodness. Let's find change environments that don't amplify *Cognitive Traps*, thinking errors, and harmful mistakes.

Having systems, structures, and organizations that engender kindness, compassion, and personal responsibility will make mankind wiser and safer. Ralph Waldo Emerson said, "There need but one wise man in a company and all are wise, so rapid is the contagion."[24] Psychologists already know the power of what's called an *Emotional Contagion,* as mentioned earlier. An emotion can be transmitted to others around a person. And they who are infected can transmit it on, and so forth and so forth. A wise person, group, or government would ask themselves, "Do I want to transmit fear, anger, sadness, revenge, etc., only to make the world feel more of the same? Or do I want love, joy, satisfaction, compassion, forgiveness, etc., to infect the world?" This is "integrity."

Wars, prisons, and other violence only transmit a Fear-based contagion. One of the first steps is to rid ourselves of *Negativity Bias. Negativity Bias* can be described as seeing everything as a threat or danger. As with many of our thinking errors, *Negativity Bias* worked well for our ancestors on the savannas of Africa or the mountains of Europe and Asia where they were always surveying for dangers. Their instincts kept them alive for their genetics to pass on to us. But we no longer live in an environment where our very survival is at stake. Yes, bad things happen, mistakes are made, and people get hurt. As Dale Atkins stated, "Everyday each one of us is an accident trying not to happen."[25] That being said, by opening ourselves up to see and experience the good in the world, we're able to transmit gratitude. We become a positive Emotional Contagion.

Phillip Zimbardo, the author of the 1971 Stanford Prison experiment we've discussed earlier, has spent decades studying goodness. On his website, Greater Good in Action (ggia.berkely.edu), he wrote, "The two lines of research aren't as different as they might seem; they're actually two sides of the same coin . . . Some people argue humans are born good or born bad; I think that's nonsense. We are all born with this tremendous capacity to be anything, and we get shaped by our circumstances—by the family or the culture or the time period in which we happen to grow up, which are accidents of birth; whether we grow up in a war zone versus peace; if we grow up in poverty rather than prosperity."[26] Zimbardo is reflecting what we've already discussed—people (all people) are redeemable, and evil can be replaced with good . . . true for convicts, ex-cons, or you.

The reader may have snickered to themselves when they read number 7 from my list above. The reader may have thought to themselves, "Mindfulness training courses for criminals? How ridiculous." But I'm here to tell you mindfulness works! It effects positive, meaningful, and transformative change. Paul Condon and his colleagues of Northeastern University conducted a study where they put the test subjects through an eight-week mindfulness course. At the end of the course, the experiment began. The mindful mediators were sent into a waiting room, where they filled up all the seats. Then a woman experiment collaborator came in the room on crutches and leaned against the wall. What would the mindful test subjects do? Of course, there was also a control group with the same setup. What the experiment showed is that people who'd been through mindfulness training were *five times* as likely to give up their seat to the woman on crutches . . . Mindfulness engendered kindness and compassion.[27] What would you do? (WWYDE reminder). Mindfulness helps any and all of us. It generates an environment where people can change themselves, fighting the *Cognitive Traps* we've been discussing throughout this book.

We each need to change ourselves in one way or another. People with criminal tendencies can change; they can be rehabilitated, either before they commit a crime or afterwards. There rarely is a dire need to make the perpetrator another victim of the toxic and inhumane. The victim really doesn't want that, especially if they're using their higher-order, Love-based thinking. It's fear that engenders the fight-or-flight tendencies. It's fear that is the source of the emotions surrounding regret and revenge. As Nelson Mandela stated, "As we are liberated from our own fears, our presence automatically liberates others."[28] Helping people see the need to change themselves is the first step. Bullying them to change will only make things worse in the long run for them and for others too. There will be people who are so dangerous to family, friends, community, and society that prison is the right course of action to prevent people from getting hurt (clear and present danger). However, that isn't the case with the vast majority of people who commit crimes. Remember, we're all capable of committing crimes...*The Lucifer Effect.* Nor is it right, or effective, to imprison anyone any longer than absolutely necessary. At a minimum, let's follow Europe's example.

In Dr. Covey's course, we teach about being a "transition person."[29] This is a person who breaks with the conditioning of family, youth, culture, or society to take personal responsibility to do the right things, to be proactive, to think long term, to know and do what's most important, to understand others, to have others' best interest at heart, and to find the best solutions to life's many problems. As my trial ended, my lawyer, who was intimately familiar with all the circumstances and facts of my case, said these final words to me. His words were to the effect: "Go in that prison and be the strong leader I know you are. You're an honorable man, and you have much to offer. You'll make a difference." He knew of my years' worth of honorable amelioration efforts and the courage it took to seek and get help, to plead guilty to what I knew to be true, and to testify against myself. He considered me a transition person, and he expected me to lead and help my fellow prisoners. I do try despite the toxic, anti-personal responsibility, bullying others environment.

Please be aware prison takes anyone, higher functioning or lower, and throws them into survival mode. It creates an environment that sucks out what's fair, what's right, and some people's compassion. It sucks out what's good. Prison makes things worse even for those who need it for the safety and security of society. I ask that no one ever be abandoned to prison, as everyone can and will change, even the person who commits heinous, reprehensible acts. We all need to help criminals change for the better, to change evil for good. Please take the opportunity to join a prison fellowship, ministry, pen pal, or visitation program. You'll find that you'll make a big difference. Your perspective will change toward these people. You'll be compassionate and wise.

Personal responsibility and transformational growth should be our universal goal. I ask for those people who are "crying for help" where there's another way to initiate the catalyst for change . . . another more conducive, positive environment, let that be society's first option. Help people have as many keys to open doors as possible. Being an convict and ex-convict closes doors and keeps them locked for so many. Conversely, our societies and cultures can help everyone heal . . . victims or perpetrators. I challenge you, the readers, to join me in taking the steps to be that "transition person," to help people everyone involved heal. We all need to follow Thuben Chadron's definition of *Sense of Integrity*: "Where we abandon doing what's destructive out of self-respect."[30] I, for one, am committed to help everyone heal and avoid destruction. In closing, I share a quote that sums up my definition of personal responsibility. Marcus Aurelius wrote, "If someone can prove me wrong and show me my mistake in any thought or action, I shall gladly change. I seek the truth which never harmed anyone. The harm is to persist in one's own self-deception and ignorance."[31] We all can adopt this wise Roman emperor's thinking and attitude.

EVERYONE'S PERSONAL RESPONSIBILITY

One night, not too long ago, there was another fight. This time, the aggressor, while going through treatment, had reported to the prison counselor (who's also a cop, and thus, there's no patient confidentiality) that he'd been sexually assaulted by a fellow inmate a few years earlier. With this information, the prison started an investigation that soon, everyone in GenPop knew about. For context, Congress recently has passed an act titled the Prison Rape Elimination Act (PREA), and the prison I'm in has followed numerous steps required by law to eliminate sexual assaults in prison. So the alleged perpetrator was questioned to get his side of the story, and of course, he denied the allegation. Since some time had passed, the evidence was very slight, and so the alleged perpetrator wasn't charged. For the prison administration, the issue was considered closed. But for the prisoners, the issue had just started. The alleged perpetrator rallied his friends and made fun and bullied the person who reported the illegal act (note: he already was a victim of prison bullying). With nowhere to go, the taunting took place almost every day for many months. Now he was victimized yet again for coming forward. The administration of PREA made the situation worse.

As mentioned earlier, in prison, you're with people 24 hours a days, 365 days a year. You see the person in the dining hall, or at work, or in the pod. In GenPop, there's nowhere to go to get away from bullies and other perpetrators. One may have wondered why crimes like rape or assaults are not reported in prison. Now I think it's obvious why. Even if the incident is real, telling someone is just signing up for more trouble. "Snitches get stitches" is alive and well in prison. It's great that Congress wants to eliminate the crime in prison, but how do they prosecute it without endangering the person even more? Per the PREA law, the prison has a confidential hotline; but once it's reported, the information is going to get out somehow. You can't separate people to make it go away. As I've already attested, prison just makes more victims. It's a toxic environment and isn't conducive to meaningful change that will rehabilitate. It just hurts people more. Especially, if to cope, the person turns into a bully. It's not the change society is hoping for.

So after months of taunting from the alleged perpetrator (whom I believe did commit the act, considering what I know of him) and all his friends, the victim finally had enough. The two individuals (the alleged perpetrator and victim) lived in different pods, and even though that was supposed to help solve the problem of close contact, it didn't. One pod had been called to the medication window for the inmates to get there "Meds," and the other pod was heading back after they'd received their "Meds." So the two individuals were passing each other, heading in opposite directions, when the alleged perpetrator taunted the victim again. However, this time the victim decided to lash out, and the fight ensued. Yes, the prison could have put the victim in protective custody and transferred him to another prison, but that doesn't solve anything either. The victim is now even being punished more for telling the truth. Trust me, word gets to the next prison, and the person will be bullied there too. So the victims remain in protective custody all their sentence . . . most times, for years. Prison creates and keeps them victims, not much of a motivation for prisoners to eliminate prison crime. Again, as a reader's personal empathy check, ask yourself, do you have compassion for them, or do you feel it's just part of the price they pay to society?

I mention this story to show that prison doesn't create an environment to stop crimes. It creates a place where more crimes take place, and those same people will eventually be released into society with their open wounds and poor *Coping* skills. Likely, they'll just commit more crime like they've been conditioned to do before and during their incarceration. It's no surprise to me that many prisoners are "radicalized" (as in radical Islamic terrorist) in prison. Prison creates an environment that teaches people that external influences drive their life. It teaches the antithesis of personal responsibility. It teaches the opposite of love, respect for human dignity, and peace.

We ended the last chapter discussing the fact that creating an environment where people learn to take personal responsibility for their actions and where people can change evil into good is the best way to help the victims of crimes, and other such hurtful actions. It's the best way to help society in the long run. A reminder is in order to state again that compassion, care, and concern for the victim is of the highest order of individual, familial, and societal responsibilities. This includes the perpetrator of the crime or hurtful action. The personal change we all want to happen should be based on remorse (which is Love-based), not regret (which is Fear-based). Getting caught and punished generates regret, not remorse. Restitution and retribution are best served by prevention and, if that's not possible, by rehabilitation with punishment being the last option, when there is no other choice. Otherwise, punishment, serving as revenge, isn't really what the victim or perpetrator needs to heal or to change . . . though that's the message of the media and governmental, political institutions. We've already learned that making more victims doesn't solve anything, but only makes things worse. Or as taught in the ancient Japanese story, *The Ronin,*[1] "None seemed to know that justice never rights a wrong, but only extends the pain to at least one more." Remorse and personal responsibility turn wrong into right, and turn poison into medicine.

So how do we get people, including ourselves, to learn and to change? How do we find the right environment? How do we make the change due to remorse, not regret? The right environment is one here something catches our attention . . . where loving kindness is the change driver. There are many natural consequences that'll help with that. One guarantee: Life is going to teach us lessons. Life provides the "change" environment naturally. If we're open to and ready for them, it's a positive experiential learning boon (as we've discussed in chapters 2 and 10). The teacher may be another person, a relationship, a coworker, a boss, an event, a crisis, or a disaster. The key to positive learning is to help people be open to the lessons and be changeable, which sets in motion the first two stages of the Transtheoretical Model: *Preconception and Conception* (as discussed in the last chapter). We don't necessarily need man-made manifestations of fear to solve people's problem. We need Love-based solutions using natural consequences as a catalyst.

Science tells us again and again that we've been conditioned because of past context, circumstances, and environment. Because of this, most of the time, we aren't open to life's lessons and change even when those lessons are beating down our door. We let ourselves be subject to the past and to the many *Cognitive Traps* that will likely be barriers to our learning. Deepak Chopra taught, "When the pain of being the same becomes greater than the pain to be different, you change."[2] He was discussing when personal responsibility meets a natural consequence, then real change will occur. There are still plenty of ways to use life's crisis as the environment for change with the proper guidance. Our correction systems should be focused on this guidance. Life itself is our teacher, and we'll learn no matter our state of mind, but does the lesson produce wholesome changes? Proper guidance is very important, but even with proper guidance, the lessons we learn are up to us . . . It's our personal responsibility. Just like coming to prison, it has been my choice to work to be "Better, not Bitter." That's not the case with the majority of my prison peers. Prison just made them bitter, blaming everything else. Proper guidance engenders personal responsibility.

Our natural inclination is to be bitter and to blame everyone and everything else for the problems and crises we face. This is our Fear-based response. Fear-based solutions only engender more fear over and above the natural consequences. Jill Fredston stated, "It is not a new phenomenon to feel the need to blame in the face of a crisis."[3] The challenges in life do not naturally teach us about personal responsibility, but that takes higher-order thinking. This is because so much of life happens outside of our control. Maya Angelou put it nicely when she wrote, "Nature has no mercy at all. Nature says, 'I'm going to snow. If you have on a bikini and no snowshoes, that's tough. I'm going to snow anyway.'"[4] We can't control nature. Will Durrant, a historian, stated, "Civilization exists by geological consent; subject to change without notice,"[5] meaning various disasters and painful experiences are only a heartbeat away. Nature is trying to kill us. To be more correct, nature will kill us. We can't control other people's thoughts, attitudes, and actions either. Life lessons are only a matter of time . . . Our opportunities to learn are numerous. It's said over 2,600 years ago the Buddha taught his Five Remembrances[6] (I'll only share four right now):

(1) I'm of the nature to grow old . . . I cannot escape old age;

(2) I'm of the nature to have ill health . . . I cannot escape ill health;

(3) I'm of the nature to die . . . I cannot escape death; and

(4) All that is dear to me and everyone I love are of the nature to change . . . There is no way to escape being separated from them . . . I cannot keep anything . . . I come empty-handed, and I go empty-handed.

As mentioned, not that it's the best environment, but coming to prison is a time when all four of the above "remembrances" seem to hit a person head-on. As I stated in my introduction, I've died many deaths since coming to prison. I've seen other people die many deaths too, some literally. When freedom and liberty are taken from you, when your position and status are brought to nothing, when your every action is monitored and questioned, when you're called a liar and worse, and when relationships are strained or broken, the prisoner is experiencing all the loss and grief that the "remembrances" describe. As listed previously, there are better options. I've already shared with you how heartbroken I am with my losses. I've also shared about other people's loss and how it's just made things worse for everyone concerned. I'll share another such story now.

One man shared with me how he has lost his familial relationships. Years have passed, and he is very sad with the loss. However, he's been embarrassed by his incarceration, and that embarrassment is the biggest barrier to reunification. He shared that after many years, he was going to call his siblings to reconnect with them. He called his sister and explained why he was in prison. She listened and accepted him and told him she still supported him. However, his call to his brother didn't go well, and it hurt him more as his brother hung up on him. He got angry and removed his brother from his call list. His heart was broken yet again. His self-image crushed more. He felt devalued and rejected. He didn't even try calling the rest of his brothers because it hurt so bad. I talked to him about how it made him feel about himself. He could see how it made him feel like less of a person and how he felt helpless and hopeless toward his family. Ties have been severed . . . the very ties he needs to reintegrate back into society in a few years. He naturally blamed his brother for the way he was feeling . . . He took his brother's rejection very personally. Now he's more bitter, and when he gets out, he doesn't have as strong a support structure, so he'll likely commit crime or purposely come back to prison, where he doesn't have to face his brothers.

Because life is so big and vast, because we can't really control anything, and because life conditions us to feel helpless, it's no wonder we naturally blame everything on something external. We can't stop old age (we've slowed it down a little), we can't stop illness (we've had some outstanding success with certain illness, but not all), we can't stop death, and we can't stop change. Most of life is external to us, and thus, we naturally are conditioned to think like lower life forms. *Negativity Bias* does have some truth to it . . . There *are* threats and dangers. That's why *Negativity Bias* is so pervasive. It rings true even when it's not true. Ironically, it seems some people sail along through life, and nothing bad happens to them, but it will. Eventually for all of us, something will go wrong. Someone will get hurt, including you or me. Then we're all left to ask "Why me?" "What have I done to deserve this?" "Isn't life supposed to be fair?" British playwright Toni Stoppard put it like this: "Life is a gamble at terrible odds—if it was a bet, you wouldn't take it."[7] If natural disasters don't get us, we'll be hurt in other ways and we'll be hurt by other people. This leads me to **my Fear-based insight,** which lines up with the first four of Buddha's Five Remembrances: **Life *is tough for everyone . . . No one gets through unscathed . . . Life is not fair!***

Despite tons of evidence to the contrary, we naturally believe the world is fair. In psychology, this is what's called the *Just-World* theory,[8] where we assume the world to be a good place. We see the world as just and meaningful. We intuitively believe good and bad events somehow distribute fairly and justly. Bad things happen to bad people, and good things happen to good people. We believe that people get what they deserve. According to this theory, we also assume bad things won't happen to us because of our *Optimism Bias* (we see ourselves as being good and therefore not deserving of bad events). So when bad things happen to us, which inevitably will happen, a *Dissonance* occurs. Leon Festinger coined the term in 1957 to mean "When what we know contradicts what we believe, we can either change our belief to fit the facts or change the facts to fit our beliefs."[9] We are then asking, "Why me?" The Buddha created his "Remembrances" to counter the *Just-World* theory's stated tendencies. By remembering, we reduce the *Dissonance*. We see we're not the only ones experiencing pain and loss. We can see the world isn't fair and just, and we'll not expect it to be so. We're less likely to get caught on the *Hedonic Treadmill*, which causes people to be dissatisfied enough to hurt someone else to get what's desired.

Despite the unjust, unfair world, to have "personal responsibility" means holding one's self accountable for what one's choices are. If so much of what happens to us is done by external forces, is there really such a thing as personal responsibility? Some neuroscientists argue that there's no such thing as "free will." This is because we are a sum of our conditioning and thinking. They say the way we're wired and conditioned is the true cause of all our actions, and many scientific studies do prove their point. Interestingly, many of the ancient masters agree with that point. For example, Buddha taught, "All that we are is a result of what we have thought."[10] However, the Buddha's fifth remembrance explains we can change our thinking . . . We've a personal responsibility to do so. We have a choice. Per the Buddha, personal responsibility is as follows:

> (5) My actions are my only true belongings . . . I cannot escape the consequences of my actions . . . My actions are the ground on which I stand (note: this is karma).

With this wisdom, we see that the personal responsibility we speak of are of the things we actually control. That concept is what Albert Ellis, Stephen Covey, Viktor Frankl, and others have taught in modern times. They've reflected what the Buddha told us . . . We can change our thinking, attitudes, and actions . . . We can choose. Nelson Mandela stated, "I realized that they could take everything from me except my mind and my heart. They could not take those things. Those things I still had control over; and I decided not to give them away."[11] We can continue to act and react according to our old conditioning, or we can be a "transition person" as we've discussed in the last chapter. Jean-Paul Sartre, the French philosopher, stated, "Freedom is what you do with what's been done to you."[12] The "free will" is our conscious effort to change our conditioning through our thoughts, attitudes, and actions (choices) . . . through mindfulness *(Metacognition)*. We can *recondition* ourselves using our own thoughts, attitudes, and actions as the catalyst . . . That's what mindfulness training is all about. To be a transition person, we need to practice mindfulness. Because it's not natural, we'll likely need guidance to obtain mindfulness. We need to understand that we have choice. That may sound obvious, but with the hundreds of people I've helped in the *7 Habits* course, I've been surprised how many blame everything on external circumstances. Personal responsibility starts on the inside.

As mentioned, my *Cognitive Trap*, all those years ago, was the *Scarcity Mentality*. I was looking for love outside of myself, so I shouldn't be surprised by people blaming the external forces for the consequences of their choices and actions. I did it too. Life's disasters and crises cause our lower life form thinking to naturally kick in gear, and *Negativity Bias* can dominate our thinking; though, our higher-order minds are capable of much more. Being mindful enables us to avoid *Cognitive Traps*. Shunryo Suzuki spoke of higher-order mind by saying, "Wisdom is not something to learn. Wisdom is something which comes out of our mindfulness . . . observe things."[13]

To bring in some more social science, when we were very young, we all started out as assimilators using what are called *Assimilation Cognitive Schema*. *Cognitive Schema* are little shortcuts we all employ throughout our day to fit each experience into a category with what we already think we know. As a small child, each new experience we had was tested to see how it fit into what we already knew (our existing schema). A plane in the sky was "a bird" or vice versa. When we were young we filed each new experience away in an already existing schema. As we grew older, when the new information didn't fit into the schema we already had, we made room for a new concept (i.e., birds fly and sing. That thing flies and makes noise . . . "Hey! They can't be the same thing."). Therefore, we accommodated the new experience, creating a new category, or what psychologists call a new *Accommodation Cognitive Schema* (i.e., it makes noise and flies; it's a plane). As children, our worldview was exploding with new experiences, and new schemas were being added all the time. Our worldview conditioned us to see a lot "out there," external to us.

As adults, we also have schemas (in other words, beliefs, assumptions, and expectations) based mostly on what's "out there." Though we too have new experiences all the time, they seem less novel because we assimilate them more readily into our broader array of experiences accumulated in our lifetime. We use *Confirmation Bias*, as we've already discussed, to reinforce our existing schemas. We've seen a lot "out there," and anything new has had to be processed quickly, so we use schema. We're exposed to an estimated two billion bits of information per second, yet we process only an estimated two thousand bits per second.[14] Shortcuts are a survival mechanism, especially in our modern, information-saturated age. Another psychology term like schema that we use is *Heuristics*, which means shortcuts we use to assess patterns and data to make judgments. In each experience we have, we use the shortcuts of schemas and heuristics to process the data. These are filters or lenses we use to view life. Together, they create our paradigms. So to take "personal responsibility" really means holding one's self accountable for what one's choices are given the current circumstances and context and given our schemas and heuristics. As we keep discussing, even though we don't control the world around us, we do control our choices—what is our attitude, what we think about, and what actions we take. We determine what schemas and heuristics we use to experience life . . . We can control ourselves through mindfulness.

In Buddhist philosophy, we hear repeatedly to combat the "ego." In our prison Buddhist group, we had a discussion that the ego discussed in Buddhism wasn't the same as what's taught in modern psychology and Psychoanalytical Theory. I voiced that they were the same. So I did a little research using the dictionary. Per *Merriam-Webster's* dictionary, the ego "serves as the organized conscious mediator between a person's perceptions and reality." It's further defined as "the self, as contrasted with another self or the world." Specifically, in Psychoanalytical Theory, it is one of the divisions of the psyche (mind), coupled with the "Id" and "Superego." After reading the definition, to me, it's the same "ego" in both Buddhism and psychology. However, I'd like to add that the ego is also directly tied to use of our schemas and heuristic tendencies. Why I discuss this now is to make sure we're all using the same definition when quotes about the ego come up.

"Fighting the ego" then is fighting our natural tendencies and thinking, to include all the *Cognitive Traps* we've been discussing. One more point about Buddhism's use of the word "ego" (or sense of self) is Buddhist philosophy teaches there's no separate self . . . In other words, "No-self." Does this counter the "personal responsibility" we've been discussing? No. Buddhism recognizes that we're all individuals, but really, we're all the same when it comes to our natural thinking tendencies with every action we do impacting everyone else. Also, as William James taught, we are all connected "like islands." Leonardo da Vinci stated, "Realize everything connects to everything else."[15] The point of the no self-concept is that we're all interrelated. Interbeing and No-self are similar concepts. What affects one affects all. By taking personal responsibility, one person is benefiting everyone. However, to do so, one must fight the ego. The self, or ego, is discussed as if it were a little separate being living inside us. Early Western philosophers came up with an idea of the "homunculus." A homunculus was used to describe the feeling we've that a little person is in our heads observing life as if on a movie screen. The recent Disney cartoon *Inside Out* was built on this premise as our emotions were represented as little beings running a control room in our head. It may be helpful to visualize these little beings, or the ego as something separate from ourselves, so that we can realize we can ignore them to make the changes necessary for personal responsibility, personal meaning, personal learning, and personal wholesome changes.

However, in reality, there's no little homunculus being or little emotional beings in our head, driving our thoughts, attitudes, and actions. It's us. It's our natural tendencies, conditioning, schema, heuristics, thinking errors, paradigms, etc., that make up who we are . . . that make up our ego. While it's helpful to blame the ego for the Fear-based actions and reactions, it's really us too. We're responsible. We all want to heal (most of us want others to heal too), and being responsible is the first step in the *Precognition* and *Cognition* stages of change. We've already discussed the insight in chapter 9 that we need to love, to have compassion for, and to forgive ourselves. This chapter is about the personal responsibility we all have, as Dr. Jampolsky taught, to forgive everyone and everything. **My Love-based insight** is as follows: *It's our personal responsibility to forgive everyone and everything . . . to let go!*

Forgiveness is taught and discussed in all of the world's major religions and spiritual traditions. Have we been discussing something radically new? No, not at all. However, I'll assert that I think that forgiveness is life's biggest lesson, and it's what really brings peace of mind. I'll also assert that I feel *forgiveness is the ultimate act of personal responsibility and love.* Lastly, I'll also assert that *forgiveness is the answer to every problem.* So I'm not going to introduce something radically new because the ancient masters already have, and religious and spiritual traditions were built around this important concept. Yet the ego doesn't want us to forgive, and it puts up barriers to forgiveness. We can justify not forgiving very easily, or even just "partially forgive," which is not really forgiving at all. The first question we must ask ourselves is this: is there some act that you feel is unforgivable? If you or I answer "yes," then we really don't believe in forgiveness. That said, we'll miss out on life's most important lesson. Yet we hear it all the time. "What so and so did is unforgivable." The *Happiness Hypothesis* introduced in chapter 8 reinforces the belief that in life, the scale can be tipped too far in the bad direction; and therefore, a person can't be forgiven or redeemed. Even by me writing that statement, many readers will naturally feel inside that it's a true statement. However, that lower-level feeling violates the principle of forgiveness.

Though I've seen many people in prison who are mean, nasty, mentally ill, hurtful, dangerous, and violent, I'm here to testify that *no one* is irredeemable! No one is beyond help and change! One man, who has a life sentence for murder, was taking the *7 Habits on the Inside* course. He's slated to be in prison for the rest of his life . . . He has no future to speak of. Yet he signed up for the course voluntarily, which should tell you something right there. One day I was teaching Dr. Covey's second habit: "Begin with the End in Mind"[16] when this man's anger and frustration with the fact he has no chance of ever getting out of prison came to a head. He lashed out at me as I was teaching, stating that what I was talking about had nothing to offer him. He stated words to the effect, "What you're teaching means nothing to a guy like me. I have a life-without-parole sentence! What future do I have?" How would you respond to such a statement? How do you teach personal responsibility to a person for whom "thinking of the end" means dying in prison? Is he irredeemable? Society and the legal courts stated he isn't redeemable. While no one would condone his actions, does forgiving him mean we do? I certainly don't condone my hurtful actions. I'd never expect anyone else to either. Forgiving someone doesn't minimize the hurt the person has caused. It doesn't excuse or condone their actions, nor does it change the past. However, it can and will change the future. The ego wants revenge. It wants to hurt the person who hurt us, or someone we love. We assimilate the person's actions using our schema and heuristic thinking. We discount him or her as a human being. We title them irredeemable or their actions as unforgivable. We lock people away, "throwing away the key," because of ego's vengeance.

As adults, *Assimilation* is likely a Fear-based *Cognitive Schema*. This schema is closed and judgmental. *Assimilation Cognitive Schemas* do not enable learning, growth, or wholesome change. *Accommodation Cognitive Schemas* are Love-based as we accept, make room for, and enable learning, growth, and wholesome change . . . ours and other people. An *Accommodation Cognitive Schema* even requires a person who's committed an extremely hurtful act or crime to accept their personal responsibility to change. We each can turn hurtful actions into good and wholesome actions. Remember the story of the Buddha and Augulimala or of Jesus and the harlot. These and other masters have taught that no one is beyond redemption or rehabilitation. As Buddha taught, it just takes "skillful means," in other words, the right environment with the right guidance. With skillful means (love), everyone can be taught, be changed, and be redeemed.

Ken Wert taught, "Unforgiving people cannot know the level of happiness, the peace, joy, and pleasure of releasing others from the prisons of their unforgiveness that forgiving people regularly experience. It's the very bars that keep other imprisoned in our hearts that keeps happiness far away, at a distance, peering in at best. It's time we free ourselves by letting old pain dissipate into the darkness so new opportunities can take us to greater heights of joy."[17] With that stated wisdom, even if it's supporting what society views as "unforgivable" or "to serve justice," we're unforgiving. We're supporting Fear-based strategies versus Love-based strategies.

I've brought up in past chapters examples of unforgiveness. I've stated that the people still holding on to justice as revenge are only hurting themselves. While that certainly is true, they are also hurting the perpetrator and, ultimately, humanity. Robert Muller stated, "To forgive is the highest, most beautiful form of love. In return, you will receive untold peace and happiness."[18] I submit, and so will humanity receive this peace and happiness. The reason I've tied the concept of personal responsibility and forgiveness together is because forgiveness is the ultimate act of love and personal responsibility. Also, because the fact we are all interconnected, forgiveness can bring everyone peace of mind, you and me. A world of peace! While this isn't a new concept or teaching, and it all sounds truly utopian, it starts with us individually . . . with you and me.

The ego (our sense of self with its biases, schemas, heuristics, and paradigms) tells us that we must protect ourselves because we've been hurt in the past using the *Precautionary Principle*. It tells us not to forgive for many, many reasons. The ego tells us to withhold our love, to make the other person pay for what they've done . . . thinking transactionally. However, that strategy never brings happiness or joy. That's *Loss Aversion* working at its fullest. If you'll recall, *Loss Aversion* is where we're so determined not to lose that we're willing to sacrifice everything even ours or others' peace of mind. The ego thrives on the *Scarcity Mentality,* as my offending history attests.

The ego uses *Hindsight Bias (The Rule of Typical Things), Availability Bias, Generalization (Stereotyping),* and *Fundamental Attribution Errors* to condemn, as irredeemable, everyone who commits a crime or hurts someone. Our ego tells us *Theory X* is true, and people have to be forced to be good. The ego tells us that *Theory Y* is for softies and is just going to open us up to being hurt again and again. The ego uses *Pain Avoidance* and *Loss Aversion* to justify hurting someone else as long as we don't get hurt, not realizing that it'll boomerang back around sooner or later. The ego takes the short-term thinking using *Confirmation Bias, Availability Bias,* and *Creeping Determinism* as its justification. In short, the ego doesn't want to forgive. The ego believes "revenge is sweet, forgiveness divine." And it tells us "we aren't divine." It even tells us we're arrogant if we tell someone we forgive them because by doing so, it implies, we think we're better than them. Likely, anyone's egos would get offended and defensive when someone forgives us. You may have experienced that reaction. I know I have. Yet that reaction is Fear-based.

Dr. Jampolsky wrote, "It is difficult to forgive when we listen to the advice of the ego, which tells us that we are doing the healthy thing by punishing the person who has hurt us and withholding our love from them. It is difficult to forgive because we have stubborn egos which attempt to convince us that it is better to hate than to love."[19] Dr. Jampolsky then taught that we have a choice to listen or not listen to our ego. Using my words for ego, I say we can "follow our lower life form thinking" or choose our higher-order thinking based on love, a choice that can give us long-range, wholesome, skillful thinking. *Forgiving is the highest-order thinking available.* As I've already stated, forgiveness is the solution to every problem and the key to everyone's peace of mind. We all have the ability to be "divine," to show real and meaningful love to one another. It's not arrogant to tell someone your forgive them. It's telling them that you really love them.

Trust me, the ego can come up with a myriad of reasons not to forgive. In Dr. Jampolsky's book *Forgiveness: The Greatest Healer of All,* he does a great job listing twenty common reasons we tell ourselves not to forgive. Our ego is the great justifier. The counselors work really hard to break the cycles that our egos put in place to justify our hurtful actions. Greg, my counselor, did the same for me over a dozen years ago. Our ego tells us to deny, deny, deny. It tells us to rationalize our hurtful actions or to minimize them, all in order to maintain our *Optimism Bias*: the view that we are good (not to be confused with an *Optimistic Disposition*, which is our positive view of the future, or *Theory Y*, which states our nature is good, not necessarily our actions). As we keep stating, we can, do, or will make mistakes. We can, do, or have hurt other people. We too are in need of forgiveness. We're also in need of forgiving . . . sometimes the harder of the two.

A powerful teaching from Dr. Jampolsky is to change our view of other people, specifically the people who have hurt us. He wrote, "Rather than seeing people as attacking you, see them as fearful and giving you a call for love. Be willing to see the light of an innocent child in everyone you meet, regardless of the costumes they wear and regardless of the terrible things that they have done."[20] It's easier to forgive when one thinks the other party just misunderstands, there's been a miscommunication, they were and are fearful, or they're crying out for love. Again, neither Dr. Jampolsky nor I are saying to condone the hurtful actions of others. But being able to forgive ourselves and others will likely require us to change our view of people. Geneviene Behrend said, "We all possess more power and greater possibilities than we realize, and visualizing is one of the greatest of these powers . . . everyone visualizes whether we know it or not. Visualizing is the great secret of success."[21] We can forgive even the worst offender even if to do so means we have to visualize and use our imagination. The Zen master Iyeyasu stated, "The life of man is like going a long distance with a heavy load upon the shoulders. Haste not . . . reproach none, but be forever watchful of thine own shortcomings . . . Forbearance is the basis of the length of days."[22] We're all like Sisyphus, pushing a bolder up life's hill. Then why not forgive? Everyone is "just like me."

Dr. Jampolsky wrote, "It is only through forgiveness can we stop the cycles of destruction and pain on our planet." He went on to say "It becomes easier to forgive when we choose to no longer believe we are victims . . . We can begin by letting go of the ego's belief that we must find someone to blame whenever something goes wrong. We can take these beliefs into our hearts, ones that allow us to see the value of letting go of self-condemnation and the condemnation of others and surrendering to love . . . forgiveness is a continuous process, not something we do just once or twice." These words remind me of the Mother Theresa quote from earlier. Finally, my last quote from Dr. Jampolsky is this: "The laws of love essentially amount to accepting people as they are, listening to them with understanding, respecting their feelings, and patiently and caringly build relationships."[23] Just think, if people were treated this way more often, there would be less hurt, pain, and suffering in the world. There'd be less crime and criminals. People would feel wanted for the right reasons. The way to prevent crime is to help all people understand and fight our ego, our *Cognitive Traps*, and our lower level life form thinking. If I'd understood my fear of abandonment and my narrow view of love being scarce, I could've taken steps to build myself up and shore up my defense against my ego's hurtful messages. I could've prevented my crimes. For all of us, Love-based thinking, attitudes, and actions are key to prevention . . . to society's protection.

In this book, I've shared a lot of my own pain and hurt that has been caused by others, the government, and society (both inside and outside of prison). I've done so not to complain but to make points needed to explain my insights, my lessons learned, and my personal growth. I don't feel I'm a victim; I'm a survivor! I've forgiven myself for being selfish when I should've been stronger. I've forgiven myself for not understanding love's power fully and for being fearful and using my Fear-based thinking, attitude, and actions to hurt someone else. I've forgiven My Sweetheart, knowing she loved me, but she was in too much pain and was fearful for her future. I've forgiven my family and friends who've felt the need to shun, abandon, and use *Relational Aggression* on me. I'm not sure why they've acted the way they did, but I'm giving them the benefit of the doubt that it wasn't meant to be malicious. I've forgiven the people who perjured themselves at my trial. I've forgiven the government lawyers who created evidence against me, both at my trial and for my appeals. I've forgiven the judge and the appeals courts for not protecting my constitutional rights. I've forgiven the prison bullies because they misunderstand many things; also, they're in pain and fearful. I've forgiven the guards for the times that there's been a misunderstanding or miscommunication. I've forgiven those who've committed crimes against me, both before prison and in prison. We all were acting out of fear . . . thus, my love to all!

As previously discussed, we go through life hoping others give us the benefit of any doubt, but life is not fair or just. Many times, we'll not be given the benefit of the doubt, or we'll hurt people, and people will hurt us. The Five Remembrances apply to all of us, to include being responsible for our thoughts, attitudes, and actions. We can't control anything but ourselves. We've the choice of what we think, our attitude, and our actions, to include who we love and who we forgive. We want others to give us a break . . . to give us the benefit of the doubt. Let's first give ourselves a break, give others a break, and be ready when life does or doesn't give us a break.

In chapter 9, I told you of an incident where I was on the phone, and the PA system didn't work to notify me about count. Since the time of that writing, I've had my disciplinary board, and I'm happy to report I was given the benefit of the doubt. I did work hard collecting evidence to back up my claim that the PA system malfunctioned, and though I did my best effort to explain the context and circumstance, it still could have gone either way. I was prepared for both outcomes. I was prepared to forgive yet again . . . myself and others. My peace of mind was at stake, and that's more valuable than my clean prison record. Mahatma Gandhi stated, "It is a million times better to appear untrue before the world than to be untrue to ourselves."[24] Forgiveness is the ultimate healer because by forgiving everyone, including ourselves and everything, we're able to be true to ourselves. Let us join together to use our higher-order thinking to take personal responsibility for our thoughts, attitudes, and actions, doing so with a focus on love and forgiveness.

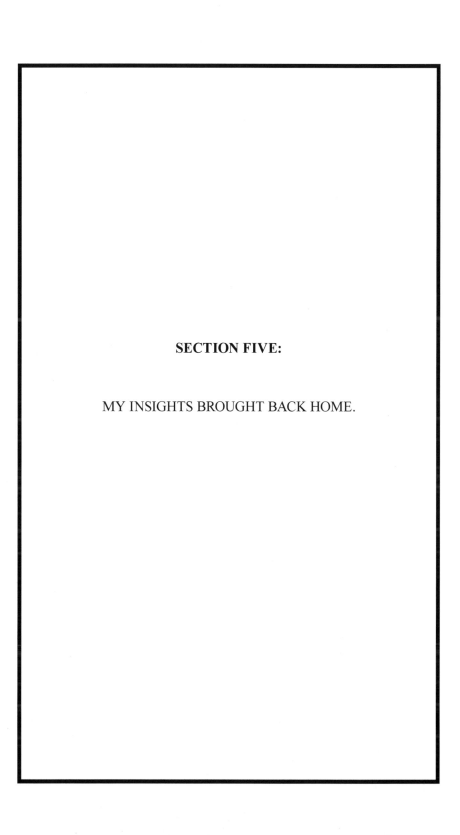

SECTION FIVE:

MY INSIGHTS BROUGHT BACK HOME.

TRUE KNOWLEDGE

A number of years ago, one inmate went into another inmate's cell and pummeled the cell's occupant very badly. I don't know why it happened, or much of how since it all happened on the other side of the pod. INN let me know it happened, that the aggressor was a very popular prison figure (a heavy), and the victim was an odd sort of fellow. Fights are a regular occurrence and sometimes when a fight happens, it's just a signal to affirm the pecking order. In that case, the bully or bullies just punch the victim's body so that the bruising is covered by the clothes, and the guards can't tell the fight happened. The message has been sent and received. However, hitting someone in the face likely occurs when the aggressor just doesn't care if they get caught, or they're so angry that they forget the likely outcome. Well, with this pummeling, the aggressor smashed the guy's face so badly that it looked like he might lose an eye. After the incident, the rest of the pod went into cover-up mode to avoid a lockdown. Lockdowns are the standard operating procedure for a fight in the pod. The victim was told not to come out of his cell and that people would bring him food so that the damage wouldn't be discovered. I'd not witnessed the fight nor was really involved in the cover-up. During the various "counts," he was to wear glasses and not to show his face. Somehow this worked for many days, but finally, a guard looked in and saw his black-and-blue swollen face with an eye ready to pop out. The lockdown ensued soon thereafter.

As mentioned, I didn't even know the fight happened when it was happening. But I was informed about it with everyone else, and I did my very small part to keep the incident under wraps, as one does when in prison. Once we were under the lockdown, the investigation took place. Each person from the pod was taken into an interrogation room and questioned as to what they knew. When it came to my turn, I acted ignorant, which I really mostly was. The investigator asked if I knew why we were locked down. I answered that I didn't, which was true. I didn't "know" why. It was only after we were locked down, and people were yelling through their doors, guessing about the guard discovering the victim, that I'd an inkling why we were locked down. But I'd no direct knowledge even though I suspected the yelled reason was, in fact, the reason. After the investigator's explanation of why he was questioning me, I stated I didn't see any fight because I normally stay to myself in my cell. I told him I didn't witness anything, and I knew no details that would help his investigation. By the way, even if I knew anything, I would've kept it to myself for reasons very obvious when one is in prison . . . to keep myself safe. I was escorted back to my cell; and finally, after a few days, we were let out after the perpetrator was led away in cuffs for a stay in solitary confinement. How the guards found out who it was that did the pummeling was beyond me, and still is to this day. A couple of weeks later, I "made custody" and was moved to another pod, and I didn't spend a moment thinking about past events.

My move to a higher custody level was based on my staying out of trouble and the amount of time I'd spent in the facility. Simply put, it was my normal time to move up in custody. To clarify, "down in custody" means more restrictions and "up" means less. A long time later, after the pummeler had come back to GenPop from his stay in solitary confinement, he wouldn't talk to me when we saw each other out on the recreation field. I was surprised, as before he went to solitary, we spoke politely to each other in passing. We were not friends, but we'd been cordial to each other. Though I was surprised, I just keep to myself and did my normal things, and we never really interacted. So there wasn't real chance that we'd speak for me to get understanding.

He went into solitary again for some other reason and, after a short time back in GenPop, went into solitary confinement yet again. Still, each time he was in GenPop, I'd see him in passing; and I'd say "Hi." Still, he wouldn't respond. One day I was talking to another person who was the pummeler's friend and was also kind of my friend. We were talking about something else, and the pummeler's name came up. I asked if he was okay, mentioning that he never responds when I say "Hi." I was then informed that the reason he wouldn't speak to me is because he thought I was the person who snitched on him. He had no proof but thought that because I'd made custody quickly after he went into solitary, I'd received special favor for snitching on him. Lucky for me, my friend had convinced the pummeler that I wouldn't snitch. Otherwise, I would've likely been the recipient of a cell visit myself. My point in bringing this story up is to say things are rarely as they seem. In fact, we really don't know much . . . For all of us, our search for clues is normally flawed.

It was really by chance that I wasn't the recipient of my own pummeling. Physicist Max Born stated, "Chance is a more fundamental conception than causality. We all owe more to chance than people realize."[1] Physicist Michael Faraday also clarified, "Human perception is not a direct consequence of reality, but an act of imagination."[2] The facts concerning my involvement with the pummeler going to solitary confinement were, in fact, all in his imagination. Sure, there was a chance that I could've been the one who snitched, and circumstances may have made it seem as though I had. Still, it wasn't proof. One big thing I've learned since my trial is there is a *huge* difference between "evidence" and "proof." I've *Experientially Learned* that principle! Many times, we as humans equate evidence with proof. When we do, things usually really get messed up. If my "kind of friend" hadn't vouchsafed for me, there may have been enough evidence for the pummeler to pummel again, or have someone else pummel for him . . . Either way, bad for me.

I ended the last chapter stating that one way to help us be more forgiving is to view the persons who hurt us as sending out a cry for love, as misunderstanding the situation, as being subject to a miscommunication, and as feeling so much hurt themselves that they're lashing out. Most times, even if perceived facts and evidence say otherwise, we really don't know anything for sure. Thus, giving everyone a break makes sense when we realize we just don't know. As previously discussed, we go through life wanting others to give us the benefit of any doubt; but most of the time, we're not willing to give others that same benefit. We need to stop thinking like the fictional character Sherlock Holmes who said, "When you have eliminated the impossible, whatever remains, however improbable, must be the truth."[3] Or stop leaning on Occam's Razor, which stated, "The simplest explanation is most likely the truth."[4] This kind of thinking leads to shortsightedness and hurtful actions due to misunderstandings and miscommunications. The example of the pummeler speaks to our innate ability to not know. **My Fear-based insight** is as follows: *we don't really* *know what we don't really know, and we don't really know much of anything.*

Philosophy has developed two constructs to use when one argues one's perspective. The first is called *Induction* and the other *Deduction*. With *Induction (Inductive Reasoning)*, the philosopher starts with an observation of one instance or system and then works to apply the inference, reasoning, or proposition to things generally. For example, I'll use my Fear-based insight from the last chapter that "life is tough for everyone." I know it's hard for me and others I've directly observed; therefore, I propose that it's hard for everybody. Another example is "prison makes things worse." Well, it's true for me and others I've talked to; so therefore, it makes things worse for all prisoners and their families. With *Deduction (Deductive Reasoning)*, on the other hand, the philosopher starts with a general observation, demonstration, or proposition and applies it specifically or narrowly to one instance or person. For example, "all prisoners are bad people and can't really be redeemed, so therefore, Prisoner X cannot be redeemed." Another example from my chapter 9 Love-based insight is everyone "needs to love, to have compassion for, and to forgive ourselves"; therefore, I must love, have compassion for, and forgive myself.

As mentioned, these forms of reasoning are man-made constructs developed to enable people to communicate ideas. They're not truths in or of themselves. Many times, we make the words or ideas as the truth (verbal or written). I've mentioned the Buddhists way of visualizing this idea is they say, "Don't mistake the finger pointing at the Moon for the Moon." Again, this points to the analogy that experiencing something is the truth, at least the truth for us . . . a subjective truth. Even the word "moon" doesn't adequately help us with the experience of looking up at the moon.

More often than not, our ego uses the reasoning that best supports its fearful position. Sometimes the ego uses *Deductive Reasoning*, and sometimes it uses *Inductive Reasoning*. The ego uses the *Precautionary Principle* in either form to make fear more motivational than love. The ego uses reason and logic to distort the truth, enabling fear to trump love. Ben Franklin stated the same thing this way: "So convenient a thing it is to be a reasonable creature since it enables one to find or make a reason everything one has a mind to."[5] Immanuel Kant put it another way when he said, "The oftener and more steadily we reflect on our own moral decisions, the more moral those decisions become."[6] The point is we envision everything *as* fixed and solid (including the truth). However, the more we learn, the more we realize truth is ever changing, thus creating uncertainty.

We humans don't like uncertainty. Most people fear uncertainty, and that fear causes problems in their lives. An interesting example of this from prison is how people who were not religious now become religious. The fear of uncertainty is the reason the old adage "There are no Atheist in foxholes" exists. I've witnessed as people become "Bible-" or "Koran-thumpers" (a term told to me when I arrived in prison) when they come to prison. Most of these people weren't religious before, and they never would've gone to a Bible study group in their spare time, like the ones held weekly in the pods. By the way, I feel odds are they won't go to a Bible study once they get out of prison. Interestingly, I've heard many of these same people express many times the sentiment, "I don't know why I'm here, but it must be for some reason that only God/Allah knows. So I'll turn it all over to God/Allah. I'll become his instrument." From what I can tell, they're using religion to quell their uncertainty. Now, I'm not critiquing religion. I'm pointing out our innate fear of uncertainty and that we're more easily able to turn things over to a "Higher Power" than concede things to chance or consequences. Uncertainty and chance make us uncomfortable. Either way, "we really don't know." Sir Roger Bacon said, "The first essential for advancement in knowledge is for me to be willing to say, 'we don't know.'"[7] Well, I don't know! I personally see uncertainty all around me every day. I recognize uncertainty exists before, during, and after.

Though I'd been raised a Christian, as the majority of the United States have been. I came to prison in the state of an "Agnostic." To many Bible- and Koran-thumpers, agnostic people are "fence-sitters" and are subject to ridicule. The term "agnostic" was coined by Thomas Huxley, the peer of Charles Darwin. He stated, "Agnosticism is not a creed but a method, the essence of which lies in the vigorous application of a single principle. Positively, the principle may be expressed in the matters of intellect, follow your reason as far as it can take you without considerations. And, negatively, in matters of intellect, do not pretend that matters are certain that are not demonstrated or demonstrable."[8] More simply put, don't say we know something unless you can prove it. Many religious discussions are circular arguments where the proof is "because scriptures say so."

For an example of this, one inmate I was talking to. I asked him what his proof was for his belief. He cited his scripture. I then asked him to explain how his scriptures proved his point of view when they're just evidence and, in fact, are the only evidence. I pointed out about all the thousands of scrolls lost throughout history and that "history is always written by the victor." I mentioned that the problem with depending on written proof is that any contrary document, scroll, or book was destroyed by the victor. What we have left is only what has survived millennia of book burnings. He got upset and stormed off. Now mind you, he's not a person to get angry, as his temper is why he's in prison . . . for killing someone in a very violent, bloody manner. As to the point about the lost documents, scholars have estimated that even now, we only have less than 10 percent of all the documents (books, scrolls, tablets, plates, papers, etc.) that have ever been written by man.[9] Part of the reason for the loss is age, of course. However, the biggest reason is mankind has destroyed anything that didn't support their point of view . . . their own *Confirmation Bias*. Book burnings are thousands of years old. Conquerors destroyed anything that didn't match their beliefs (schema, heuristics, and paradigms). My point is we really "don't know" even with documented evidence . . . Written or spoken words aren't truths anyway; they just point to truths.

I read a book by an atheist, and in his first chapter, he railed on religious or theistic people for believing in something that can't be proven.[10] But in all the rest of his book, he was stating that there was "no God." He wrote as if it were fact and that there was all this proof, giving his interpretation of scientific *evidence as proof.* So while starting with the premise that others are using evidence as proof, he turned right around and did the same thing from his polemic perspective. More ironic, he was slamming people who have "faith in God" when he himself was demonstrating his faith in his point of view of no God and his faith in science. All the evidence he was citing was evidence he gleaned using his own *Confirmation Bias*. He was *Coping* with his own battle with uncertainty by making it a certainty that there was no God. There are also people in prison who use the fact that they're in prison as proof that there is no God, and they ridicule the Bible- and Koran-thumpers. In my prison, we've even had a group of guys start a Satanist chapel group. Talking to some of the guys in that group, it's not as much a belief in Satan as it's a way to poke at the people who are Christian and Muslim. Again, my point isn't to support religion or antireligion but to point out the way we as humans deal with uncertainty. Norman B. Anderson said, "Religion is used by many as a way of interpreting both positive and negative events so that they are more easily assimilated."[11] The same can be said for antireligion. Religion and antireligion are both ways of *Coping* with life's craziness . . . with life's uncertainty.

Sir Francis Bacon stated, "The human understanding, once it has adapted an opinion, collects any instances that confirm it, and though contrary instances may be numerous and more weighty, it either does not notice them or rejects them, in order that this opinion remains unshaken."[12] Sir Bacon was no psychologist, but his insight demonstrates an understanding of *Confirmation Bias*. To confirm (pun intended) a thought that may have crossed the readers' mind as you read the above statements—"So science itself (even the social sciences) is subject to the *Confirmation Bias* trap?"— yes, there's no question that science and scientist can and do fall into the many biases and *Cognitive Traps*. However, scientists are more likely to admit that they do so and work hard to try and avoid doing so through the "peer-review process" and standardization of the scientific method.

Yet scientist can be, and are many times, wrong (or at least not right). There are many, many examples. The following example about medical doctors is but one example I could use: To me, it is amazing that only about 150 years ago (in 1857 to be exact, Louis Pasteur rediscovered bacteria), doctors didn't know about germs (virus and bacteria); and bloodletting was still a common practice. I read a book that told how back in history, doctors *wouldn't* change their smock or apron between surgeries. They'd go from one operation to another, wearing the same blood-soaked smock or apron day after day. The blood on the smock was how the doctor demonstrated that he was experienced. The newer the doctor, the cleaner the smocks; and the more experienced the doctor, the bloodier. To us today, this sounds crazy; but without understanding germs, it made sense, at least to the doctors. Laurence Gonzales said, "The word 'experienced' often refers to someone who's gotten away with doing the wrong thing more frequently than others."[13] And Jill Fredston stated, "We think of experience as a classroom, yet it can also be a prison."[14] Jamie Holmes wrote, "Uncertainty is an adverse state we avoid if we can . . . feelings of uncertainty bias us against new things, makes us prefer familiarity, and stops us from recognizing creative ideas."[15] Other than revenge, why we lock people up, alienate them, abandon them, and put them out-of-sight, out-of-mind is because of *fear of uncertainty*. We feel we can't predict what the criminal will do, so we victimize them. Fear only drives more victimization.

To cope with uncertainty, we use various *Cognitive Traps*. For example, the term *Fundamental Asymmetry of Past and Future* means "it seems relatively easy to see what happened and the causes or chance occurrences that led up to the situation, after the fact." You can do this with any historical event—Pearl Harbor, 9/11 attacks, etc. Daniel Gardner stated, "*Hindsight Bias* drains the uncertainty out of history. Not only do we know what happened in the past, we feel that what happened was likely to happen. What's more, we think it was predictable. In fact, we knew it all along."[16] Numerous social scientific studies confirm what Gardner stated. We can make meaning where there's no meaning, we can make fact where there's no fact, and we can prove where there's no proof. *Confirmation Bias* for physicist Leonard Mlodinow means "instead of searching for ways to prove our ideas wrong, we usually attempt to prove them correct . . . this applies to new ideas and existing illusions."[17] Daniel Gardner talks about *Confirmation Bias* when he stated, "We all do it. Once a belief is in place, we screen what we see and hear in a biased way that ensures our beliefs are 'proven' correct."[18] The book you've been reading is also subject to *Confirmation Bias . . .* mine! While I want this book to be meaningful to you, the reader, I adamantly state that these are my insights and my philosophy and are subject to my biases. I don't really know anything, but I believe these things. I've *Experientially Learned* many of these insights as my truths.

The Buddha, on his deathbed, told his disciples words to the effect not to take his words and teachings as fact but to explore them with their own experience. The Buddha was telling his followers that what he knew was not something they could know without experiencing it for themselves. In fact, earlier, he'd stated he had one hundred thousand different teachings for each of the various people he met. Other than for himself, he was stating that he "did not know." In Dr. Covey's *7 Habits* course, we discuss how, when we communicate, we normally use what he calls Autobiographical Responses.[19] Most of the time, we frame what we're saying to others using what we think, feel, and have experienced as our default. His point is we never really get to know the other person if we're projecting ourselves onto them. David Foster Wallace stated, "There's no experience you've had that you were not the absolute center of. We each are the lord of our own skull-sized kingdom."[20] Yet we forget that sentiment; and we know what others think, feel, and experience because that's how we'd think and feel . . . matching all to our experience.

At the end of the last chapter, I told you I'd been cleared of the charge against me. I explained that I'd collected evidence that gave a very plausible reason why I didn't hear the count calls and why I was out of my cell when count started. As if to prove my point of this chapter, the success of my efforts have created an unintended consequence. Since I've been cleared, people in my pod have been distant or rude to me. I even had one guy "get all up in my face" and threaten me. He told me he "hates me." I did my best to be Gandhi-ish, and I stood there calmly, speaking in a very cordial manner. This just got him more upset, and two other people pulled him away from me. I didn't understand why people became frosty to me as I'd really done nothing wrong.

Or had I? The next day, I was outside jogging when the senior guy in the pod pulled me aside to talk to me. I was informed that because it's so rare for anyone to "beat a charge" in prison, the people in the pod deduced (used *Deductive Reasoning*) that I was a "snitch" and had received some special favor. They were using evidence as if it were fact or proof. They were uncertain why I'd been acquitted when it's so rare. So they worked to resolve their uncertainty by filling in their gaps of knowledge with speculation. We as humans do this process all the time, day after day. It's how we *Cope* with uncertainty. We create beliefs and belief systems to manage the uncertainty. We then align ourselves with people who think and feel the way we do. We then tell each other stories to make sense of life's uncertainties even if those stories only have a small thread of evidence. We jump to conclusions using many of our various *Cognitive Traps* in order to make sense out of nonsense. The result is more misunderstandings and miscommunications.

In prison, as in all environments, religions and belief systems are used to determine who we can trust. We more likely trust people who think and feel the way we do. Obviously, this was an evolutionary advantage over the millennia. However, it also has led to wars and other horrific man-made disasters. Social scientists have a term to describe another trap, *Group Polarization*, which, according to Daniel Gardner, "means that when people who share beliefs get together in groups, they become more convinced that their beliefs are right and they become more extreme in their views. *Confirmation Bias* plus *Group Polarization*, and culture equals crazy views" (capitalization and italics mine).[21] These are all people who are afraid to say "I don't know." Knowing or thinking we *do* know creates closed-mindedness and judgmental thinking and enables violence and revenge. Think of the Nazis, the KKK, and many more examples. It has been said that the majority of wars are fought for religious reasons; however, wars are fought over *beliefs.*

While we see it today in the form of radical Islam, which is more about a radical belief system than religion, Nazism and Communism weren't directly religiously motivated, but their horrific actions were in defense of their closed-minded and unforgiving belief systems. Can culture, *Group Polarization*, and *Confirmation Bias* affect us today? One ironic fact is the United States, a mostly Judeo-Christian country, has the "highest incarceration rate in the world . . . that has gone up 600 percent since 1970 . . . while violent crime rate stands the same"[22] per Natalie Pompilio's recent Associated Press news article. Yet Jesus taught forgiveness. Mahatma Gandhi said, "If then I had to face only the Sermon on the Mount and my own interpretation of it, I should not hesitate to say 'Oh, yes I am Christian' . . . but negatively I can tell you that much of what passes as Christianity is a negation of the Sermon on the Mount."[23] I agree with Gandhi. Jesus's teaching of love, compassion, and forgiveness is a principle that I strive to emulate. **My Love-based insight** that applies to both religious and nonreligious conditions is as follows: ***the more we learn, the less we know.*** This insight is not new. Over 2,600 years ago, Lao-tzu stated, "The farther one goes, the less one knows."[24]

This insight is about love because it accepts everyone for who they are, what they think and feel, and how they act and react. It accepts uncertainty. As already discussed, we really don't know very much. We can have faith and believe many things, and all those things are right and true for us. For example, "nature" may prove God to a religious person and also disprove God to an Atheist. Both are right and true for those respective people. If we accept that we don't know everything, we're more likely to accept and love those who think and feel differently than we do. We can even love and care for people who've committed crimes, etc. We don't know other people's intentions. We don't know their thinking and feelings even when they tell us their thinking and feelings. This is so because words cannot truly communicate what's in the person's heart and mind. However, we can and should have empathy, but it's still filtering someone else's experience through our experience. This principle is as the Buddha taught many millennia ago.

I tell this story when I teach the *7 Habit* course as an example of one of my many paradigm shifts. When I was a boy, we had a milkman deliver our milk. (I know for some readers that is saying I lived in horse-and-buggy days.) Every time the milkman saw me, he'd call me Suzy. I'd no idea why, but I didn't like being called a girl's name. So I decided to trade insults, and I called him Mary or some other ladies' name. His reply was always "You can call me anything you like, but just don't call me 'later for dinner.'" In my young mind, I took this statement literally; and from then on, I traded insults by calling him Late for Dinner. Looking back, I think he must have thought I was a bit slow and probably drove away laughing. When I grew older, I realized my milkman was using a play on words. Sadly, it's too late to show him I'm not mentally challenged, realizing what he was really saying was a paradigm shift to me. Being older, I understand the world of double meanings of words and phrases. Context really matters as we gather evidence.

My simple mind had the same problem with the above-stated Love-based insight: "The more I learn, the less I know." This proverbial statement never really made much sense to me until I started to learn more, and I realized that the more I learned, *the less I really knew.* Truly, I now see that I don't know much of anything and can therefore accept everything! For this book, I've written hundreds of pages thus far; and really, what I'm sharing with you, the reader, are things I've learned and insights I've gained . . . They tell you about me and how I've been conditioned. However, I really know nothing, in the literal sense, other than the fact that "I don't know." Prison has only reinforced that I don't know. I have many beliefs; and my beliefs, though sharable, are very personal. I respect everyone else's beliefs as their own and, therefore, as not subject to my true understanding. Being Love-based, I accept everyone's perceptions as real and true for them and that my perceptions are my own. I see the wisdom in physicist David Bohm's words: "We are all linked by a fabric of unseen connections. This fabric is constantly changing and evolving. This field is directly structured and influenced by our behavior and by our understanding."[25] As Stephen Covey stated, "We see the world, not as it is, but as we are conditioned to see it."[26]

When we accept that we really don't know, then we open ourselves up to new experiences. We realize that there isn't just one way but many. There are trillions and trillions of teachings, and lesson, and teachers. We become accepting and open-minded. We're more able to forgive and to have compassion for everyone. We're able to love everyone. By accepting that we don't know and *cherishing that fact* rather than being fearful, we open ourselves up to having a "beginner's mind" as taught by Zen master Shunryo Suzuki. All the masters taught acceptance. Jesus was teaching that sinners are people too. Think of the story of the Good Samaritan or the harlot. Jesus was breaking with hundreds of years of traditions and religious dogma. The Buddha accepted everyone into his order, breaking the highly discriminatory Indian caste system, by teaching that everyone is a Buddha in need of awakening. Gandhi fought the Indian caste system that still exists.

When I came to prison, I determined to study all the religions that I could. Not all religions are represented in our prison chapel, so some I could only read about. I attended all the services and study groups I could, to include the religion of which I was raised. I opened myself up to them and their teachings. I read as many books on different religions as was possible. I love and accept all religions and antireligions. I've gleaned the shared principles from all the belief systems; and I've held close the ones who engender love, peace, compassion, and acceptance. All the principles are truths; but yet they still mean, even if ever so slightly, something different to different people. We're all experiencing principles and truths in our own unique manner. Physicist Neils Bohr stated, "The opposite of a correct statement is a false statement, but the opposite of a profound truth may well be another profound truth."[27] With this experience, I've been blessed by different prison ministries, especially the ones that espouse love, acceptance, and forgiveness.

Lately, there have been many studies on memory. Every article I've read states that we envision our memory is like a movie camera, and what's recorded is etched in stone, so to speak. Rick Hansen speaks of memory like this: "Memories are recalled (including its emotional associations) from a few key elements and then it is reconstructed with the things of the 'state of mind' when you recalled it the last time."[28] So each time we recall a memory, we change it and restore (as in filing it away) it with the emotional associations (i.e., fear or love) of our current state of mind. We can't count on our memories to be factual. In fact, we can say they aren't factual.

Since this is the case, how can we be sure of anything? We can be sure of how we are feeling, thinking, and acting right now. That's the only truth we can be sure of, and since each moment is subject to change, we can only be sure we are experiencing "right now" for what it is. Aristotle said, "It is the mark of an educated mind to be able to entertain a thought without accepting it."[29] A "beginner's mind" means we're experiencing right now and seeing it as new because we've never been in this exact moment before. We've already learned that chance plays a bigger portion of our lives than we might feel comfortable with. We've learned that uncertainty can scare us, or we can choose to love the fact that nothing is ever the same and never will be. Albert Einstein stated, "The most beautiful thing we can experience is mystery. He who does not know it, and does not marvel at it is, one might say, dead, and his vision extinct."[30] Every moment I'm feeling life's mystery . . . Join me.

The old adage "You can never go home" is true because we can never get things to be the same. Sure, we can get things close, but there'll always be differences. Our ego hates it that we don't know . . . It raises all sorts of fears. As Leonard Mlodinow put it, "We have a need to understand the situation in the terms of cause and effect."[31] Our ego wants cause and effect. We want the same surety with our memories. "This happened which led to this happening." Yet as we've learned, we only perceive a tiny fraction of all that happens around us in every given second. What happens to the rest of the data? We miss it. Then each time we remember something, we change it and its meaning. The more we remember it, the more it changes. Vincent Carroll, a *Denver Post* columnist, recently wrote an article titled "Can You Believe Your Eyes? In the article, he stated, "Prosecutors, defense attorneys and scholars have long known that eyewitness testimony can be problematic. Not only can it be colored by suggestion and prompts but also by people's natural tendency, according to Stanford law professor and former prosecutor George Fisher, to 'tailor their stories—and thus their memories—to the interests of their first listeners.'" Vincent Carroll goes on to say "And yet eyewitness testimony is indispensable in convicting many criminals . . . But, ultimately we're at the mercy of fallible humans."[32] Not so comforting, is it? We only know more uncertainty.

In a 2014 *The New Yorker* article by Michael Specter, I read about psychologist Elizabeth Loftus of University of California, Irvine. She's been working for decades, showing how "misleading information can insinuate itself into one's memory." I read about Loftus's famous study where she gave twenty-four people a journal filled with details of three events from their childhood. She solicited the help of family members to make the journals as accurate and compelling as possible. She then added a completely fictional experience of being lost in a mall at the age of five. The false memory was given many plausible details of the event to make it seem more likely. Then she interviewed the subjects, and 25 percent told of their experience of being lost at the mall. They even gave very specific details as if it really happened because *now it had*. Specter wrote, "These assertions were delivered with a precision that few people could have doubted . . ." Loftus had successfully seeded some subjects' memories with completely false memories.[33]

In a March 2012 *Wired* magazine article about a medication that can rewrite memories, the author, Jonah Lehrer, wrote, "Even though every memory feels like an honest representation, that sense of authenticity is the biggest lie of all." He goes on to tell of a study conducted by psychologist William Hirst and Elizabeth Phelps. In their study, they surveyed hundreds of people, very shortly after the September 11 terrorist attacks, concerning their memories of the awful events. They then repeated the surveys over time and watched as people's memories changed, sometime with wholesale changes of where they were and who they were with. One year later, 37 percent of the people's stories changed; and three years later, around 50 percent had changed their stories. Elizabeth Phelps stated, "What's most troubling, of course, is that these people have no idea their memories have changed that much." Lehrer then wrote, "Reconsolidation provides a mechanistic explanation for these errors. It's why eyewitness testimony shouldn't be trusted (even though it's central to our justice system) and why it's disturbingly easy to implant false recollections." The article goes on to say "The psychologist Elizabeth Loftus has repeatedly demonstrated that nearly a third of subjects *can be tricked into claiming* a *made-up memory as their own*. It takes only *one single exposure to a new fiction* for it to be reconsolidated as fact" (italics mine).[34] Numerous studies[35] show memory changes over time. People, as they repeat the story, add or drop details. People even add details they learned after the fact. We can't trust our mind to give us proof, just some evidence. Our memories aren't a tape recorder or video camera . . . They're subject to influence and are fallible. Our brain is subject to conditioning traps.

Being Love-based means that we accept everyone for who they are right now in this moment. That being said, it seems that most people are trying to change the other person to conform to their worldview, their paradigm.

We see it all the time among religious people. There always seems to be an effort to convert someone else to their belief. Notwithstanding, unconditional love isn't based on someone's performance, belief, or actions but only because they're human beings, just like us. Meister Eckhart put things nicely when he wrote, "The eye through which I see God and the eye through which God sees me is the same."[36] Unconditional love is inclusive, not exclusive. It's beyond right and wrong, good and bad, light and dark, "I and you," "I and it," etc. When we create opposites, poles, or duality, we create division and exclusiveness. The key point to not knowing is you and I admit that the divisions are man-made constructs, many times leading to an "us versus them" mentality. We don't and can't know the future. We can't see the unintended consequences of any of our actions. We can't see the final impact of any given action or circumstance. For example, my teenage sons are growing up without their father in their lives. Is that a good or bad thing? Time will tell. However, even if you or I take a snapshot in some future time, we still can't know if it is or was good or bad. All we know is "It is what it is," and "It'll be what it'll be." It might be generations to see the outcome of my sons' current circumstance. But even then, that's still not the end . . . The outcome is still never final. The decision to marry my wife, was it a good or bad decision? Really, that's a pointless question because I did marry her. I did have children with her, and we divorced and are estranged. "It is what it is," and looking back is an exercise in futility. *Hindsight Bias*, *The Fundamental Asymmetry of Past and Future,* and *Creeping Determinism* are all terms for how our mind and our ego deal with the concept of time. Yet past and future are still only in our imaginations, our perceptions, and our fallible memories.

We don't know that what we remember is completely true, and we can't rely on the past to be real. We need to live in the present, letting go of the past, letting go of past fears, letting go of past hurt, and letting go of grudges and vengeful wishes. We don't know what we don't know, or what we do know. We have to live right because it's the right thing to do and nothing else. We need to realize we don't know the outcome of our actions, but they're our actions, and we own them as the Buddha taught. Still, we don't know the unintended consequences of any given act. We can't determine where the cascade of events, actions, and conditions will lead. We need to let go of the concern for the outcome of our actions and focus on doing our best to do things right. That stated, we can do "the right thing," and it could still turn out hurtful and harmful to someone or something. So we just do our best always. Ethics, morality, principles, values, and religious teachings are skillful guides to doing right actions *that likely cause less harm*. But we still don't know. Now we can see why forgiveness is so important . . . We really don't know. Since we *all* will be victims from someone's thoughtless and malicious actions, inactions, or words and we *all* will be victims of hurtful conditions or circumstances, forgiveness is a tool that enables each of us to Be Better, Not Bitter. I'm working, every day and every hour, to forgive. Not really knowing gives more validity and credence to everyone's personal responsibility to forgive . . . to let go. With love in our hearts and peace and wisdom in our intentions, we step into the future, ready to forgive.

HEROES AND REAL FREEDOM

What makes someone a hero? What's the definition? According to *Merriam-Webster's* dictionary, a hero "is an illustrious warrior; a man (or woman) with great strength or ability; a man (or woman) admired for his (her) achievements and noble qualities; and one that shows great courage." I'll add, and I'm sure you'll agree, that a hero is a person willing to put their life on the line for others. The word's Greek origin means "protector." With me being in a military prison, I'm surrounded by heroes. With my many prison stories about bullying, crimes, and other lower life form actions that occur every day around me, it may surprise you to read my words about these men being heroes. However, these men are the same type of men who are written about in books and shown in war movies like *Lone Survivor, Black Hawk Down, American Sniper*, etc. The only difference between those heroes in books and movies and the men surrounding me in prison is they made a mistake and committed a crime. It might surprise you to learn that many of my fellow prisoners served multiple tours in Iraq and Afghanistan, or in some other locale in support of those and other wars. Many had served their country, voluntarily, for many decades. All, if not directly but indirectly, killed for the United States, for your freedom and for democracy throughout the world. Many had impeccable military records, and their *only* mistake is the one that brought them to military prison. Like ancient Greek heroes, who'd committed grievous acts, these heroes have their battle with their dual divinity and humanness. As stated before, the majority are first-time offenders; but because of the seriousness of their crime, there was no second chance offered or given by the military. Many, if not all, were having mental and relationship issues related to overwork, stress, separation anxiety, post-traumatic stress, and combat. If you'd met these men before their court-martial, you would've considered them heroes. You would've thanked them for their military service when you saw them in uniform at the airport. Now they're just forgotten warriors, whose service to their country is in the past. These many heroes are no longer considered heroes, but now wear the title of convict. Does the title change who they are, heroes? No. Does it take away their heroic actions, lives dedicated to serving our country, and veteran status? Sadly, yes, it does.

When I was a kid, I watched a *Perry Mason* TV episode in which the defendant was a military man. He'd committed the crime, but the military jury was asked to take into account his heroism when determining his sentence. The defense then read off all his many heroic acts in the service of our nation, and his sentence was lessened because of his outstanding military record. As a boy, I remember thinking how fair that was for a person who was defending me and my country to receive extra mercy. While the Manual for Courts-Martial still allows that process to take place, it's a very weak, meaningless act, mostly ignored by judge and jury. If the defense submits the person's military record, it may even be read aloud to the judge or jury, but it doesn't help like it used to. The reason this is now the case is judged mostly because of political reasons. In fact, having an outstanding record is now likely a detriment to the defendant, as it's used as a demonstration for just how "far the hero has fallen." The anecdotal evidence states the military judicial system discounts, minimizes, and forgets any great, heroic, and honorable thing done for our country.

I see the reason as twofold: First, the military now is so worried about their image with the public that any hint of mitigation, even in the form of an outstanding military record, is sacrificed in the name of what's good for the military's image (politics). The fact that the person was a military veteran who committed a crime means the person embarrassed the military's good name and is now an "embarrassment to all people who wear the uniform." Of note, the military judges and juries are made up of people who wear that uniform . . . the person's peers. Furthermore, a "jury of peers" in the military is a very selective population, all who believe the axiom that "we're held to a higher standard." Only 1 percent of the U.S. population serves in the military, voluntarily I might add. Additionally, because so few military members commit serious crimes (I'd estimate less than 1 percent), the few who do are looked upon with ire and treated with disdain and disgust. The higher standard creates a constitutional injustice. By volunteering to serve our country, our rights are taken away.

Second, the military institution has an "attrition mentality," the same "attrition mentality" that, historically, has sent millions of people into combat to die in the trench warfare of WWI, the jungles of Vietnam, etc. The "attrition mentality" can be defined like this: "People are needed, but some will be lost along the way through death or some other factor. Not to worry, we'll just recruit or draft more people to replace the losses." So what comes into play judicially is an unfair and unjust legal standard set in the back of the minds of the military judge and military jury. This in addition to *Cognitive Traps* and the lower life form tendency to separate, abandon, and ostracize. Of note, mercy is not a military "core value." However, we've all heard of *military discipline*.

Legal scholars have a phrase for when a jury is unduly influenced by the prosecution. They state the "prosecution inflamed the passions and prejudices of the jury." I feel that certainly was the case with my court-martial. The result of the overzealous military justice system averages around a 95 percent conviction rate compared to around a 85 percent civilian rate.[1] Also, military members get harsher sentences than their civilians counterpart (as mentioned earlier, many times triple the civilian sentence). Yet heroes can, and do, make mistakes too. Heroes deserve *fairness and mercy* too. Sadly, not just with me, the whole of the person's record is forgotten or ignored; and *Availability Bias, Contamination Effects,* and *Negativity Bias* are encouraged and free to take place to protect the military's image . . . in military terms, "to promote good order and discipline."

A recent study, unrelated to the military, demonstrated that it's best to have one's parole board first thing in the morning or right after lunch because the board members are refreshed and are more likely to grant parole.[2] What does this tell us? Being well fed changes how we make decisions. Curiously, my sentencing hearing went from five o'clock until eleven o'clock on a Friday night before a long Autumn holiday. Do you think that affected the jury's decision? Did it have an effect on my sentence? Likely, the jury, consciously or subconsciously, was trying to go home, camping, etc.

We all think reason reigns supreme, but a little thing like low blood sugar or impatience to go on holiday can affect our higher-order thinking processes, let alone all the *Cognitive Traps* already in play, influencing people's lives for the worse. Even our reasoning processes, of *Induction* and *Deduction*, can cause unfair results as they're based on the *Generalization* thinking error in one direction, or the other. We tell ourselves that judges and juries are objective and fair, but they too are subject to emotions and thinking errors. All judges and juries are going to have their passions and prejudices inflamed . . . The prosecution knows this, and they push things to get away with as much inflaming as possible. That's what they get paid to do . . . to imprison people. O. J.'s lawyer, Alan Dershowitz, said, "The courtroom oath—'to tell the truth the whole truth and nothing but the truth'—is applicable *only* to witnesses. Defense attorney's prosecutors, and judges don't take this oath . . . indeed, it is fair to say the American Justice System is built on a foundation of not telling the truth."[3] We already know that juries and the people Mr. Dershowitz mentioned are subject to the various *Cognitive Traps* we've been discussing, even if there are no nefarious intents or actions. We know legal arguments rely on *Inductive* and *Deductive Reasoning*, which may include untruths here and there, to ensure a win. Added to the fact that the only people who are required to tell the truth have fallible memories (discussed previously), and it's no wonder *any* legal system is flawed.

We've all seen the TV drama where the defense yells, "Objection, Your Honor," and the judge will "disallow the evidence" or what has been said and instructs the jury to "forget what you just saw or heard." But it's *already too late.* The jury has already been influenced by the *Anchoring Effect.* The *Anchoring Effect* is where a meaningless bit of information (an anchor) influences the person's subsequent decision, completely unbeknownst to the person. The prosecution knows about the *Anchoring Effect,* even if they don't know the psychological term. Why do you think they made that false or inadmissible statement in the first place? To the lawyers, it's gamesmanship.

Daniel Gardner cites an example of *Anchoring Effect* from a German study in his book *The Science of Fear*, where some judges are called on the phone during a break while deliberating the person's sentence and asked by a reporter if the sentence will be some very low number of years. Other judges are also called conversely, and asked about the possibility of a very high number of years for the sentence. In both cases, the judges do what they're supposed to do and refuse to answer the question and hang up. However, when the sentence is pronounced, the meaningless number given by the reporter has influenced the judge's decision compared to the study's control group, where no reporter called.[4] Legal scholar Frederick Schauer said, "Painting with a broad brush is an often inevitable and frequently desirable dimension of our decision making lives."[5] This may be true, but be prepared for many mistakes when one *Generalizes*. There's no true objectivity when people are involved. All people, and their institutions are full of foibles and follies. I state all this to introduce **my Fear-based insight:** *honor, courage, and other good acts are quickly forgotten, or heavily minimized and discounted until those acts are meaningless.*

While it's very, very hurtful when this happens, maybe it'll soften the blow if we understand why this happens. It has for me. Humans and their institutions are ruled by the human brain. In 2002, psychologist Daniel Kahneman stated that every human brain has two systems at work every moment of the day.[6] *System One* is *Feeling*, and it works on a lightning-fast subconscious level using snap judgments, hunches, intuitions, and emotions. If we say to ourselves, "I don't know why, but I just feel this way," we are experiencing *System One. System One* is tied to our Limbic System (as described by French neurologist Paul Broca in 1878)[7] or the older portions, evolutionary speaking that I mentioned back in chapter 4. In this book, I've referred to the Limbic System's processes as lower life form thinking; and while the Limbic System is very, very important to our survival, it makes many mistakes. *System Two* is *Reason*; and it works slowly as it examines evidence, calculates odds, and considers options. We know we're using *System Two* if we can easily put the "why" into words. *System Two* or what's called higher-order thinking makes better decisions that are less reliant on the many *Cognitive Traps*. That said, *System Two* is also subject to making mistakes when it depends on and utilizes thinking errors. In fact, social science has also demonstrated that overthinking things can only make things worse, imprisoning us and others with a constant didactic voice in our head. If our bloodstream has low blood sugar, required for higher-order thinking (our brain is a calorie hog), or at eleven o'clock on a Friday night, before a long Autumn holiday weekend, which system is the most powerful? We know we can't control others or circumstances and contexts. So then how do we combat either system's tendency to discount and minimize another's good, honorable, and courageous actions? How do we balance between two systems (Reason and Feeling) to make mistake-free decisions?

The first and most powerful answer is with love as our watchword, recognizing the fact that fear plays a big part of both *Systems One* and *Two*. Realizing this foible allows us to create a more loving and compassionate mind-set. It enables us to realize that "Forgiveness is our function,"[8] to quote Dr. Jampolsky. Second, we admit to ourselves that we really "don't know" as we've discussed in the last chapter. Not knowing doesn't mean we have failed. It means we recognize that even with the best evidence, there still will be many unforeseen and unintentional outcomes. Realizing that we truly "do not know helps" us genuinely forgive ourselves and others. It helps us realize that the same applies to others as well. Third, we recognize our tendency toward the various *Cognitive Traps*. By doing so, we'll make less errors, we'll hurt others less, and we'll be hurt less by ourselves and others. These three mindfulness factors help us understand that all of ours and others' honorable, courageous, and good actions can be quickly forgotten or minimized . . . by us, as well as others toward us. Having a flexible mind-set allows better human understanding. With *Metacognition*, we're more willing to give everyone a break . . . a second or even a third chance.

A visualization tool in the management of our two systems, as we've discussed in chapter 8, from Dr. Covey is a metaphorical concept, the "Emotional Bank Account." In his concept, there are two types of interpersonal transactions: "a deposit" or "a withdrawal." Examples of deposits are telling the truth, seeking to understand the person, keeping your word, etc. Examples of withdrawals are lying, arrogance, breaking promises, etc. In Dr. Covey's metaphor, deposits and withdrawals happen all the time in every relationship. He counseled us to put our efforts to make more deposits than withdrawals. He also states that many times, withdrawals, if serious enough, can bankrupt the account . . . Withdrawals are more powerful than deposits.

Covey's metaphor, coupled with psychologist Phillip Jackson's words quoted in chapter 4: the "strategy of psychological withdrawal"[9] (not to be confused with account withdrawals), look at relationships as transactional, not transformational. In other words, once we feel the Emotional Bank Account is broke, we all can stop compassionately caring for someone. That being recognized, is that the skillful course of action? Is it the Love-based, wise, and compassionate course of action, or the Fear-based response? I know there are times when abandonment seems like the only solution; but as we've learned, it fails to take into account contexts, circumstances, conditions, conditioning, and potential. We've also discussed that abandonment is shortsighted thinking. It looks at *relationships as obligations, not opportunities.* We, being Love-based, are long-sighted. We're seeking to have our love be "unconditional love." Any "psychological withdrawal" from a relationship is *Relational Aggression* by another name—conditional love.

We're working not to make attribution errors. *Fundamental Attribution Error* is described by Leonard Mlodinow this way: "We cannot see a person's potential, only his or her results. So, we often misjudge people thinking that the result must reflect the person."[10] In short, we don't know. I see shortsightedness on deciding that anyone's Emotional Bank Account is ever really bankrupt. We all can and will make major withdrawals with everyone, looking transactionally. Our own arrogance, our tendency to judge, and many other *Cognitive Traps* disable our wisdom and compassion toward others. We think we know when we really don't. Considering an account "bankrupt" means we think *we do know.* Viktor Frankl wrote, "Men will be guided back to the commonplace truth that no one has the right to do wrong, not even if wrong has been done to them."[11] Dr. Covey, when writing about deposits, stated, "How you treat the one reveals how you regard the many, because everyone is ultimately a one."[12] Mahatma Gandhi's words reflect a long-term mind-set (a deposit) when he stated, "It is always possible by correct conduct to lessen an evil and eventually bring good out of evil."[13] Everyone has the potential for correct conduct . . . No *one's* account is totally bankrupt. For us all, unconditional love takes higher-order thinking and feeling.

An example of not really knowing and our tendencies toward *Cognitive Traps* was recently written about in my prison's newsletter. The article was about exoneration. Interestingly, in 2015, a record showed fifty-eight U.S. people were exonerated based on DNA evidence (cases of murder and rape).[14] Sadly, after decades in prison, many states don't have the money to compensate the freed individual. So after years in prison, being made indigent and derelict, the person is released to society to live on Social Security with a minimum-wage job. These were people the judge or jury *were convinced* were guilty based on the evidence. These convicts were sent to spend decades in prison but were lucky that they were cleared based on more substantial evidence. Of note, there were many convictions where there was no physical evidence used to convict . . . only an accusation. Hardly 100 percent proof! Sadly, more and more convictions are based *solely* on very fallible witness testimony. It's hard to be exonerated when only memories are involved. While DNA, fingerprints, and other hard evidence help us "know" to a greater certainty, even then, it isn't foolproof either.

An unforeseen, unintended consequence, according to one exoneree, is even though he's innocent, people now judge him because they feel "prison turned him into a bad person."[15] His statement itself is very telling. There are many innocent people and first-time offenders in prison who will become "bad people" because they were sent to the toxic environment, which is prison. If they don't become bitter and hardened, people will still feel they have because of the experience. Is that what we want? People are afraid of ex-cons. They're afraid to hire them or to live next door to them, just because they've been convicted of a crime; and the added expectation is that prison has made them worse, not better. Yet prison was society's chosen solution to the offenses. The high recidivism rate can be partially blamed on fearful people who are looking for reasons to judge. As George Orwell wrote, "Everyone in this world has someone else whom he can look down on."[16] Society has created vehicles, enabling people to discriminate and withhold love, calling it justice.

Speaking of looking down on a person, societal solutions, and second chances, I'll ask the following question: Is it more compassionate and humane to lock a person away for life or to execute them? People who state they are fighting the death penalty are doing so for humane reasons, and I respect them for their efforts. On the other hand, have they had to face a life in prison? People against the death penalty state they value life, yet they're willing to let someone live a miserable, tortuous life for all their remaining days. Why is that okay? To punish? Yes, to punish. How many times have you and I heard the sentiment, "Let them rot in prison." To me, that is just Fear-based revenge. Having lived in prison, I think and feel it's no more inhumane to make someone live out the rest of their life as a trapped animal, than to execute them.

In my opinion, it's more merciful to kill someone than have them suffer more pain and anguish. Remember, the reason they committed their heinous crimes was because they were in pain and suffering, or they are psychopathic . . . Either way, they needed help prior to their criminal act. Maybe, many of the same well-intentioned, anti-death penalty people would advocate for assisted suicide because it's a humane way to end someone's suffering. How about assisted suicide as an option for prisoners serving life-without-the-possibility-of-parole sentences? My friend who has a life-without-the-possibility-of-parole sentence for murdering his wife told me, "It feels like I'm very slowly and painfully dying every day with my eyes open." I say let the prisoner choose death over torture. People who argue otherwise likely think of justice as retribution . . . eye for an eye. While it's okay to make someone suffer and be miserable for the rest of their lives, because they committed a heinous crime, it's not okay to kill them. That doesn't make, Love-based, sense to me.

From a different perspective, could it be we, as a society, don't trust the legal system to convict only the guilty? How many innocent people are suffering in prison? Or could it be we subconsciously know the vast majority of people are inherently good and capable of change; but we, as a society, are too shortsighted to find more humane solutions than locking someone up for the rest of their "miserable" life? If human life is valuable, as the proponents against the death penalty advocate, then let's find solutions that recognize people can change to be good. Let's find humane ways to give the majority of the people, even ones guilty of the worst, a second chance.

While I still believe everyone is redeemable, even the worst of the worst, if society deems that the convict is too dangerous to live in society, then why is executing or helping them commit suicide an issue? We "put down" dangerous animals once they've shown they're willing to attack and kill people. While I recognize it's very hard to give serial rapist and killers, mass murders, etc., an extra chance or be left in society, I feel the humane thing to do is to let them be executed, or assist with their suicide. Let death be a merciful option for the worst of the worst who'll never leave prison.

Interestingly, speaking of wisdom and compassion, in many European countries, the longest sentence a person can get is twenty years.[17] Yet Europe's crime rates aren't soaring. It goes back to what was mentioned in the last chapter, a criminal isn't choosing, in the overwhelmingly majority of the cases, to commit crime using rational, logical means. The criminal isn't doing a cost-benefit analysis as he or she decides whether to commit the crime. In fact, emotions, past conditioning, mental health, contexts, conditions, and circumstances are at play. As mentioned, many European countries obviously recognize that people can change. They're wise to the downside of escalating prison sentences in the false hope that the crazy-long sentence will reduce crime. Europe recognizes the empirical, not emotional, evidence from the many social studies that show longer sentences don't reduce crime. I think if the death penalty was reserved for the worst of the worst, too dangerous for society (i.e., Jeffrey Daumer and Charles Manson), and the rest got a maximum of twenty years to give them time to rehabilitate using effective programs, it would enable prevention and real restitution. It would show that we really do value all humans, even criminals.

Renowned psychiatrist Dr. Daniel Amen talks about one of the many conditions that factor into criminal decision-making. He wrote, "Judges and defense attorneys sought our help in trying to understand criminal behavior. To date we have scanned (the brains of) over five hundred convicted felons, including ninety murders. Our work taught us that **many people who do bad things often have bad brains . . . that was not a surprise . . . but what did surprise us was that many of these people had brains that could be rehabilitated**. Here is a radical idea I recently discussed with a group of judges in Georgia. What if we evaluated and treated troubled brains, rather than simply warehousing them in toxic, stressful environments?" (bold in original) Dr. Amen goes on to say "In my experience, we could potentially save tremendous amounts of money by making a significant percentage of these people more functional, so that when they got out of prison (if they had to be put there in the first place) they could work, support their families, and pay taxes. Dostoyevsky once said, 'A society should be judged not by how it treats its outstanding citizens, but by how it treats its criminals.' Instead of just crime and punishment, SPECT imaging taught me that we should also be thinking about crime, evaluation, and. treatment."[18]

Note: SPECT stands for single-photon emission computed tomography, a type of brain scan. When I read this, my first thoughts were "I wonder what was wrong with my brain during the time I committed my crime . . . my anomalous actions," "Could I have been helped earlier so I did not hurt my victims?" and "What damage did my actions cause my victims, and how can their brains be rehabilitated too?" Again, like DNA evidence, brain scans provide better evidence. Obviously, we want to make better, more informed decisions to reduce the chances for unseen and unintended consequences. Prison is "toxic," I can attest to that fact! It's very encouraging to know we can find better ways to prevent or rehabilitate crime with better technology. Biofeedback has been proven to be a very effective tool in many ways. Think of how much money could be saved if we spent it on brain scans, for example, rather than spending $28,000 to $50,000 per year per person to warehouse them.[19] Think of the humane aspect of the value of a mentally healthy human being.

However, even with better technology, more wise and compassionate thinking, and more reasoned decisions, mistakes will still happen. There'll be unforeseen and unintended consequences. Heroes and honorable and innocent people will be imprisoned, figuratively and literally. Societies, institutions, justice systems, communities, families, and individuals are all fallible with inherent foibles. As we've already stated, we're going to get hurt, and we're going to hurt other people. Life will never be fair. So what do we individually do to cope with the uncertainty . . . with life's unfairness? How do we deal with others declaring any of our Emotional Bank Accounts bankrupt? How do we deal with others treating us like an "it"? How do *we* deal with our rights being violated and our human dignity being minimized, discounted, or taken away? Or our freedom taken away?

We have some choices in ways to cope with the unfairness that we encounter. One way to cope is to look to a fair afterlife. Many believe life isn't fair, but heaven will be; and this belief helps soften the blows of life's impermanence, life's unfairness, and life's uncertainty. Another way to cope is to see the randomness of life and not to take it all so personally. "Stuff happens . . . It's just our turn." Realizing this helps people feel less like a victim, but for some, this evokes more fear. Don Miguel Ruiz stated, "Nothing other people do is because of you. It is because of themselves. All people live in their own dream, in their own mind; they are in a completely different world than the one we live in."[20] Also, Denis Waitley said, "Life is the movie you see with your own eyes. It makes little difference what's happening out there. It's how you take it that counts."[21] In ancient history, the Greeks and Romans believed in "The Fates," three goddesses that made the decisions of what happens to each person. One can still believe in fate or destiny as a way to cope with uncertainty. Whether it's belief in God, fate, or chance, the highest strategy to cope is to prepare for whatever is coming and not expect life to be fair. We can avoid falling for the *Just-World Theory* trap, knowing both good and bad things can and will happen to us. Leonard Mlodinow's advice is as follows: "We can focus on the ability to react to events rather than rely on the ability to predict them. We can focus on qualities like flexibility, confidence, courage, and perseverance."[22] From my bad days, I remember what my wise father says, "Life is not a still picture. What you see today will not be the same tomorrow." That's why I do my best to focus on now, which is difficult.

Almost as wise as my father, Viktor Frankl wrote, "To invoke an analogy, consider a movie: it consists of thousands upon thousands of individual pictures, and each of them make sense and carries meaning. Yet, the meaning of the whole film cannot be seen before its last sequence is shown. However, we cannot understand the whole film without having first understood each of its components, each individual picture. Isn't it the same with life? Doesn't the final meaning of life, too, reveal itself, if at all, only at its end, on the verge of death? And doesn't this final meaning, too, depend on whether or not the potential meaning of each single situation has been actualized to the best of the respective individual's knowledge and belief?"[23] In other words, we just have to do our best in every situation using the "qualities" that Leonard Mlodinow mentioned and many others that he didn't mention. In the end, it may or may not make sense to us. I know I've seen movies where at the end, I still didn't understand. Life may never reveal its full meaning to us.

A few pages ago, we've discussed how we balance between two systems (Reason and Feeling) to make mistake-free decisions. In summary, when we're love-focused, we recognize we really don't know; and we are mindful of our *Cognitive Trap* tendencies. As counter to these three Love-based strategies, *Egoistic Hedonism* is an ethical theory stating that "achieving one's *own* happiness is the proper goal of all conduct." Similarly, *Egoism* is a doctrine stating that "an individual's self-interest is the actual motive of all conscious action and the valid end of all action." In summary of the two, our own pursuit of happiness is our highest motivation. We've also talked about *Happiness Hypothesis*, where life is viewed as a scale with good things on one side and bad things on the other. Even the Emotional Bank Account we've been discussing is ego-focused. We or the other person decide what's a deposit and what's a withdrawal to our ego's emotional account. We're naturally and habitually looking at the relationship as transactional and love as conditional.

As if to support *Egoistic Hedonism*, *Egoism*, and *Happiness Hypothesis*, we're the center of all our perceptions, including our dreams; life makes it feel that way. What other people do isn't about us; it's about them. Just like what we do is about us ourselves, right? "We're the lord of our own skull-sized kingdom" as David Wallace stated earlier. Our direct observations state we're central to life. Is our own happiness the true objective? Is our own happiness the path to true freedom? While the above theories and doctrine do ring of some truth, they also counter what I've learned experientially and what we've discussed previously. In chapter 7, we've discussed how to be happy. We found that focusing on one's self will only make us unhappy. Paradoxically, we found that reaching outside one's self brought "true happiness." We've read many quotes from wise people who've experientially learned that self-centeredness is the main contributor to unhappiness and most of life's problems. Yet, we're only responsible and accountable for our own thoughts, attitudes, and actions . . . It's the only control we have. The only freedom we have is to choose, and naturally, we tend to choose for ourselves and our own happiness. Paradoxically, as stated before, "It isn't about you, but it all starts with you." This mind-set/mantra is how we balance our two systems.

Does this mind-set help with our quest for "true freedom?" How's our true freedom linked to everyone else? My answer is this: our perspective doesn't create our direction. Many times, one may mistake one's perspective for the direction one must go, and that's when one becomes unhappy because then, one is really going in a circle and not getting anywhere. The above-stated mind-set/mantra does provide us direction. Counter to *Egoistic Hedonism*, *Egoism*, and *Happiness Hypothesis*, our own happiness is not the goal of life. As Dr. Jampolsky wrote, "Peace of mind as our single goal is the most potent motivating force we can have. To have inner peace we need to be consistent in having peace of mind as our single goal."[24] I know I've reflected that sentiment many times throughout this book. Our own happiness isn't our single goal if we want inner joy and peace. **My Love-based insight** then is this: *one's peace of mind is the real and ultimate goal in life, leading us to true freedom.*

The Buddha gave us his prescription to end life's suffering and dissatisfaction with his Fourth Noble Truth. The Fourth Noble Truth is to follow the Eightfold Path—Right View, Right Thinking, Right Speech, Right Action, Right Livelihood, Right Diligence, Right Mindfulness, and Right Concentration.[25] I'll not expound on the Eightfold Path in this book as there are many others on the subject. My point in bringing up the Eightfold Path is to state there are paths laid out already for one's own peace of mind, no matter your worldview, or religious belief. Any path that focuses on being selfless, mindful, wise, and compassionate is equivalent to the Buddha's Eightfold Path.

To me, the Buddha was instructing us on our attitude and intent, which leads to the path to true freedom, or as the Buddha put it, "the end of suffering and dissatisfaction." We're always free to choose our attitude and intents. Our peace of mind is directly affected by our attitude and intents. Charles Swindall wrote, "The longer I live, the more I realize the impact of attitude on life. Attitude, to me, is more important than facts. It is more important than the past, than education, than money, than circumstance, than failures, than successes, than what other people think or say or do. It is more important than appearance, giftedness or skill. It will make or break a company . . . a church . . . a home. The remarkable thing is we have a choice every day regarding the attitude we will embrace for that day. We cannot change the fact that people will act in a certain way. We cannot change the inevitable. The only thing we can do is play on the one string we have, and that is our attitude . . . I am convinced that life is 10 percent what happens to me and 90 percent how I react to it. And so it is with you . . . We are in charge of our attitudes."[26] The Dalai Lama stated something similar when he wrote, "If we have a positive mental attitude, then even when surrounded by hostility, we shall not lack inner peace. On the other hand, if our mental attitude is more negative, influenced by fear, suspicion, helplessness, or self-loathing, then even when surrounded by our own best friends, in a nice atmosphere and comfortable surroundings, we shall not be happy. So mental attitude is very important; it makes a real difference to our state of happiness."[27] In short, we control our mind-set: "It's not about you, but it all starts with you."

With love as our watchword, we need to live right, not out of fear or for reward in this life or the next but because it's the right thing to do. By doing so, we drastically reduce our *Cognitive Dissonance* and the other thinking errors that lead to wrongful actions. We also rid ourselves of self-serving motivations and intent. This is true no matter what system or path our mind is using. We need to give service, not because it makes us feel good but because it's the right thing to do. We need to stop judging and to forgive ourselves and others, not because it alleviates our own suffering but because it's the right thing to do. We need to be spiritual and religious, not because of some reward in this life, or the hereafter, but because it is the right thing to do. We need to live honorable, integritous, and courageous lives. We need to correct our mistakes as best we can, not because to avoid prosecution or stay out of prison, but because it's the right thing to do. Robert M. Pirsig wrote, "Peace of mind produces right values and right values produce right thoughts. Right thoughts produce right actions and thus right works which will be a material reflection for others to see of the serenity at the center of it all."[28] Our heart knows what's right. We've just got to be still enough to listen. That's what being mindful, spiritual, and religious is really about . . . to bring us peace of mind through right attitude and intent (reminder: WWYDE), which leads us to right actions.

As I brought up in chapter 11, I developed a course for the prison's informal mindfulness training group based on Dr. Alex Lickerman's book. In his book, *The Undefeated Mind*,[28] he gives his version of a prescription to peace of mind, which I'll paraphrase for this book as the following: to redefine success or victory to mean inner peace; to find purpose and meaning in life; to make and keep commitments; to expect life to be full of challenges; to take personal responsibility for your thoughts, attitudes, and actions; to choose to accept pain, but to choose not to suffer; to be grateful for life's wonder and beauty, looking for the life's serendipities and celebrating them; to reach outside yourself to serve others; and to work all your days so that you make a difference. To me, Dr. Lickerman provides a very powerful list for living in the present moment. By following his guidance, one can have an undefeatable mind, or peace of mind.

No matter if it's the Buddha's Eightfold Path, Moses's Ten Commandments, Jesus's Beatitudes or Two Commandments, or Dr. Lickerman's guidance for an undefeated mind; no matter what's our spiritual path; no matter what gives us a perspective that doesn't circle back around to us and our own self-centeredness; and no matter what principles and values lead us to right, principled action, the key is to have peace of mind as our only goal.

Having peace of mind as our ultimate goal automatically generates a desire to do the right, skillful action. Also, having peace of mind as a goal is the antidote for when people judge us using any one of the numerous *Cognitive Traps*. It's the antidote to when we're bullied, used, or victimized in one way or another. It's the antidote for when others discount and minimize our honorable, courageous, and good acts. It's the antidote when people consider our interpersonal "Emotional Bank Account" bankrupt; and they psychologically withdraw to abandon us, put us out-of-sight and out-of-mind, and ostracize us. It's the antidote to times others misunderstand or discount our amelioration, restitution, and retributive efforts. It's the antidote to the pain that happens from an unjust, unfair world where people and nature itself are bound to hurt us eventually.

Additionally, we've learned that focusing on our own happiness will lead to self-centeredness and will more likely cause us to hurt ourselves and others. Also, peace of mind is the antidote for the times that we've been selfless, and those selfless actions are misunderstood or misrepresented by others. That said, we still should have a desire for everyone's happiness, including ourselves. That too is part of having peace of mind as our only goal. Having personal happiness isn't wrong; it's just a by-product of our inner peace, of having peace of mind as our only goal. Having peace of mind as our only goal is what ultimately converts relationships from being an obligation to an opportunity, from being transactional to transformational, and from being Fear-based to Love-based.

In the end, we've got to live with ourselves no matter what action we've taken, what belief system we aspire to, and what other people think of us. We're the one who'll die knowing our attitude and our intentions. We're the only one who knows if our actions taken meet our intentions. We're the only one who knows our first and second scores, meaning how you ameliorated the mistakes and errors committed against us and by us. We're the only one who knows our life's "GPA." We're the only one who knows how we've handled all of life's challenges. Our real freedom comes from knowing ourselves well enough to control our thinking, attitude, intentions, and actions. The outcome is our sense of inner peace or our peace of mind. That's how heroes and nonheroes can find true freedom despite a mis-aligned *Happiness Hypothesis* scale. That's how we balance between two systems (Reason and Feeling) to make error-free decisions. With peace of mind as our goal, we'll be Love-based and love-focused and will act mindfully, reducing our chances of injuring ourselves and others. We'll have a beginner's mind, recognizing that we don't really know the final outcome or consequence. We'll be mindfully watching, using *Metacognition*, to minimize any of our naturally occurring *Cognitive Traps* . . . taking advantage of the WWYDE. Peace of mind engenders true freedom, even in a literal prison.

PRISON IS TOUGH: WHY NOT GIVE UP?

This book has given a few examples of prison life; it has my description of the toxic environment, the difficulties, the struggles, and the human interactions. You've read others' and my words relating how tough the experience really is. Yet, it's very hard for you, the reader, to really understand what prison is like unless you've experienced it for yourself. Yet, there's no need for you to come to prison to learn the life lessons it teaches. There's no reason for you to feel the innate helplessness that pervades one's prison experience, and the longer one's sentence, the more helpless and hopeless one feels. Most days, it's very hard to find motivation to go on. As I've witnessed, some choose to kill themselves because of what this toxic, damaging environment does to them. If offered, I'm sure there would be a lot of assisted suicides for prisoners with a life without-parole sentence or super long sentences. With my relatively short sentence (and it's not short . . . believe me), I look at people with very long sentences (life-without parole, 55 years, 109 years, etc.), and I'm amazed that they've not killed themselves. I'm sure many coldhearted people could read those words and only think about the money saved.

As we've discussed, prison ruins the majority of people, causing more social ills than it helps eliminate. At a very deeply personal level, each prisoner has to ask him or herself, "Why not just give up?" Of note, each one of us, prisoner or not, asks ourselves that same question, especially in times of crisis or difficulty. That's what this chapter is about: my answer to that question. In addition, I intend to use this closing chapter to tie things together and to leave the reader with their own motivation to press forward despite whatever life's challenges lie ahead. Prison is a very painful challenge with palpable physical, emotional, and mental experiences. I see prison as a microcosm of society and life. Life itself provides each of us many various challenges, trials, and crucibles for us to go through, to learn from, to grow from, or to fall further into deep despair.

Early in the book, we talked about the effects of being abandoned and being alienated. Back in the spring of 1991, Dr. Richard A. Gardner published a legal paper about Parental Alienation Syndrome (PAS),[1] which is an alienation that affects many prisoners and nonprisoners alike. According to Reena Sommer, "PAS is the deliberate attempt by one parent (and/or guardian/significant other) to distance his or her children from the other parent. In doing so, the parent engages the children in the process of destroying the affectional ties and familial bonds that once existed." In his study, Dr. Gardner identified *children* of the alienator as the ones being afflicted . . . They're the true victims. I first found out about PAS in 2010 (the year after my trial) when My Sweetheart sent me a newspaper article by Mary Winters of the *Denver Post*.[2] The article was the first step in my understanding of why things surrounding my trial and convictions had happened as they did. Before the article, I was truly baffled why my children, in the middle of a divorce, would seek to estrange themselves from me. PAS is common and well-documented even though few people have ever really heard of it. A 2003 study of seven hundred "high conflict" divorce cases over a twelve-year period found elements of parental alienation in the vast majority. Experts estimate two hundred thousand U.S. children have this disorder, similar to the number of children with autism, per Drs. Glenn Sacks and Ned Holstein, author of *Fathers and Families*. Mary Winters quoted Judith Ray, a family therapist, saying, "Their (alienating parent) hatred for their ex-spouse is stronger than their instinct to protect their children."[3] I've witnessed this firsthand with my children and my divorce.

While it's true that people who go to prison, in the majority of the cases, have done something wrong and while there are some who are a direct danger to their family, specifically their children, that's not the case for the majority of prisoners. As we've discussed, almost all prisoners were having problems and issues *Coping* with something traumatic in their lives, and their emotional state was a main factor in their committing a crime . . . They were "crying for help." We've discussed that very few convicts are irredeemable. Yet the crime and conviction is used by the alienating parent as a reason to abandon the other parent. Of the 2.5 million people incarcerated, *over half of the incarcerated parents* report never having received a personal visit from their children.[4] Some of this can be attributed to financial barriers or physical distance. However, much can be attributed to PAS. Again, there may be valid reasons to protect the child from a violent parent, but it could also be the alienating parent is using the context and circumstances to hurt the "ex" through *Relational Aggression*. The effect of PAS on an incarcerated person is a feeling of loss and helplessness. Many times, the legal system emboldens PAS for the sake of the few cases where protection of the children is warranted, using the *Precautionary Principle* as rationalization.

After reading the *Winter's* article, I was lucky enough to find a prison counselor who'd professional experience with PAS. She helped me understand that children of alienators don't really understand what they're doing. They see themselves as protecting and helping the alienating parent. Many children go so far as to report false accusations to bolster their attacks on the alienated parent, which was the case with the main subject, the father, in the *Winter's* article. Dan Ariely explains that many of his studies showed that *altruism can generate dishonesty*. In his words, "We found that knowing others will benefit from our action does indeed motivate people to cheat more . . . Altruism is a powerful rationalization."[5] To please and to protect the alienating parent or their siblings from a perceived threat, children will tell untruths about the alienated parent. We've already discussed in the last chapter how malleable memories are and how easy it is to justify alienation and abandonment of an incarcerated parent . . . either factual, fabricated, or merely exaggerated. PAS is a manifestation of Fear-based, lower life form, *System One* thinking.

The last time I saw my two youngest sons is a personal example . . . a very painful one to recall and to write about. The following is a brief version of that story: Because of our pending divorce, my wife had cut off my communication with my two young sons. The alienation started a year and a half prior and was unrelated to my trial. At the time of the trial, they, living in a different state, came to town for my trial. At the time of my greatest struggle, I'd been instructed to avoid my family because of the fact that some were possible witnesses against me. Any contact by me could be seen as trying to influence their testimony. I was to report incidental contact immediately to my lawyers.

One day during the week of my trial, I'd parked in the lot where the court-martial was taking place. Next to the parking lot was a set of public restrooms. As I made my way toward the building, I stopped at the restroom. No one else was around when I went in. As I was walking out the door to the parking lot, I could hear the voices of children playing outside. I thought nothing of it, and I opened the door to leave. There in front of the restroom entrance were my two young sons, whom I'd not seen or talked to in a year and half. They were jumping on some concrete barriers that separated the parking lot from the sidewalk. There on the sidewalk to my left was my soon-to-be ex-wife. I immediately froze as I realized who they were and the peril of the situation. My eyes locked with my sons, but I couldn't say or do anything to greet them. I couldn't hug them. I couldn't even voice to them how much I love them. I quickly spun on my heels and went back in the restroom. There, *my heart shattered*! I broke down, slumping against the wall, and sobbed. From inside the restroom, I heard my wife corral the boys and head into the building. Luckily, no one was there in the restroom to witness the crazy man slumped in a corner with tears streaming down his face and his head in his hands. That was well over seven years ago as I write, and I've not been able to communicate with them to explain or even be able to tell them I dearly love them. It haunts me that my sons' last memory of me is my turning my back to them and slinking away. I've been kept from communicating with them for all these years.

Do they still wonder why I'd treat them so coldly? Did they understand why I acted the way I did, or did my soon-to-be ex-wife use the opportunity to further denigrate me in their eyes? Did they feel rejected and unloved? Did they feel offended and hurt that I would turn my back to them? Do they still feel that I don't care about them? Do they resent me for my actions that day? As you can read, there are many questions and no answers. Sadly, according to Dr. Gardner, PAS is usually permanent; and it robs the child of more than just the alienated parent. According to Judith Ray, "They lose half their heritage. They lose their grandparents, they lose their aunts and uncles, they lose their cousins."[6] I can attest that's the case with my children. How do I deal with this traumatic event in my life? Statistics justify my fear: I'll never be reunited with my children. My children were my reason to go forward, to get help, and to testify against myself at trial. Well, I can always "hope" things will get better. Is that the right attitude? **My Fear-based insight** is this: ***Hope is an illusion and is directly linked to fear. Hope and Fear are two sides of the same coin.***

While understanding PAS has helped me frame the context and circumstances of my children's thinking, attitudes, and actions, I still don't know anything. However, being informed about PAS can generate and exacerbate my fear, which then spawns my hope, which is the ego's solution to the feeling of fear. I bring up PAS and my last interaction with my youngest sons to highlight the uncertainty and to highlight the fear and hope dynamic. Also, PAS is another type of *Cognitive Trap* that affects parents and ensnares children, causing all concerned additional hurt and pain. PAS generates many more victims. With PAS, no one knows anything, but the fearful and hopeful reactions associated surely don't help the situation. There's much uncertainty. As with PAS, the same is true in our current world situation, where there are wars, terrorist attacks, financial crisis, refugee crisis, etc. Humans deal with uncertainty and with fear and hope . . . not Love-based reactions.

In our Western society, hope is touted as a good thing. However, in Buddhist wisdom and Eastern philosophy, we're taught otherwise. We're taught that the ego is using fear and hope to generate grasping and clinging. Both hope and fear are rooted in the future, rather than the present moment. Hope is normally addressed when speaking of some expectation in the future, for example, "I hope that my sons and I are reunited," even if we're speaking of the past. Another example, "I hope my sons weren't wounded by my actions related to that day described above." By acknowledging hope for the future, we also acknowledge and give life to the fear that something will or will not happen. In this case, "my sons will be wounded, and we'll remain estranged." As taught by Lama Dorje, "So while hope generally has a positive connotation, it is in fact a desire for something other than what we have at the moment. This is really a sort of mental poverty—of thinking the current situation is not good enough."[7] The ego projects fear (hope) into the future, and anything future-related is something we really don't know.

As Victor Frankl wrote, "A victim of a hopeless situation, facing a fate he cannot change, may rise above himself, may grow beyond himself, and by doing so change himself. He may turn a personal tragedy into a triumph."[8] Norman Vincent Peale stated, "The tests in life are not meant to break you, but to make you."[9] The majority of our fears are unfounded, stress-inducing, and counterproductive . . . Our hopes are too. When we're fearful, ruminating about the future, we're living in the fear in our mind. Mark Twain said, concerning fear, "Some of the worst things in my life never happened."[10] If what we feared actually happened, then we've *lived it twice.* However, if it doesn't turn out like we envisioned, we've now *lived two* different troubling situations. For our mind, real and imagined events produce the same neurological, hormonal, and emotional reaction. Science has shown that our brain's reactions to real or imagined fears produce the same neurotransmissions and chemical releases. Both hope and fear require negative visualizations of an imagined future, impacting our brain. Do we really want to live bad events twice or increase our mind's negative experiences? Again, our hope gives life to a fearful, uncertain future.

How do we come up with these Fear-based thoughts? The answer is we will most likely use many of the *Cognitive Traps* that we've been discussing in this book. If we discuss just a few as an example, it may be a helpful reminder. For example, with *Availability Bias*, we use information readily available to us, failing to take into account *all* factors and conditions. *Hindsight Bias* causes us to attach higher probabilities to events after it's happened than what's true before the event happened . . . We think something is typical when it isn't. Also, we learned about the *Anchoring Effect* in the last chapter. It's where a meaningless bit of information subconsciously influences our decisions. Lastly, *Fundamental Attribution Error* causes us to think people have fixed characteristics, either good or bad; and we base our Fear-based decision with those "fixed" characteristics in mind. Hope and, its flip side, fear are both based on our judgment; and as we know, our judgment can easily be flawed or influenced by misinformation and misunderstandings.

Hope is a cause of suffering. That statement maybe news to the reader, but it's true. For example, I keep hoping that my request for clemency and parole will come to fruition, or that my estranged loved ones will contact me, and we'll be reunited, or I keep hoping for fair and true justice concerning my legal case. I keep envisioning a future where what I want to happen happens. Or, I envision a future where it doesn't happen . . . Fear sneaks in through a back door. Life isn't fair, and people and systems will fail us . . . They've failed me. My hoping has only made me suffer more as I keep having unfulfilled expectations. This doesn't mean I shouldn't try for clemency and parole, or work to be reunited with my loved ones, or fight for true justice. It means I must focus on the now . . . the present moment. I must focus on *what is* and on what actions I can take now . . . That's not hope; that's action. The Dalai Lama has stated, "Why worry about something? If you can change it, you will. And if you can't, then why worry about it?"[11] I tell myself all the time "Today is the tomorrow of yesterday . . . Focus on today." Not working in the present may cause us to miss opportunities because we're focused on the past or the future. Where we put our focus and effort is either past or future (Fear-based) or now in the present (Love-based).

Life is about effort and opportunities. Where we spend our resources (i.e., time and money) states our priorities and focuses our effort. Stanford psychologist Carol Dweck stated, "Effort is one of the things that gives life meaning. Effort means you care about something, that something is important to you and you are willing to work for it. It would be an impoverished existence if you were not willing to value things and commit yourself to working toward them."[12] Spiritual master, Kristnamurti taught, "We all want to be famous people, and the moment we want something, we are no longer free."[13] While it may seem that these two statements counter each other, they don't. The key is "opportunity." The Buddha taught that suffering comes from "grasping and clinging," which is the same as wanting. Is wanting the same an opportunity? No. Lama Dorje passed along a great analogy to teach this point. He asked, "How do you hold a coin (something of value to you) without grasping it?" He then held the coin with his open palm, face up, rather than the coin in a closed fist, facedown. Opportunity is palm open, receiving and appreciating. Wanting is a closed fist, grasping so hard one can't even see the coin.

When Lama Dorje was teaching me this point, my mind immediately pictured how one approaches an unfamiliar dog or catches a falcon or an eagle. If one tries to grab the animal, either the animal or human is going to get hurt, or be afraid. However, if one holds out their hand or arm, for the other to take the opportunity for contact, it shows respect for the individual's freedom and allows intimacy to take place. This is true with all our relationships. They are opportunities.

When I was first married, I worked at a meatpacking plant. For a time, I was in the hamburger patty making section. During my breaks, I'd go outside in the warm sunshine (the packing rooms are refrigerated) and sit. I still had on my dirty apron, and my hands were caked with fat. As I would sit there, bees would come and land on my hands to eat the fat. I would have hundreds of bees on my hands, calmly nibbling away. I could even feel their pincers on my skin as they scraped off the fat. When it was time to go into work, I'd gently and slowly get up, and all the bees would depart. Neither of us were fearful. We both shared a wonderful, intimate opportunity.

We go through life with a learned concept of possession using words like *my*, *mine*, and *ours*. Or we explain our role using titles like father, mother, son, daughter, husband, wife, etc.; and while these words help convey meaning, they also give a false sense of ownership. Ownership is a man-made construct to explain a relationship, but we're tricked into thinking the relationship is an entity unto itself. Put another way, the relationship exists *because* of us. This is our ego again, asserting its own importance; and while we've roles and responsibilities to perform, the function of those roles will go on with or without us filling those roles. Every role isn't person-dependent. While I'm in prison, someone else is filling my father role to my two youngest sons. I've been replaced by someone. Our ego assumes or desires that we're important and irreplaceable, but that assumption is false. I don't possess my sons. Albert Einstein is quoted as saying, "Possessions, outward success, public luxury . . . to me these have always been contemptible. I believe that a simple unassuming manner of life is best for everyone, best for both the body and the mind."[14]

Relationships are healthy and important. As we've already discussed, they can be the source of our greatest joy and pain. Social science has proven that we'd die without other human contact. We do need each other for our survival. Without the support we've discussed in chapter 8 (emotional, instrumental, financial, and appraisal support), we'd all die out very quickly. The classic example was a thirteenth-century study done under the directive of the Prussian emperor Frederick II. He wanted to know what was the natural language and words a child would speak without conditioning. He had infants taken immediately from birth and put them in homes to shelter and feed them with strict instructions not to touch, cuddle, or talk to them. The experiment was a failure because no original language was ever discovered. Why? None of the babies ever spoke a word because they were all dead before they were old enough to speak. Salimbene, a historian who lived at the time of the experiment in 1248, stated, "They could not live without petting."[15] Not "grasping or clinging" doesn't mean we never have a relationship or care for another person. It means relationships are not possession, or ownership, and/or obligation . . .

only the opportunity to love and be loved. We do very much need each other, but we don't own or possess each other.

Not "grasping or clinging" doesn't mean we don't have vision, mission statements, goals, or objectives. It doesn't mean we never plan for the future. It does mean planning isn't the end all, be all. Planning and its related processes are the "finger pointing at the Moon." It's pointing toward opportunities and experiences that really are unexpected, unforeseeable, unpredictable, and not experienceable until the present, until the now. Planning and setting goals and objectives do happen in the present moment, and we can have the experience of planning and goal setting. However, they are a direction, a guide, a vector, and an intention. As previously stated, in the *7 Habits* course, we teach Dr. Covey's principle of "Beginning with the End in Mind." However, the "end" is unknowable; and even though visions, goals, and objectives can come to fruition, it'll still not be exactly as envisioned because of life's many variables, randomness, and unintended consequences. Economist Albert O. Hirshman came up with a term to explain how planning and goal setting are affected by life's randomness, which he calls The Principle of the Hiding Hand. He describes this principle as "paradoxes: Plans that did not turn out the way they were supposed to—to unintended consequences and perverse outcomes and the puzzling fact that the shortest line between two points is often a dead end."[16] I find his point on paradoxes truly profound. Think back how many times a dead end was just what you needed.

How do we prepare for life's randomness? What do we teach our children? L. R. Knost said, "It's not our job to toughen our children to face a cruel and heartless world. It's our job to raise children who will make the world a little less cruel and heartless."[17] Put another way, Jean-Jacques Rousseau taught, "The first thing a child should learn is how to endure. It is what he will have most need to know."[18] Also, I like Malcolm Gladwell's words when he stated, "There is more courage and heroism in defying the human impulse (the various *Cognitive Traps*) and taking the purposeful and painful steps to prepare for the unimaginable."[19] Learning, teaching, planning, and preparing are all actions of living in the present moment while being aware that the future is unknowable and truly unpredictable. There will be dead ends and unimaginable outcomes. There will be opportunities that we could've never predicted and must remain open to experiencing.

Viktor Frankl, as a way of survival, envisioned himself in a future where he was lecturing people on the principles and lessons he'd learned while being a prisoner in Nazi concentration camps, still didn't know how things would turn out. He envisioned the *opportunity*, not the final outcome. In fact, the final outcome is still not final, as his principles and teachings are still multiplying exponentially even as you read my words, quoting him. Frankl taught a powerful principle to get through even the toughest of life's experiences. He taught that having *purpose and meaning* can and will pull you through. Determining and acting upon, in the present moment, our life's purpose and meaning will provide us opportunities that will pull us though life's randomness. **My Love-based insight** is exactly that *we don't know; therefore, we must not ever give up!*

Viktor Frankl taught that there are three possible sources of meaning: (1) meaning in work . . . doing something significant, (2) meaning in love . . . caring for another person(s), and (3) meaning in courage during difficult times . . . how one deals or copes with adversity, pain, and suffering. Here is a Frankl quote for each: (1) "Everyone has his own specific vocation or mission in life to carry out a concrete assignment which demands fulfillment. Therein he cannot be replaced, nor can his life be repeated. Thus, everyone's task is as unique as is his specific opportunity to implement it." (2) "The more one forgets himself—by giving himself to a cause to serve another or another person to love—the more human he is and the more he actualizes himself . . . self-actualization is possible only as a side effect of self-transcendence." And (3) "Life can retain its potential meaning in spite of its tragic aspects. Life is potentially meaningful under any conditions, even those which are most miserable."[20] Notice the words *opportunity* and *potential*. That's where our choice comes in. We may be replaced in roles as discussed above; however, we're not replaceable because only we can live the life we actually live and make the choices we choose. Again, in context, we control our thoughts, attitudes, and actions. We choose to love or to fear. We choose to press on or give up. The following are a litany of motivational quotes to support Dr. Frankl's teachings:

Bill Strickland wrote, "The value of life can be measured by one's ability to affect the destiny of one less advantaged. Since death is an absolute, certainly for everyone, the important variable is the quality of life one leads between the times of birth and death."[21]

Football coach and congressman Tom Osborne said, "Adversity is not always your enemy. Adversity in many ways is your friend, and most growth and progress occurs through adverse circumstances. It depends on your orientation."[22]

Dr. Crystal Park stated, "Using the experience as a catalyst for positive changes in one's life is one of the more adaptive strategies that a person can take to make meaning."[23]

Peter Koestenbaum said, "Anxiety is the experience of growth itself . . . Anxiety that is denied makes us ill; anxiety that is fully confronted and fully lived through converts itself into joy, security, strength, centeredness, character. The practical formula is go where the pain is."[24]

Author Eckhart Tolle wrote, "Emotion in itself is not unhappiness. Only emotion plus an unhappy story is unhappiness . . . Don't seek happiness. If you seek it, you won't find it, because seeking it is the antithesis of happiness. Happiness is ever elusive, but freedom from unhappiness is attainable now, by facing what is."[25]

Author Malcolm Gladwell stated, "Obstacles lead to frustration, and frustration to anxiety. No one wants to be anxious. But anxiety is the most powerful motivation—the emotion capable of driving even the most reluctant party towards some kind of solution."[26]

While I agree with Gladwell that anxiety is a strong motivation, the downside to it is anxiety is also fear-driven. There's no question that sometimes we need lesser motivations to stoke the fire of change; however, the highest-order motivator is self-actualization. As Dr. Frankl wrote, "Self actualization is possible only as a side effect of self-transcendence."[27] In other words, love, care, and compassion for others lead to self-actualization. We've discussed that we must first have love, care, and compassion for one's self to be able to truly show love, care, and compassion for others. One must first learn to love one's self to transcend one's self. Our connection to others has been proven to lengthen one's life. Social scientists call it *Social Immunity*, which, according to Dr. Norman Anderson, "provides us with a level of ongoing protection against illness and often increasing one's activity during emergencies."[28] *Social Immunity* is dependent on our connection to others. Again, Love-based thinking and choices, such as care, consideration, and compassion, enable self-actualization and growth. Even with tragedy, being Love-based makes life meaningful.

The key to stories like Viktor Frankl, Nelson Mandela, Cornelia ten Boom, Phakyab Rinpoche, and other prisoners and other tragedies is they didn't give up. Their stories are examples of resiliency and determination. They had or found Love-based meaning and purpose. They let it drive them to finish their race, so to speak. They looked at life as an opportunity. They've generated positive unforeseen, unintended consequences that continue to multiply to this day and beyond. Why not give up? My answer is because *Love endures.* Also, when we allow ourselves to be, we all are embodiments of love. Sogyal Rinpoche taught, "Spiritual mastery is the attainment of a level of consciousness that knows no conflict with the Divine, so that one's own choices are the same *as* Divine choices."[29] Finding Love-based meaning and purpose in life transcends us to higher-order thinking. Higher-order thinking is divine because it generates compassion, consideration, and care for ourselves and others. Fear-based, ego thinking is selfish and leads to despair when things are tough, difficult, and beyond our ability to affect change.

Mistakenly, hope is seen as a positive emotion. A person is more likely to give up when one is using hope and its flip side, fear, as motivation. Hopes can be dashed on the rocks of life. Transcending one's self leads to self-actualization, to love, to care, to compassion, etc. These are the divine choices. I'm constantly fighting my lifelong conditioning of depending on hope as my motivator. It takes my concerted effort to shift focus to love, care, and compassion for everyone.

Physical or *Relation Aggression,* vengeance, *Precautionary Principle, Fundamental Attribution Error, Generalization, Stereotyping,* and other mental traps are not divine choices and aren't Love based. Fear-based thinking multiplies as an *Emotional Contagion* and does have lasting effects, experienced as mostly negative, unwholesome outcomes. When one is Fear-based, one's consciousness isn't in sync with the divine. Love-based thinking and love-filled actions will also be an *Emotional Contagion* to lead us as a species to live divine, love-filled lives. We need to transcend the normal human ego tendencies and *Cognitive Traps.* We have to find ways to cope with life's challenges and tragedies that join rather than separate, that learn from mistakes, that make changes honorably and spontaneously out of concern for others, and that encourage personal responsibility. We need to forgive ourselves and others, leading us to love ourselves and others spontaneously. We need to find ways to resolve inner conflict (*schema, biases, heuristics,* and *Cognitive Dissonance*) not based on rationalizing, judging, minimizing, discounting, and condemning. We need to resolve both inner and outer conflicts using forgiveness (i.e., letting go).

Forgiveness is easier if we recognize that despite one's good core nature, we'll all make mistakes. We need to recognize that, as taught by Zen master Shunryo Suzuki, "We can find perfect existence through imperfect existence."[30] We need to decide ahead of time "what we would do" given a circumstance. We, of course, can't foresee what's coming; but we can establish that our reactions will be Love-based versus Fear-based. We need to recognize that ostracization, alienation, and abandonment are disabling, Fear-based *Coping* strategies that damage *Social Immunity* and *Utility* rather than helping it, degrading lives and social systems in the long run. Our life is not really about us but transcends us through service, care, concern, consideration, and compassion for others. Pain and suffering are inevitable, but we each can do our part to reduce rather than add to pain and suffering. We don't possess anyone, but we can fill roles to reduce another's pain or suffering. We need to live in such a way to make a difference in others' lives.

Fear is very powerful; and bullying, either by an individual, group, or nation, only perpetuates more fear, more pain, and more suffering. We all are capable of bullying, but we are also capable of Love-based, higher-order thinking and actions. We are all capable of kindness and compassion in any given situation. We just need to choose to be Love-based and decide what we will do before the situation arises. Then we're more likely to react with love rather than fear. We need to realize we *all* are more alike than different. We need to seek ways to avoid an "us and them" mentality. We need to realize that through familiarity of others, we're better able to understand and feel compassion for everyone. *The Extended Contact Effect* of meeting and becoming familiar with others is natural. Discounting the power of familiarity is the ego's method of generating an "I, it" relationship instead of an "I, you" one. South Africa's Apartheid and the United States's "Jim Crow laws" are some more examples of people making other people into an "it," not a "you."

Using people will not make us happy. Our happiness is directly tied to helping others . . . in *Social Utility*. Seeking our own happiness isn't going to make us happy. Having peace of mind as our only goal and Love-based actions toward others will. Friends and family may let you down, or vice versa. As with any relationship, there's bound to be pain and hurt. However, we choose the meaning of others' actions (deposits or withdrawals) and even the meaning of what nature does to us. We need to perceive pain from others, or the circumstances, as our teacher. We can turn *any* poison into medicine. We can gain meaning from the process of turning poison into medicine itself. Through mindfulness practice, let's learn about our own character. We can see how we transform life's challenges into life lessons. Through mindfulness, we can turn any circumstance, prison, illness, loss, etc., into something that makes us stronger and more resilient.

By being Love-based, we are able to see that vengeance is short-term, shortsighted thinking and action, leading to more victims. By being Love-based, we're able to see that prisons, wars, and other methods of punishment, exile, or exclusion only cause more pain and suffering. We need to teach personal responsibility. We need to find ways and environments for meaningful, positive changes to take place, which also enable personal responsibility, not personal debilitation, dereliction, or *Learned Helplessness*. There are many Love-based solutions. Yes, they may take more time and effort, they may cost more money initially, but in the long run, they benefit both the society and the individual. Life will not be fair, but we can help soften the blows and stand for what's fair, right, and compassionate. Justice in the form of revenge doesn't heal. Anger and hate don't heal. Only love and forgiveness can heal! Letting go of past hurts and eliminating the thoughts of possible future hurts enable us to live in the present moment with love and compassion. The Dalai Lama stated, "The essence of compassion is a desire to alleviate the suffering of others and to promote their well-being."[31] Seeing everyone as hurting, seeking to alleviate their own pain, enables our wisdom and compassion for and toward everyone.

We really don't know anything. We don't know what people are really going through. We don't know their conditioning, their circumstances, and the context of any given situation. We don't even fully know those things about ourselves, which is why mindfulness training is so valuable. We can't rely on memories for complete truths, as they're changeable and malleable. We can't rely on perceptions as we miss most of what's going on around us. We know we're subject to *schema, biases, heuristics,* and many thinking errors as are others. We need to give ourselves and others a break, we need to forgive everyone even ourselves, and we need to realize everyone is "just like me." It's very possible that all the good things we've done may be forgotten. Our "Emotional Bank Accounts" may be dropped to next to nothing, all in a blink of an eye. Others will never know our true intentions, only we will. Others may be biased, prejudiced, or mistaken in some way and are judging, discounting, and minimizing us accordingly. We can't count on people or life being fair. We can't count on others' understanding. We can count on forgiveness to alleviate pain and suffering. Forgiving ourselves and others gives us breathing room so that we can mindfully see what we're experiencing and make insightful choices with this information. Forgiveness is self-transcending, which leads to self-actualization. Forgiving only for our own benefit isn't self-transcending or self-actualizing. It's the ego using a Love-based principle for selfish purposes.

We need to commit to *peace of mind* as our ultimate goal. Peace of mind leads to true freedom for a prisoner, or anyone else, trapped in a dead-end situation. Peace of mind enables us to find purpose and meaning in every and in any given situation. Peace of mind enables us to carry on even when we only can see the dead end, the wall, the barrier, and people at their worst. Love-based thinking, attitudes, and actions are the basis of peace of mind. It's following the Buddha's Eightfold Path, or living the core Jewish, Christian, Muslim, Hindu, Sikhs, and other religion's teachings that reinforce love, compassion, and forgiveness as the highest principles. Peace of mind comes from living a principle-centered life. Love-based focus' natural consequence is our peace of mind.

We need to realize that we each are love personified, embodied, and we need act accordingly. Let love radiate to others. For some, it may not seem natural at first, but mindfulness teaches us that we're all love deep inside. No one is irredeemable. No one should be forsaken or forgotten. We don't really know anything but one thing: "love always wins." Everything else is just a distraction, a dead end, a barrier, or a shield. Everything else is what's blocking what's really important . . . our love for others. We never really know the outcome of any action; all we know is our thinking, our attitude, and our intentions. If we're Love-based, even when we're mistaken, misunderstood, misinformed, and when miscommunications happen, we can feel remorse (not regret) and repent. We expect pain but choose not to suffer and help others with the same task. We can do our best to make things right because it's the right thing to do. Where change is needed, it'll come from love, from taking personal responsibility, and by holding one's self accountable. Then we forgive, forgive, forgive. Then we never give up on anyone or anything.

The prince of Mito is quoted as saying, "To rush into the thick of battle, and be slain in it is easy enough, and the worst churl is equal to the task; but it is true courage to live when it is right to live and to die only when it is right to die."[32] Put another way, Master Lao-tzu stated, "He who knows how to live can walk abroad without fear of rhinoceros or tiger. He will not be wounded in battle. For in him rhinoceros can find no place to thrust their horn, tiger no place to use their claws, and weapons no place to pierce. Why is this so? Because he has no place for death to enter."[33] To me, these quotes describe peace of mind, the peace of mind from a life well lived . . . not giving up!

Mahatma Mohandas Gandhi wrote about what it means to be a Karma Yogi (a person who's lived life well). He wrote, "He is a devotee who is jealous of none, who is a fount of mercy, who is without egotism, who is selfless, who treats alike cold and heat, happiness and misery, who is ever forgiving, who is always contented, whose resolutions are firm, who has dedicated mind and soul to God, who causes no dread, who is not afraid of others, who is free from exultation, sorrow and fear, who is pure, who is versed in action yet remains unaffected by it, who renounces all fruit, good or bad, who treats friend and foe alike, who is untouched by respect or disrespect, who is not puffed up by praise, who does not go under when people speak ill of him, who loves silence and solitude, and who has disciplined reason. Such devotion is inconsistent with the existence at the same time of strong attachments."[34] What Gandhi describes is a tall order for anyone of us, but we can do our best and have peace of mind that we're Love-based in all our actions, reactions, and repentance efforts. We can't give up working to be a Yogi, Christlike, a Buddha, a Muslim, etc., to be self-actualized. We can use this mantra: "It isn't about you, but it all starts with you."

Again, I invite you to join me in my effort not to quit . . . to keep going in the face of adversity. When I was turned down for parole, my friend sent me a poem, "Don't Quit," by an unknown author. It goes like this:

> When things go wrong as they sometimes will, when the road you're trudging seems all up hill,
>
> When funds are low and the debts are high, and you want to smile but you have to sigh,
>
> When care is pressing you down a bit; rest, if you must, but don't you quit.
>
> Life is queer with its twist and turns, as everyone of us sometimes learns,
>
> And many a failure turns about when we might have won had he stuck it out,
>
> Don't give up though the pace is slow—you may succeed with another blow.
>
> Success is failure turned inside out—the silver tint of the clouds of doubt,
>
> And you can never can tell how close you are, it may be near when it seems so far.
>
> So stick to the fight when you're hardest hit—it's when things seem worst that you must not quit.

In this chapter, we've discussed how hope is really the flip side of fear and isn't really a helpful emotion because it engenders grasping and clinging. What then do we do to prepare for the future? How then do we not give up? During a crisis or tragedy, many people will say, "Don't give up hope!" They're saying these words to motivate and soothe. When it's said to me, I tell the person that "their kind, compassionate sentiment is appreciated." However, I'm not hoping (which takes my constant, concerted effort). I'm living life, now, so that future opportunities can be realized. When I say I'll never give up on my loved ones, I'm not hoping that things will get better, and I'm not pining for the past. I'm living my life so that if and when an opportunity arises, I'm living the best life I can . . . to be ready to capitalize on opportunities presented. Constantly checking my attitude and my effort, I'm living to have "doors open" to me, a life that leads to peace of mind.

For clarification, anytime I've wrote the word "we" in this book, I was talking to myself; and I was inviting you to join me with my realizations, intentions, attitudes, and efforts toward Yogihood. I'm doing my very best to be Love-based and love-focused. I know opportunities will arise, and I know all experiences can be my teachers. I'm choosing to view all experiences that way . . . to make vitamins and medicine of every moment. Gandhi stated, "Live like you will die tomorrow, but learn like you will live forever."[35] I close this book sending you, the reader, my best wishes for many wonderful opportunities. May love fill *all* our existence. May *all* have peace of mind!

THIRTY LIFE LESSONS

FEAR-BASED INSIGHTS	LOVE-BASED INSIGHTS
1) Fear is very, very powerful and scary!	2) Unconditional love is hard to do, but it's attainable and lasts.
3) The majority of people in prison "don't like their cell mate;" most people don't like themselves.	4) Accepting one's self for who one is and having love and compassion for one's self lead to naturally liking one's self.
5) People are very quick to judge, discount, minimize, and condemn and are slow to seek to understand the whole story.	6) We all make mistakes, but everyone's core nature is good.
7) The "out-of-sight, out-of-mind" reaction is very common. Abandonment still seems to be the norm.	8) It isn't about you, but it all starts with you.
9) Bullying works because fear is such a powerful emotion.	10) Kindness compassion, and love are more powerful and effective in relating to and influencing bullies.
11) Our primitive instincts and Fear-based thinking are what drive us to segregate and discriminate.	12) Familiarity with others and an open mind breed understanding and compassion.
13) People who use people are not happy.	14) Reaching outside yourself is the key to true happiness.

15) Coming to prison, one finds out the true character of one's friends and family.

16) Pain happens, but suffering is a choice; both pain and loss are our teachers.

17) Prison and other difficult life experiences enable a person to really find out their true character.

18) We need to love, to have compassion for, and to forgive ourselves continuously.

19) Locking someone up is really just institutional, or societal revenge.

20) Only wisdom, compassion, and forgiveness can bring peace to victims, perpetrators, and society.

21) Anecdotal evidence seems to say people don't believe in rehabilitation, or a criminal's ability to change for good.

22) Taking "personal responsibility" is the best reason to change.

23) Life is tough for everyone . . . No one gets through unscathed . . . Life is not fair!

24) It's our personal responsibility to forgive everyone and everything . . . to let go!

25) We don't really know what we don't really know, and we don't really know much of anything.

26) The more we learn, the less we know.

27) Honor, courage, and other good acts are quickly forgotten, or can be heavily minimized and discounted until those acts are meaningless.

28) One's peace of mind is the real and ultimate goal in life, leading us to true freedom.

29) Hope is an illusion and is directly linked to fear; hope and fear are two sides of the same coin.

30) We don't know; therefore, we must not ever give up!

GLOSSARY

Abundance Mentality: A mindset where there is an unlimited amount of a given resource. This mindset then determines the decision one makes and what action one takes.

Accommodation: Educational Psychology term used to describe how one handles a new or unfamiliar experience. With accommodation, one makes room for a new schema, creating a new category.

Anchoring Effect: Psychological term (cognitive trap) used to describe the tendency to allow a meaningless anchor (event, thought, data, or feeling) to have an unconscious, strong impact on one's subsequent decision.

Anterior Cingulate Cortex/Gyrus: Neurological term describing a portion of the brain that registers the interpretation and meaning of a given sensation (i.e. pain).

Assimilation: Educational Psychology term used to describe how one handles a new or unfamiliar experience. With assimilation, one places the experience in an already existing schema that fits what ones think they know.

Attrition Mentality: Military term used to describe the leadership's view of their human and non-human resources. Simply put, people will die and things will be destroyed in order to reach some military (political) objective. Resources will be attrited (used up) in order to fulfill the required goal.

Autobiographical Memory: Educational Psychology term used to describe an Explicit Memory subdivision that stores our life's memories. We are able to describe when and where we got the memory.

Availability Bias: Psychological term (cognitive trap) meaning when one uses the most recent or most available (easiest to obtain) information to make judgment and/or decision about something or someone. In Economics, this is known as The Rule of Typical Things.

Aversion Reaction: Psychological term (cognitive trap) used when one, due to anxiety or offense, casts off another perceived offending person.

Beginner's Mind: Buddhist term used to describe the optimum mental state as one approaches the world. The term addresses the fundamental fact that we really do not know anything. Every situation or condition of each given moment is new and has never been experienced before.

Bodhisattva: A Buddhist word to describe a being who was on the verge of obtaining Nirvana, but voluntarily remained to help all other beings to become enlightened.

Bodhichitta: A Buddhist word to describe a loving heart and mind that is focused on compassion for all sentient beings.

Brothers Section: A prison construct where people of the African heritage (black race) congregate. It uses physical appearance and similar upbringing as justification to segregate from other prison population members. The group became the basis of a prison gang or gang-type identity.

Capitalization Learning: Educational Psychology term used to describe the sub category of Experiential Learning, where the experience is easy and obvious...one seems to have a talent for it.

Cognitive Dissonance: Psychological term used to describe a disconnect between our thoughts and feelings...from what we tell ourselves and how we really feel.

Cognitive Schema: Psychological term used to describe how one creates a new category when experiencing something new. There two types of cognitive schema used with the new experience; either we assimilate the experience into an already existing schema or we make room to accommodate the experience into a new schema.

Cognitive Traps (Distortions): Psychological terms used to described ways, shortcuts, and mind states in which the mind works and causes problems in ways one experiences the world.

Compensation Learning: Educational Psychology term used to describe the sub category of Experiential Learning, where the experience is really hard and one has had to scramble, adapt, and confront perceived limitations.

Confirmation Bias: Psychological term (cognitive trap) used to describe when one is inclined to look for confirming evidence of an initial hypothesis, belief, or belief system; rather than look for any falsifying evidence that would disprove it; the tendency to screen what we see and hear in a biased way that ensures one's beliefs are proven correct. Using selective attention, perception, and retention we screen out data that would prove our belief(s) wrong.

Coping: Psychological term used to describe what things people do to reduce the negative emotional, psychological, and physical fall out of stressful life circumstances and daily travails.

Cred (Credit): Prison term for trust or expectations built between prisoners. Cred is earned from favors and transactions for services, reputation from the time before the person was locked up (previous prison time or their crime), and/or for bullying (most are violent) actions.

Creeping Determinism: Term (cognitive trap) used to described the sense that grows on a person, in retrospect, that what has happened was actually inevitable. Looking back one tends to reconstruct the probability to make it less surprising that the event/occurrence happened than what the real, original probability was before the event/occurrence. (aka: Hindsight Bias)

Cro-Magnon Man: The name given to our direct ancestors from prehistoric times. Though history of these people exists, through genetics and Anthropology, we know they are genetically modern man's

DNA match. They had the same genetic capabilities of historic and modern man.

Culture of Fear: Where fear is used by politicians to motivate people to follow or allow a certain course of action; by the media to sell and generate revenue; and by individuals to justify one's thoughts, attitudes, and actions towards a person (people, culture, race), place, or thing.

Custody-level: Prison term for levels of trust and privilege for prisoners. In the U.S., the prison system has five levels of custody. The largest number equals the least trust and privilege and the smallest number equals the most. Each level also has a term associated: 5 = Maximum or Death Row, 4 = Medium, 3 = Minimum Inside, 2 = Minimum Outside, and 1 = Trustee There is a lower level of custody titled parole, where the person is living back in society, with supervision.

Deduction/Deductive Reasoning: Philosophical term used to determine and argue one's perspective and method of reasoning, given the evidence. For Deduction, the philosopher starts with a general observation, demonstration, or proposition and applies it specifically or narrowly to one instance or person.

Denisovan Man: An archaic humanoid life form that lived for millions of years. Not thought to be modern man's direct ancestor, but many modern humans (mostly East Asian heritage) do have a very small amount of Denisovan DNA.

Dissonance: Psychological term (cognitive trap) used to describe when what one knows contradicts what one believes, one can either change one's belief to fit the facts or change the facts to fit one's beliefs.

Dispositional Optimism: Psychological term used to describe a person's natural disposition of a positive expectation for their future. This term is used for people who, the majority of the time, feel and act as if life will turn out positive, even in the face of adversity.

Dispositional Pessimist: Psychological term used to describe a person's natural disposition of a negative expectation for their future. This term is used for people who, the majority of the time, feel and act as if life will turn out negative, even in the face of adversity.

Doing Dirt: Prison term for breaking the prison rules (favors or service transaction) to help another inmate, usually in exchange for some benefit to themselves.

Egoism: Merriam-Webster Dictionary Definition: An individual's self-interest is the actual motive of all conscious action and the valid end of all action.

Egoistic Hedonism: Merriam-Webster Dictionary Definition: Achieving one's own happiness is the proper goal of all conduct.

Emotional Bank Account: Term coined by Dr. Stephen Covey to describe human relation transactions. One's actions are considered by the receiver as either a deposit or withdrawal.

Emotional Contagion: Psychological term used to describe the fact that emotions can be contagious, just like a virus or bacteria, between many individuals. The emotion can be positive (Love-based) or negative (Fear-based). How other people feel can many times become the way we feel, without us being cognitively aware of the transfer.

Experiential Learning: Educational Psychology term used to describe when one "learns by experience." This can be both a conscious (Explicit Learning) or subconscious (Implicit Learning) level. Experiential Learning is broken down into two sub categories: Capitalization Learning and Compensation Learning.

Explanatory Style: Psychological term used to describe the stories one tells one's self concerning past experiences and possible future event. These stories are framed as either negative or positive.

Explicit Learning: Educational Psychology term used to describe when a person consciously learns a sequence which is stored in one's Explicit Memory.

Explicit Memory: Educational Psychology term used to describe where our mind (long-term memory) stores information we can verbalize. It has two subdivisions: Semantic Memory and Autobiographical Memory.

Extended-contact Effect: Psychology term to describe "Familiarity" with a person, place, or thing. Extended contact breaks down fears, enables compassion and concern, and stops an "Us versus them" mentality. With people influenced by the Extended Contact Effect, mutualism was between the parties.

Fear-based Insight: A realization by the author that is connected with fearful thoughts, attitudes, and actions. Fear-based insights demonstrate handicaps to one living life fully.

Follower Bully: Term coined by the author to describe when a person bullies someone else at the direction of, or to get in the good graces of the actual bully (the person who is more naturally malicious). The follower bully bullies, not because they are intending to be malicious, but because they see and desire the security derived from bullying.

Fundamental Asymmetry of Past and Present: Scientific term used (like Hindsight Bias and Creeping Determinism) to describe the tendency one has, after the fact, to surmise what happened and the causes or chance occurrences that led up to the situation or event despite the inability to prognosticate what would have happened in the future due to multitude of data.

Fundamental Attribution Error: Psychological term (cognitive trap) meaning when one uses the most quick, uninformed, arbitrary and capricious judgment towards another person; that one has a tendency to fixate on supposedly stable character trait (good or bad; positive or negative) and overlook the influence of context.

Generalization: Psychological term (cognitive trap) meaning when one uses stereotypes or general categories to view other people, places, or things. Allows one to ignore each person's place or things individuality and uniqueness.

General Population: A term coined by prison officials to describe where the majority of the prison population lives and works. Prisoner coined the term GenPop by shortening the formal term.

Group Polarization: Psychological term (cognitive trap) used to describe the tendency that when people with shared beliefs get together in groups, they become more convinced that their beliefs are right and they become more extreme in their views. Seeing that one is not the only one who thinks, believes, or feels a certain way emboldens the individual and, ultimately the group.

Happiness Hypothesis: Psychological term (cognitive trap) describing when one believes that one can only be happy if one's life has more positive experiences than negative ones. This person feels that life is a scale and if one does bad, it can be made up (balanced) by transactions of doing a lot of good.

Heavies: A term coined at the author's prison to describe the inmates who wield the most power over other prisoners, usually derived by a "might makes right" environment. Mental manipulation is also a common tool of the "Heavy." Another way to describe them is as "prison bullies."

Hedonic Treadmill: A cognitive trap where a person adapts to a given scenario and always wants more. (i.e. if one earns more, then one adapts and then desires more). This applies to many things, not just money.

Heuristics: Scientific term used to describe shortcuts one employs in assessing patterns in data. In turn, one makes judgments using these shortcuts, especially when one is confronted with uncertainty.

Hindsight Bias: Psychological term (cognitive trap) used to describe when a person attaches a higher probabilities to an event(s) after they it has happened (ex post) than was probable before the event(s) happened (ex ante).

Hispanic Section: A prison construct where people of the Hispanic heritage/cultures (Spanish speakers) congregate. Cultural and physical appearance is used as justification to segregate from other prison population members. The group becomes the basis of a prison gang or gang-type identity.

Homunculus: Philosophy term used to describe the feeling we have that a little person in our head, somewhere, observing our life and interactions on a movie screen or stage.

Implicit Learning: Educational Psychology term used to describe learning that takes place outside one's awareness (i.e. how to speak or walk, etc.) and is stored in our Implicit Memory.

Implicit Memory: Educational Psychology term used to describe where our mind (long-term memory) stores information we don't consciously know. (i.e. peddle a bike, ride a horse, drive a car, etc.).

Incarceration Nation: A term coined to describe the Fear-based phenomena of a society imprisoning millions of people (enough to be their own nation), creating a second-class person.

Induction/Inductive Reasoning: Philosophical term used to determine and argue one's perspective and method of reasoning, given the evidence. For Induction, the philosopher starts with an observation of one instance or system and then works to apply the inference reasoning, or proposition to things generally.

Institutionalized: According to Merriam-Webster dictionary, to put (a person) into the care of an institution (i.e. prison or mental hospital). However, in prison, to be institutionalized means one has given up on ever getting out or ever changing their circumstance, and so they become passive, compliant, and some become pawns of the institution (prison) itself.

Just-World Theory: Psychological term (cognitive trap) used to describe one's tendency to view the world as just and fair despite the overwhelming evidence otherwise.

Learned Helplessness: Psychological term (cognitive trap) used to describe human reactions when given a painful, stressful, uncontrollable experience, but there is no way to escape or change what's happening. The person gives up and becomes passive, even when the conditions changed and there is a way to escape or changes what's happening.

Loss Aversion: Psychological term (cognitive trap) to describe being so determined to avoid any option associated with loss that one is willing to risk everything. The judgment of the loss's importance skews the person thinking and the person will end up making harmful decisions. One is willing to risk everything...the potential loss looms much larger than possible gain.

Love-based Insight: A realization by the author that is connected with love-filled thoughts, attitudes, and actions. Love-based insights demonstrate a pathway to all of us living life fully.

Lower life form thinking: Term coined by the author to describe one's "gut reaction," or automatic response generated by the reptilian and mammalian parts of one's brain and cognitive traps; thinking generated by the evolutionary older portions.

Lucifer Effect: Psychological term to describe the potential all humans have to turn mean and hurtful. Philip Zimbardo's famous Stanford Prison Experiment was were the term was coined.

Mantra: Sanskrit word meaning mind protection: "Man" equals mind and "Tra" equals protection.

Metacognition: "Meta" is Latin for after. "Cognition" in the scientific term for thinking. Therefore, Metacognition is after thinking. A better way to understand the term is humans have the ability to become an observer of our thoughts and can mindfully shift thoughts, emotions, and attitudes.

Neanderthal Man: An archaic humanoid life form that lived for millions of years. Not thought to be modern man's direct ancestor, but many modern humans (mostly European heritage) do have a very small amount of Neanderthal DNA.

Neophobia: Fear of anything new.

Occidental: Term to describe the imperial Western (European nations and the USA) nations in relation to the Eastern or Oriental nations.

Optimism Bias: Psychological term (cognitive trap) used to describe when a person see themselves as being basically good and therefore judges their intent as being good, even if the actions leads to others harm, or is really motivated by self-interest.

Oriental: Term to describe Eastern people and their location in relation to the Western, or Occidental, imperial nations.

Pain Avoidance: Psychological term (cognitive trap) used to describe when a person is so determined to avoid pain that they will over look any positive outcomes associated with the situation.

Physical Aggression: Using physical (violence) means to harm another person: fighting, stabbing, hanging, shooting, etc.

Posterior Insula: Neurological term describing a portion of the brain that registers the actual sensation (i.e., pain).

Precautionary Principle: Term (cognitive trap) used to describe a common mindset or outlook which states we must act now if there is any chance of this happening again in the future. This can be called the knee-jerk reaction or "cover-your-ass" rule. This mindset or outlook causes one to give undue weight to a very small probability.

Principle of Legitimacy: Psychological term used to describe when people in authority (or perceived authority) want the rest to behave as if it matters that they are in charge. When, in fact, in almost all cases it really does not matter as people in authority are easily replaced and, in many cases, are ineffectual when they are in charge.

Rationalization: Psychological term (cognitive trap) used to describe the tendency to find a way to justify one's thoughts, attitudes, and actions to decrease any dissonance associated with what is real, any harm generated, or one's self-interest.

Recency Effect: Psychological term (cognitive trap) used to describe one's tendency to remember the last event, occurrence, or interaction when judging or making a decision about a person, place or thing. Put another way, it is the "What have you done for me lately" rule.

Relational Aggression: Using relations (nonphysical violence) in order to harm another person using the relationship, or lack thereof, as a weapon (i.e. abandonment, alienation, gossip, breaking off communication, etc.).

Rinpoche: Tibetan Buddhist term for a high Lama (teacher), revered for their lifelong devotion to Buddhist principles and their example of a life filled with equanimity.

Scarcity Mentality: A mind-set (cognitive trap) where there is only so much of a given resource. This mind-set then determines the decision one makes and what action one takes.

Self-actualization: Psychological term to describe a person who is living to their full potential, talents, and capacities.

Self-efficacy: Psychological term used to describe how one views one's effectiveness in dealing with the world.

Self-forgiveness: To be able to forgive one's self, having an unconditional love for everyone, including one's self.

Self-fulfilling Prophecy: Psychological term used to describe where one's thinking of a certain circumstance, scenario, or condition determines one's actions to produce the circumstance, scenario, or condition one envisioned.

Semantic Memory: Educational Psychology term used to describe an Explicit Memory subdivision that stores things "we know," but we don't know when or how we came to know them.

Sense of Integrity: Thuben Chodron's definition: Where we abandon doing what's destructive out of self-respect.

Short-term Play: Where one's thinking, attitudes, and actions are focused on immediate gains or losses, regardless of what the long-term consequences will be.

Social Immunity: Social Scientific term used to describe the effect that people taking care of people provides one with a level of ongoing protection against illness and often increasing one's survivability during emergencies.

Social Utility: Social Scientific term used to describe one's general urge to take care of others, even when doing so uses up our own resources. Negatively, this urge is naturally used by people to justify (rationalize) cheating, lying, or worse.

The Attribution Game: Term coined by the author to describe a game explained to him by his commanding general. It is played by using a term or phrase to describe people one interacts with at work or socially (i.e. he or she is "Creative").

The Law of Love: Based on an abundance mentality, we are completely filled with love all the time, and our supply is always full and running over.

The Rule of Typical Things: Economics term used to describe when one uses the plausibility of some element of the scenario to judge the likelihood of the whole scenario. In Psychology, the term Availability Bias means the same thing.

The Why Game: A term coined by the author to describe a mental boiling-down process, where one asks the "why" question until they have boiled down the issue or word meaning to its most basic level.

Theory X: Psychological term to describe a basic point of view of some people or way of thinking about the inherent nature of people. This theory states people are inherently evil and that they must be forced to be good...to do the right thing. If left alone, people will choose the most self-centered, self-serving, and evil choice the majority of the time.

Theory Y: Psychological term to describe a basic point of view of some people, or way of thinking, about the inherent nature of people. This theory states people are inherently good, but they make mistakes, or they forget their core nature, and they just need to be reminded, and they will do the right thing. If left alone, people will self-correct towards positive and good the majority of the time.

Tonglen: A Buddhist meditative practice where one visualizes breathing in the pain and suffering of others and with one's Bodhichitta or inherent Buddha Nature, the out breath releases exactly what the person or persons need to relieve the pain and suffering.

Victim Mentality: When one views him or herself as a victim and then holds onto that idea which becomes part of their identity or self-image.

"What Would You Do" Effect: Term coined by the author to address a phenomena where people see or come across a moral or ethically challenging situation and, having recently watched the TV show *What Would You Do?*, they make a better, more positive choice because they had previously asked themselves the question, "What would you do?" as the show aired.

White Section: A prison construct where people of European heritage congregate. Cultural and physical appearance is used as justification to segregate from other prison population members. The group became the basis of a gang or gang-type identity.

Xenophobia: Fear of stranger or foreigners.

RESOURCE BIBLIOGRAPHY

Amen, Daniel G. Dr. *Change Your Brain Change Your Life: the Breakthrough Program for Conquering Anxiety, Depression, Obsessiveness, Lack of Focus, Anger, and Memory Problems.* NY: Harmony Books, 2015.

Anderson, Norman B. Dr. *Emotional Longevity.* NY: Viking Books, 2003.

Ariely, Dan. *The (Honest) Truth About Dishonesty: How We Lie to Everyone—Especially Ourselves.* NY: Harper Perennial, 2013.

Batchelor, Stephen. *Buddhism Without Belief.* NY: Riverhead Books, 1997.

Bronson, Po. *Why Do I Love These People? Understanding and Creating Your Own Family.* NY: Random House, 2002.

Buruma, Ian and Margault, Avishai. *Occidentalism: the West in the Eyes of Its Enemies.* NY: Penguin Books, 2002.

Chopra, Deepak. *Why Is God Laughing? The Path to Joy and Spiritual Optimism.* NY: Three Rivers Press, 2008.

Covey, Stephen. Dr. *7 Habits of Highly Effective People: Powerful Lesson in Personal Change.* NY: Free Press, 1989.

Dispenza, Joe. *Breaking the Habit of Being Yourself: How to Lose Your Mind and Create a New One.* NY: Hay House, Inc., 2012.

Doidge, Norman, Dr. *The Brain That Changes Itself: Stories of Personal Trump from the Frontiers of Brian Science.* NY: Penguin Books, 2007.

Epstein, Greg M. *Good Without God.* NY: Harper Collins, 2009.

Frankl, Viktor E. Dr. *Man's Search for Meaning.* Boston: Beacon Press, 1959.

Fredston, Jill. *Snowstruck: in the Grip of Avalanches.* NY: Harvest Book, 2005.

Gladwell, Malcolm. *Blink: The Power of Thinking Without Thinking.* NY: Back Bay Books, 2005.

Gladwell, Malcolm. *David and Goliath: Underdogs, Misfits, and the Art of Battling Giants.* NY: Back Bay Books, 2013.

Gladwell, Malcolm. *The Tipping Point: How Little Things Can Make a Big Difference.* NY: Back Bay Books, 2008.

Gladwell, Malcolm. *What the Dog Saw: and Other Adventures.* NY: Back Bay Books, 2010.

Gardner, Daniel. *The Science of Fear: How the Culture of Fear Manipulates Your Brain.* NY: A Plume Book, 2009.

Glassner, Barry. *The Culture of Fear: Why Americans Are Afraid of the Wrong Things.* NY: Basic books, 1999.

Hanh, Thich Nhat. *Anger.* NY: Riverhead Books, 2001.

Heen, Sheila and Stone, Douglas. *Thanks for the Feedback: the Science and Art of Receiving Feedback Well.* NY: Penguin Books, 2014.

Holmes, Jamie. *Nonsense: the Power of Not Knowing.* NY: Crown Publishers, 2015.

Jampolsky, Gerald G. Dr. *Forgiveness: the Greatest Healer of All.* NY: Atria Books, 2007.

Jampolsky, Gerald G. Dr. *Love Is Letting Go of Fear.* Berkeley: Celestial Arts, 1979.

Kolbert, Elizabeth. *The Sixth Extinction: a Unnatural History.* NY: Henry Holt and Co., 201 4.

Lao-tzu. *Tao Te Ching.* trans: Mar, Victor. NY: Book of the Month Club, 1990.

Lehrer, Jonah. *How We Decide.* Boston: Mariner Books, 2009.

Levitt, Steven. *Freakonomics.* NY: Harper Perennial, 2005.

Lickerman, Alex. *The Undefeated Mind: On the Science of Constructing an Indestructible Self.* FL: Health Communications, Inc., 2012.

Millard, Candice. *The River of Doubt: Theodore Roosevelt's Darkest Journey.* NY: Anchor Books, 2005.

Mlodinow, Leonard. *The Drunkards Walk.* NY: Vintage Books, 2012.

Morris, Edmund. *The Rise of Theodore Roosevelt.* NY: Random House, 2013.

Mullane, Nancy. *Life After Murder: Five Men in Search of Redemption.* NY: Public Affairs, 2012.

Myss, Caroline, Dr. *Anatomy of the Spirit.* NY: Three Rivers Press, 1996.

Pink, Daniel. *A Whole New Mind.* NY: Riverhead Books, 2005.

Pirsig, Robert M. *Zen and the Art of Motorcycle Maintenance: an Inquiry into Values.* NY: Harper Collins Publishing, 1999.

Ruiz, Don Miguel, Dr. *The Four Agreements: a Toltec Wisdom Book.* San Rafael, CA: Amber-Allen Publishing, 1997.

Shenwar, Maya. *Locked Down, Locked Out: Why Prison Doesn't Work and How We Can Do Better.* San Francisco: Berrett-Koehler Publishers, Inc., 2014.

Selby, John. *Seven Masters, One Path.* San Francisco: Harper Collins, 2003.

Smith, Adam. *Wealth of Nations.* Great Books of the Western World. NY, 1776.

Dorje, Changchup Kunchok, (Lama). *The Basics of Buddhism: a Twelve Week Course.* Kansas: Self-Published, 2014.

Stringer, Chris. *Lone Survivors: How We Came to be the Only Humans on Earth.* NY: St. Martin Griffin, 2012.

Suzuki, Shunryo. *Zen Mind, Beginner's Mind: Informal Talks on Zen Meditation and Practice.* NY: Weatherhill, 1970.

The Buddha. *The Dhammpada.* trans: Narada, Thera. Taiwan: The Corp Body of the Buddha Ed. Foundation, 1999.

The Dalai Lama. *How to Expand Love: Widening the Circle of Loving Relationships.* NY: Atria Books, 2005.

The Dalai Lama. *The Universe in a Single Atom: the Convergence of Science and Spirituality.* NY: Three Rivers Press, 2005.

Tolle, Eckhart. *A Whole New Earth: Awaken Your Life's Purpose.* NY: A Plume Book: Penguin Group, 2006.

Tolle, Eckhart. *The Power of Now: a Guide to Spiritual Enlightenment.* Novato CA: Namaste Publishing, New World Library, 1999.

Wade, Nicholan. *Before the Dawn: Recovering the Lost History of Our Ancestors.* NY: Penguin Books, 2006.

Wallace, Alan. *The Seven-Point Mind Training.* NY: Snow Lion Publications, 1992.

CHAPTER NOTES

CHAPTER ONE: Love Versus Fear

1. Brandeis, Louis (Supreme Court Justice). *Other People's Money and How Bankers Use It*. Published in 1914.

2. Henry David Thoreau. *Walden*. Published in 1854.

3. Sine, Richard.

4. Richard M. Nixon (U.S. President). Quoted in Glassner, Barry. *The Culture of Fear* (New York: Basic Books, 1999) and http://www.brainyquote.com/quotes/quotes/r/richardmn400958.html.

5. Glassner, Barry. *The Culture of Fear* (New York: Basic Books, 1999).

6. Thomas McCurdy. *The Structure of Morale*. Published in 1943.

7. Bronson, Po. *Why Do I Love These People: Understanding and Creating Your Own family* (New York: Random House, 2006).

8. Jampolsky, Gerald. Dr. *Love Is Letting Go of Fear* (Berkley, California: Celestial Arts, 1979).

9. Tolle, Eckhart. *The Power of Now: a Guide to Spiritual Enlightenment*. (Novato, California: Namaste Publishing, 1999).

10. Dr. Elisabeth Kubler-Ross.

11. Jampolsky, Gerald. Dr. *Love Is Letting Go of Fear* (Berkley, California: Celestial Arts, 1979).

12. Chopra, Deepak. *Why Is God Laughing: the Path to Joy and Spiritual Optimism* (New York: Three Rivers Press, 2008).

13. Ibid.

14. Smiles, Samuel. Quoted in *The 7 Habits on the Inside.* Course slides. Franklin Covey. 2012.

15. Torres, Jose. *Fire & Fear: the Inside Story of Mike Tyson.* Published in 1990, citing Cus D'Amato.

16. Roosevelt, Franklin D. (U.S. President). *Inaugural Address*, March 4, 1933. Published in Rosenman, Samuel. Ed., *The Public Papers of Franklin D. Roosevelt Vol 2: the Year of Crisis* (New York: Random House, 1938).

17. The Buddha. *The Dhammapada: Yamaka Vagga* (Taiwan: The Corporate Body of the Buddha Educational Foundation, 1999).

18. Jampolsky, Gerald. Dr. *Love Is Letting Go of* Fear. (Berkley, California: Celestial Arts, 1979).

19. Hanh, Thich Nhat. *"How to Be a Bodhosattva,"* *Shambhala Sun* (January 2015).

20. Jampolsky, Gerald. Dr. *Love Is Letting Go of Fear* (Berkley, California: Celestial Arts, 1979).

21. Haanel, Charles. *The Master Key System.* Published in 1912.

22. Chogyum Trumpa Rinpoche. "How to Be a Bodhosattva," *Shambhala Sun* (January 2015).

23. Unknown. http://www.becomingminimalist.com/love.

24. Gossami, Amit. *The Self-Aware Universe* (New York: Putnam Books, 1993).

25. James, Steven. *The Knight: a Patrik Bower Thriller* (Grand Rapids, Michigan: Revell, 2009).

26. Merton, Thomas.

27. Myss, Caroline. PhD. *Anatomy of the Spirit.* (New York: Three Rivers Press, 1996).

28. Tolle, Eckhart. *The Power of Now: a Guide to Spiritual Enlightenment* (Novato, California: Namaste Publishing, 1999).

29. Levine S. http://www.goodreads.com/author/quotes/4169.Stephen_Levine.

30. Mitch Albom. *Tuesdays with Morrie: An Old Man, A Young Man, and Life's Greatest Lesson* (New York: Anchor, 1997).

CHAPTER TWO: Being Alone

1. Eddie Cantor. Quoted in *The Sun: Sunbeams* (June 2015).

2. James, Lane. http://www.brainyquotes.com/quotes/quotes/j/jameslanea194685.html.

3. Franklin, Ben. *The Autobiography of Ben Franklin* (Roslyn, New York: Walter J. Black, Inc., 1941.

4. Salter, Elizabeth. *The Last Years of* a *Rebel: a Memoir of Edith Sitwell.* Published in 1967.

5. Evans, Mike.

6. Angel, Marc. marcangel.com/2012106/08/60-quotes-change-theway-youthink.

7. Robert Baron, Van-della, and Brunsman. Eyewitness Study.

8. Ruiz, Don Miguel. *The Four Agreements: a Toltec Wisdom Book* (San Rafael, California: Amber-Allen Publishing, 1997).

9. Tokmay Sangpo. https://www.goodreads.com/author/quotes/13667281.Bodhisattva_Tokmay_Sangpo.

10. Rabbi Hillel. *Pirque Aboth*, trans. by Charles Taylor.

11. Lao-tzu. *Tao Te Ching* (New York: Book of the Month Club, 1997).

1 2. Ibid.

13. Socrates. http://www.goodreads.com/quotes/23687.

14. Shenwar, Maya. *Locked Down, Locked Out: Why Prison Doesn't Work and How We Can Do Better* (San Francisco: Berrett-Koehler Publishers, Inc., 2014).

15. Langan, Patrick A., Schmitt, Erica L., and Durose, Matthew R. "Recidivism of Sex Offenders Released from Prison in 1994," U.S. DOJ, Office of Justice Programs, Bureau of Justice Statistics. (November 2003).

16. Ten Boom, Connelia. *The Hiding Place* (Grand Rapids, Michigan: Chosen Books, 1971).

17. Brown, Daniel James. *Boys in the Boat* (New York: Penguin, 2014).

18. Chödrön, Pema. *The Pocket* (Boston: Shambala, 2008).

19. Tokmay Sangpo. https://www.goodreads.com/author/quotes/13667281. Bodhisattva_Tokmay_Sangpo.

20. Angel, Marc. marcangel.com/2012/06/08/60-quotes-change-theway-youthink.

21. *Socrates.* http://www.goodreads.com/quotes/23687.

22. Tokmay Sangpo. https://www.goodreads.com/author/quotes/13667281. Bodhisattva Tokmay Sangpo.

23. Angel, Marc. marcangel.com/2012/06i08/60-quotes-change-theway-youthink.

24. Dorje, Changchup Kunchok (Lama). *The Basics* of *Buddhism: a Twelve Week Course* (Kansas: Self-Published, 2014).

25. The Dalai Lama. *How to Expand Love: Widening the Circle* of *Loving Relationships* (New York: Atria Books, 2005).

CHAPTER THREE: People's Reactions

1. Ruiz, Don Miguel. *The Four Agreements: a Toltec Wisdom Book* (San Rafael, California: Amber-Allen Publishing, 1997).

2. Chappell -v- Wallace, 76 Ed 2d 586, 462 U.S. 296.

3. Buber, Martin. (1923–1933). *I and Thou* (Published in 1958 University of Frankfurt am Main. Charles Scribner & Sons, 1937. New York: Continuum International Publisher Group, 2004).

4. Hock, Roger R. *Forty Studies That Changed Psychology: Explorations into History of Psychological Research, 7th ed.* (New York: Pearson, 2013).

5. Nisbett, Richard.

6. Perrow, Charles.

7. Gandhi, Mohandas K. (Mahatma). Quoted in Herman, Arthur. *Gandhi and Churchill* (New York: Bantom, 2008).

8. Confucius. *The Wisdom* of *Confucius* (New York: Modern Library, 1994).

9. Ferguson, Marilyn. Quoted in *Covey,* Stephen. *The 7 Habits for Highly Effective People* (New York: Simon and Schuster, 1989).

10. Buruma, Ian and Margault, Avishai. *Accidentalism: the West in the Eyes* of *Its Enemies* (New York: Penguin Books, 2002).

11. Lao-tzu. *Tao Te Ching* (New York: Book of the Month Club, 1997).

12. Suzuki, Shunryo. *Zen Mind, Beginner's Mind: Informal Talks on Zen Meditation and Practice* (New York: Weatherhill, 1970).

13. Gladwell, Malcolm. *Blink: the Power of Thinking Without Thinking* (New York: Back Bay Books, 2010).

14. Hock, Roger R. *Forty Studies That Changed Psychology: Explorations into History of Psychological Research, 7th ed.* (New York: Pearson, 2013).

15. Wallace, Alan. *The Seven-Point Mind Training* (New York: Snow Lion Publications, 1 992).

16. Ibid.

17. Ibid.

18. Roosevelt, Theodore (U.S. President). Quoted in Morris, Edmund. *Theodore Rex* (New York: Random House, 2004).

CHAPTER FOUR: Cause and Effect of Separation

1. *The Evolutionary Layers of the Human Brain.* http//thebrain.mcgill.ca/flash/ d/d_05/d_05cr/d_05_cr_her/d) 05_cr_her.html. and Wade, Nicholan. *Before the Dawn: Recovering the Lost History of Our Ancestors* (New York: Penguin Books, 2006).

2. Kolbert, Elizabeth. *The Sixth Extinction: a Unnatural History* (New York: Henry Holt and Co., 2014).

3. Ibid.

4. Jackson, Philip.

5. The Dalai Lama. *Essential Tibetan Buddhism:* needs publisher data

6. Stringer, Chris. *Lone Survivors: How We Came to be the Only Humans on Earth* (New York: St. Martin Griffin, 2012).

7. Anderson, Norman B. *Emotional Longevity* (New York: Viking Books, 2003).

8. Campbell, Joseph.

9. King, Martin Luther. Dr.

10. The Buddha.

9. James, William. *The Principles of Psychology* (Chicago: William Benton Publisher for Encyclopaedia Britannica, Inc., 1952).

10. Darwin, Charles. *The Origins of Species by Means of Natural Selection* (Chicago: William Benton Publisher, 1952).

11. Shenwar, Maya. *Locked Down, Locked Out: Why Prison Doesn't Work and How We Can Do Better* (San Francisco: Berrett-Koehler Publishers, Inc., 2014).

12. The Buddha. *The Middle Length Discourses of the Buddha, trans.* by Bhikkhu Nanamoli. Barre Center for Buddhist Studies, 4th ed.

13. Fuller, Buckminster.

CHAPTER FIVE: Influencing Relation to Others

1. Raskin, Leo. Quoted in Stephen Covey's *The 7 Habits of Highly Effective People* (New York: Simon & Schuster, 1989).

2. Jampolsky, Gerald. Dr. *Love Is Letting Go of Fear* (Berkley, California: Celestial Arts, 1979).

3. Gandhi, Mohandas K. (Mahatma). Quoted in Herman, Arthur. *Gandhi and Churchill* (New York: Bantam, 2008).

4. Hock, Roger R. *Forty Studies That Changed Psychology: Explorations into History of Psychological Research, 7ᵗʰ Ed.* (New York: Pearson, 2013).

5. The Dalai Lama. *How to Expand Love: Widening the Circle of Loving Relationships* (New York: Atria Books, 2005).

6. Buruma, Ian. *Year Zero: a History* of *1945* (New York: Penguin Books, 2014).

7. Batchelor, Stephen. *Buddhism Without Beliefs: a Contemporary Guide to Awakening* (New York: Riverhead Books, 1997).

8. Gandhi, Mohandas K. (Mahatma). Quoted in Herman, Arthur. *Gandhi and Churchill* (New York: Bantam, 2008).

9. Shelly, Percy Bysshe. *Hellas*, trans. by Charles and James Ollier (London, 1822).

10. The Buddha. *The Dhammapada: Atta Vagga* (Taiwan: The Corporate Body of Buddha Educational Foundation, 1999).

11. Tutu, Desmond (Bishop). *God Has a Dream* (New York: Image Books, 2005).

12. Walls, Jeanett. *Half Broke Horses: a True Life Story* (New York: Scribner Books, 2011).

13. Mother Theresa.

14. The Dalai Lama. *How to Expand Love: Widening the Circle of Loving Relationships* (New York: Atria Books, 2005).

15. Moore, Thomas (Sir). *The Utopia* (New York: Walter J. Black, Inc., 1947).

16. The Dalai Lama. *How to Expand Love: Widening the Circle* of *Loving Relationships* (New York: Atria Books, 2005).

17. Ikeda, Daisaku.

18. King, Martin Luther. Dr.

19. Mead, Margaret.

20. Shaw, George Bernaud.

21. Goethe, Johann Wolfgang von. Quoted in Covey, Stephen. *The 7 Habits of Highly Effective People* (New York: Simon and Schuster, 1989).

CHAPTER SIX: Understanding Others

1. Salzberg, Sharon. "Know Your Enemy," *Shambhala Sun* (November 2013).

2. Kant, Immanuel. *The Critique of Pure reason, and other Ethical Treatises: the Critique of Judgment* (Chicago: William Benton Publisher, 1952).

3. Slazberg, Sharon. "Know Your Enemy," *Shambhala Sun* (November 2013).

4. http://100people.org.

5. National Institute for Health. National Human Genome Research Institute. http://genome.gov.

CHAPTER SEVEN: How Can I Be Happy?

1. Franklin, Ben. The Autobiography of Ben Franklin. Walter J. Black, Inc. Roslyn (NY) 1941

2. Frankl, Viktor. *Man's Search for Meaning.* Beacon Press: (Boston) 1959

3. Anderson, Norman B.. *Emotional Longevity.* Viking Books: (NY) 2003

4. Hock, Roger R.. *Forty Studies That Changed Psychology: Explorations into History of Psychological Research, 7th Ed.* Pearson: (NY) 2013

5. Wallace, Alan. *The Seven-point Mind Training.* Snow Lion Publications: (NY) 1992

6. Hanh, Thich Nhat. *Anger.* Riverhead Books: (NY) 2001

7. Wilson, Robert Anton.

8. Ali, Muhammad.

9. Gandhi, Mohandas K. (Mahatma). Quoted in: Herman, Arthur. *Gandhi and Churchill.* Bantom (NY) 2008

10. Hanh, Thich Nhat. *Anger.* Riverhead Books: (NY) 2001

11. Shatideva. *A Guide to the Bodhisattva's Way of Life.* 8th Century C.E., trans Padmakara Translation Group, rev. ed. Shambhala Publications: (Boston) 2006

12. Stanford, Chuck (Lama). *The Basics of Buddhism: A Twelve Week Course.* Self Published: (KS) 2014

13. Jung, Carl. *The Basic Writings of Carl Jung.* Modern Library (NY) 1993

14. Journal of Social Psychology: 2014

15. Journal of Happiness Studies: Harvard Business School and University of British Columbia

16. The Buddha.

17. Ruiz, Don Miguel. *The Four Agreements: A Toltec Wisdom Book.* Amber-Allen Publishing: (San Rafael, CA) 1997

18. Washington, Booker T. *Up From Slavery.* Signet Classics (NY) 2010

19. Nagarjuma. Quoted in: *The Tibetan Book of the Dead.* Fremantle, Francesca, and Chogyam Trungpa. Shambala (Boston) 1975

20. Stanford, Chuck (Lama). *Happiness.* Discussion in author's prison group

21. Frankl, Viktor. *Man's Search for Meaning.* Beacon Press: (Boston) 1959

22. Rosten, Leo.

23. Emerson, Ralph Waldo. *The Best of Ralph Waldo Emerson.* Walter J. Black, Inc. (NY) 1941

CHAPTER EIGHT: My Family and Friends' Character

1. Berkman's Alamedia Study Quoted in Anderson, Norman B.. *Emotional Longevity.* Viking Books: (NY) 2003

2. Anderson, Norman B.. *Emotional Longevity.* Viking Books: (NY) 2003

3. Haidt, Jonathan. *The Happiness Hypothesis: Finding Modern Truth in Ancient Wisdom.* Basic Books (NY) 2007

4. Covey, Stephen R. *7 Habits of Highly Effective People: Powerful Lessons in Personal Change.* Free Press: (NY) 1989

5. Mandela, Nelson. *Long Walk to Freedom.* Back Bay Books: (NY) 1994

6. Angel, Marc. *Marcangel.com/2012/06/08/60-quotes-change-theway-you-think.*

7. Ibid

8. Ibid

9. Lewis, C. S..

10. Hanh, Thich Nhat. *Anger.* Riverhead Books: (NY) 2001

11. Mother Theresa.

12. Covey, Stephen R. *7 Habits of Highly Effective People: Powerful Lessons in Personal Change.* Free Press: (NY) 1989

13. Gardner, Richard A. M.D.. *Legal and Psychotherapeutic Approaches to the 3 Types of Parental Alienation Syndrome Families; When Psychiatry & the Law Join Forces.* Court Review, Vol 28, Num 1, Spr 1991, p14-21

14. James, Steven. *Opening Moves: A Patrick Bower Thriller.* Revel: (Grand Rapids, MI) 2009

15. U.S. DOJ, Office of Justice Programs, Bureau of Justice Statistics. *Recidivism of Sex Offenders Released from Prison in 1994,* By Patrick A. Langan, Erica L. Schmitt, and Matthew R. Durose, November 2003

16. Shelton, Richard. *Crossing the Yard: Thirty Years as a Prison Volunteer.* University of Arizona Press: (Tucson) 2007

17. Stanford, Chuck (Lama). *The Basics of Buddhism: A Twelve Week Course.* Self Published: (KS) 2014 and Dharma Talk on 9 Aug, 2015

18. Lickerman, Alex Dr.. *The Undefeated Mind: The Science of Constructing an Indestructible Self.* Health Communications, Inc.: (FL) 2012

19. Tangpa, Langri.

20. Chopra, Deepak. *Why is God Laughing: The Path to Joy and Spiritual Optimism.* Three Rivers Press: (NY) 2008

21. Jobs, Steve.

22. Rumi, Jalaluddin, *The Essence of Rumi.* Chartwell Books (NY) 2005

23. Palov, Chloe M. *Ark of Fire.* Berkley Books (NY) 2008

24. Mandela, Nelson. *Long Walk to Freedom.* Back Bay Books: (NY) 1994

25. Tolle. Eckhart. *The Power of Now: A Guide to Spiritual Enlightenment.* Namaste Publishing: (Novato CA) 1999

26. Stanford, Chuck (Lama). *The Basics of Buddhism: A Twelve Week Course.* Self Published: (KS) 2014

27. Ibid

28. Myss, Caroline PH.D. *Anatomy of the Spirit.* Three Rivers Press: (NY) 1996

29. Ruiz, Don Miguel. *The Four Agreements: A Toltec Wisdom Book.* Amber-Allen Publishing: (San Rafael, CA) 1997

30. Alcorn, Alfred.

31. Unknown to me.

CHAPTER NINE: My Own Character

1. King, Martin Luther (Dr.)

2. Chatterton, John.

3. Frankl, Viktor. *Man's Search for Meaning.* Beacon Press: (Boston) 1959

4. Ibid

5. Thoreau, Henry David. *Walden.* Walter J. Black, Inc. (NY) 1942

6. Stanley, Thomas.

7. Mandela, Nelson. *Long Walk to Freedom.* Back Bay Books: (NY) 1994

8. Addison, John.

9. Nisaradatta, Sri.

10. Japolsky, Gerald Dr.. *Love is Letting Go of Fear.* Celstial Arts: (Berkley, CA) 1979

11. The Buddha. *The Dhammapadha: Atta and Sukha Vagga.* The Corporate Body of the Buddha Educational Foundation: (Tawain) 1999.

12. Patton, George (General). *Patton.* Harper Perennial (NY) 1995

13. Unknown to me.

14. Franklin, Ben. The Autobiography of Ben Franklin. Walter J. Black, Inc. Roslyn (NY) 1941

15. Buscagila, Leo.

16. Thoreau, Henry David. *Walden.* Walter J. Black, Inc. (NY) 1942

17. Ruiz, Don Miguel. *The Four Agreements: A Toltec Wisdom Book.* Amber-Allen Publishing: (San Rafael, CA) 1997

18. Hemingway, Ernest. *The Old Man and the Sea.* Scribner & Sons: (NY) 1952

19. Millma, Dan. *The Way of the Peaceful Warrior.* Random House (NY) 2007

20. Bronson, Po. *Why Do I Love These People: Understanding and Creating Your Own family.* Random House: (NY) 2006

21. Robison, Maria.

22. Heen, Sheila; Stone, Douglas. *Thanks for the Feedback: The Science and Art of Receiving Feedback Well.* Penguin Books: (NY) 2014

23. Jung, Carl. *The Basic Writings of Carl Jung.* Modern Library (NY) 1993

24. Lamore, Louis.

CHAPTER TEN: Justice Versus Peace

1. Mandela, Nelson. *Long Walk to Freedom.* Back Bay Books: (NY) 1994

2. Ibid

3. U.S. DOJ, Office of Justice Programs, Bureau of Justice Statistics. 2014: *Recidivism of Prisoners Released in 30 States in 2005: Patterns from 2005 to 2010,* By Matthew R. Durose, Alexia D. Cooper, and Howard N. Snyder

4. Drucker, Ernest. *A Plague of Prisons: The Epidemiology of Mass Incarceration is America.* New Press; (NY) 2013

5. Schenwar, Maya. *Locked down, Locked Out: Why Prison Doesn't Work and How We Can Do Better.* Berrett-Koehler Publishers, Inc: (San Francisco, CA) 2014

6. Mulane, Nancy. *Life After Murder: Five Men in Search of Redemption.* Public Affairs: (NY) 2012.

7. Ibid

8. Ariely, Dan. *The (Honest) Truth About Dishonesty: How We Lie to Everyone— Especially Ourselves.* Harper Perennial: (NY) 2013

9. Samet, Elizabeth.

10. Bush, George W. (U.S. President). *U.S. President Seeks Congressional Authorization to Attach Iraq: Pre-Emptive Strike Strategy Outlined.* Fact on File. World News Digest. Vol 62, No 3224* Sept 26, 2002

11. Bell, James. *The Sum magazine: Sunbeams:* June 2015

12. Kennedy, John F. (U.S. President).

13. Ingersoll, Robert. *The Sun magazine, Sunbeams:* June: 2015

14. King, Martin Luther (Dr.).

15. Darrow, Clarence. *The Sun magazine, Sunbeams*: June: 2015

16. Hanh, Thch Nhat. *Anger.* Riverhead Books: (NY) 2001

17. Fredston, Jill. *Snowstruck: In the Grip of Avalanches.* A Harvest Book: (NY) 2005

18. Fishoff, Baruch.

19. Gardner, Daniel. *The Science of Fear: How the Culture of Fear Manipulates Your Brain.* A Plume Book: (NY) 2009

20. Lizza, Ryan. *The Great Divide.* New Yorker Magazine: 21 March 2016

21. Ibid

22. Hanh, Thich Nhat. *Anger.* Riverhead Books: (NY) 2001

23. The Zohar. *The Sun magazine: Sunbeams:* June 2015

24. Bronson, Po. *Why do I Love These People: Understanding & Creating Your Own Family.* Random House: (NY) 2006

25. Tutu, Desmond (Bishop). *God Has A Dream.* Image Books (NY) 2005

26. Croggon, Alice. *The Sun magazine: Sunbeams:* June 2015

27. Lao Tzu. *Tao Te Ching.* Book-of-the-Month Club: (NY) 1997

28. Thoreau, Henry David. *Walden.* Walter J. Black, Inc. (NY) 1942

29. Ginzburg, Natalia. *The Sun magazine: Dog Eared Page.*

30. King, Martin Luther (Dr.)

31. Harden, Blaine. *Escape from Camp 14.* Penguin Books: (NY) 2012

32. Jampolsky, Gerald PH.D.. *Forgiveness: The Greatest Healer of All.* Atria Books: (NY) 2007

33. Nouwen, Heneri J.M.. *The Sun magazine: Sunbeams:* June 2015

34. Doe Zantamata.

35. Wiseman, Theresa. *Four Qualities of Empathy.* Journal of Advanced Nursing.

36. Hanh, Thich Nhat. *Anger.* Riverhead Books: (NY) 2001

37. The Dali Lama. *How to Expand Love: Widing the Circle of Loving Relationships.* Atria Books: (NY) 2005

38. Einstein, Albert. Quoted in Stephen Covey's: *The 7 Habits for Highly Effective People.* Simon & Schuster: (NY) 1989

39. Japolsky, Gerald Dr.. *Love is Letting Go of Fear.* Celstial Arts: (Berkley CA) 1979

CHAPTER ELEVEN: Retribution and Restitution

1. Shakespeare. *Merchant of Venice: Shakespeare I.* Britannica Great Books. William Benton, Publisher (Chicago) 1952

2. Von Clausewitz, Karl. *On War.* Princeton Press: (NY) 1977

3. Goldman, Emma.

4. Mullane, Nancy. *Life After Murder: Five Men in Search of Redemption.* Public Affairs: (NY) 2012

5. Gandhi, Mohandas K. (Mahatma). Quoted in: Herman, Arthur. *Gandhi and Churchill.* Bantom (NY) 2008

6. Hanh, Thich Nhat. *Anger.* Riverhead Books: (NY) 2001

7. Elliot, Kate.

8. Gandhi, Mohandas K. (Mahatma). Quoted in: Herman, Arthur. *Gandhi and Churchill.* Bantom (NY) 2008

9. Driver, William.

10. U.S. DOJ, Office of Justice Programs, Bureau of Justice Statistics. *Recidivism of Sex Offenders Released from Prison in 1994,* By Patrick A. Langan, Erica L. Schmitt, and Matthew R. Durose, November 2003

11. Kennedy, David. *Deterrence and Crime Prevention.* Routledge: (NY) 2008

12. Wegman, Jesse. *False Hope and a Needless Death Behind Bars.* The New York Times, 6 Sept. Vol. CLXV No. 57.347

13. Harrell, S. Kelly. *The Sun, Jan2016: Sunbeams.*

14. Solzhenitsyn, Aleksandr. *The Gulag Archipelago.* Harper (NY) 1991

15. Prochaska, J.O., & Velicer, W.F. *The Transtheoretical Model of Health Behavior Change.* American Journal of Health Promotion, 12 (1997)

16. Warhol, Andy.

17. Dubios, Charles.

18. DePree, Max.

19. Morgan, J. Peirpont.

20. Bozick, Robert; Davis, Lois; Miles, Jeremy; Saunders, Jessica; and Steele, Jennifer (sponsored by The Bureau of Justice Assistance). *Evaluating the Effectiveness of Correctional Education: A Meta-analysis of Programs That Provide Education to Incarcerated Adults.* RAND Corp: 2013

21. Pascal, Blaise. *The Provincial Letter Pensees Scientific Treatises.* William Benton Publisher (Chicago) 1952,

22. Plank, Max.

23. Smith, Adam. *The Theory of Moral Sentiments.* Modern Library: (NY) 1994

24. Emerson, Ralph Waldo. *The Best of Ralph Waldo Emerson.* Walter J. Black, Inc. (NY) 1941

25. Atkins, Dale.

26. Smith, Jeremey Adam. *You Can Count on Goodness:* Shambhala Sun Article, May 2015

27. Ibid

28. Mandela, Nelson. *Long Walk to Freedom.* Back Bay Books: (NY) 1994

29. Cover, Stephen R. *7 Habits of Highly Effective People: Powerful Lessons in Personal Change.* Free Press: (NY) 1989

30. Thuben Chodron.

31. Aurelius, Marcus. Translated by Martin Hammond. *Meditations.* Penguin Classics: (NY) 2006

CHAPTER TWELVE: Personal Responsibility

1.   Jennings, William Dale. *The Ronin.* Tuttle Publishing (Vermont) 1969

2.   Chopra, Deepak. *The Return of Merlin.* Three Rivers Press: (NY) 2009

3.   Fredston, Jill. *Snowstruck: In the Grip of Avalanches.* A Harvest Book: (NY) 2005

4.   Angelou, Maya. Quoted in: Fredston, Jill. *Snowstruck: In the Grip of Avalanches.* A Harvest Book: (NY) 2005

5.   Durrant, Will. Quoted in: Fredston, Jill. *Snowstruck: In the Grip of Avalanches.* A Harvest Book: (NY) 2005

6.   The Buddha. Translated by Bhikkhu Nanamoli. *The Middle Length Discourses of the Buddha.* Barre Center for Buddhist Studies

7.   Soppard, Toni. Quoted in: Fredston, Jill. *Snowstruck: In the Grip of Avalanches.* A Harvest Book: (NY) 2005

8.   Lerner, Melvin J. and Montada. *An Overview: Advances in Belief in a Just World Theory and Methods: in Responses to Victimizations and Belief in a Just World.* Plemun Press (NY) 1998

9.   Festinger, Leon. *A Theory of Cognitive Dissonance.* 1957

10. The Buddha. Translated by Bhikkhu Nanamoli. *The Middle Length Discourses of the Buddha.* Barre Center for Buddhist Studies

11. Mandela, Nelson. *Long Walk to Freedom.* Back Bay Books: (NY) 1994

12. Sartre, Paul.

13. Suzuki, Shunryo. *Zen Mind, Beginner's Mind: Informal Talks on Zen Meditation and Practice.* Weatherhill: (NY) 1970

14. Basicknowledge101 .com/subjects/brain...*Between 2 & 11 Billion bits per second to process; we only process between 50 and 1,000 bits per second*

15. DaVinci, Leonardo.

16. Covey, Stephen R. *7 Habits of Highly Effective People: Powerful Lessons in Personal Change.* Free Press: (NY) 1989

17. Wert, Kurt.

18. Muller, Robert.

19. Jampolsky, Gerald Dr.. *Forgiveness: The Greatest Healer of All.* Atria Books: (NY) 2007

20. Japolsky, Gerald Dr.. *Love is Letting Go of Fear.* Celestial Arts: (Berkley CA) 1979

21. Behrend, Geneviene.

22. Iyeyasu.

23. Jampolsky, Gerald Dr.. *Forgiveness: The Greatest Healer of All.* Atria Books: (NY) 2007

24. Gandhi, Mohandas K. (Mahatma). Quoted in: Herman, Arthur. *Gandhi and Churchill.* Bantom (NY) 2008

CHAPTER THIRTEEN: True Knowledge

1. Born, Max.

2. Faraday, Michael.

3. Doyle, Arthur Conin. *Sherlock Holmes: The Complete Novel & Stories.* Bantam Books (NY) 1986

4. Occam (Ockham), William of. *Summa Logices: Quaestiones in Octo libros physicorum.* Germany: 1285 to 1349. Translated by: Loux, Michael J. Notra Dame University Press (IN) 1974

5. Franklin, Ben. The Autobiography of Ben Franklin. Walter J. Black, Inc. Roslyn (NY) 1941

6. Kant, Immanuel. *The Critique of Pure reason, and other Ethical Treatises: The Critique of Judgment.* William Benton Publisher (Chicago) 1952

7. Bacon, Roger (Sir).

8. Huxley, Thomas. *Agnosticism.* 1889 Essay Published in Science and the Christian Tradition: Macmillan: (London) 1904

9. Booth, Mark. *The Secret History of the World*, Overlook Press (NY) 2008

10. Epstein, Greg M. Good Without God. HarperCollins: (NY) 2007

11. Anderson, Norman B. *Emotional Longevity.* Viking Books: (NY) 2003

12. Bacon, Roger (Sir).

13. Gonzales, Laurence. *Deep Survival.* Quoted in: Fredston, Jill. *Snowstruck: In the Grip of Avalanches.* A Harvest Book: (NY) 2005

14. Fredston, Jill. *Snowstruck: In the Grip of Avalanches.* A Harvest Book: (NY) 2005

15. Holmes, Jamie. Nonsense: *The Power of Not Knowing.* Crown Publishing: (NY) 2015

16. Gardner, Daniel. *The Science of Fear: How the Culture of Fear Manipulates Your Brain.* A Plume Book: (NY) 2009

17. Mlodinow, Leonard. *The Drunkard's Walk.* Vintage Books: (NY) 2012

18. Gardner, Daniel. *The Science of Fear: How the Culture of Fear Manipulates Your Brain.* A Plume Book: (NY) 2009

19. Covey, Stephen R. *7 Habits of Highly Effective People: Powerful Lessons in Personal Change.* Free Press: (NY) 1989

20. Wallace, David Foster.

21. Gardner, Daniel. *The Science of Fear: How the Culture of Fear Manipulates Your Brain.* A Plume Book: (NY) 2009

22. Pompilio, Natalie. *Old Prison's Transformation Offers Unvarnished Look at U.S. Crime, Punishment.* Associated Press: January 2016

23. Gandhi, Mohandas K. (Mahatma). Quoted in: Herman, Arthur. *Gandhi and Churchill.* Bantam (NY) 2008

24. Lao Tzu. *Tao Te Ching.* Book-of-the-Month Club: (NY) 1997

25. Bohrn, David.

26. Covey, Stephen R. *7 Habits of Highly Effective People: Powerful Lessons in personal Change.* Free Press: (NY) 1989

27. Bohr, Neils. Quoted in: *The Secret History of the World,* by Mark Booth. The Overlook Press (NY) 2008

28. Hansen, Rick.

29. Aristotle. *On Man in the Universe.* Walter J. Black, Inc (NY) 1943

30. Einstein, Albert.

31. Mlodinow, Leonard. *The Drunkard's Walk.* Vintage Books: (NY) 2012

32. Carrol, Vincent. Can You Believe Your Eyes. Denver Post. 2010

33. Specter, Michael. *Partial Recall: Can Neuroscience Help us Rewrite our Most Traumatic Memories?* The New Yorker magazine: May 19, 2014.

34. Lehrer, Jonah. *The Forgetting Pill.* Wired magazine: Mar 2012

35. *The Problem with Eyewitness Testimony.* Stanford Journal of Legal Studies: Nov 2015. http:agora.stanford.edu/sjls/issue%200ne/fisher &tversky.htm and *Why Science Tells Us Not to Rely of Eyewitness Accounts.* Scientific American:

36. www.scientificamerican.com/article/do-the-eyes-have-it; Hock, Roger R.. Forty Studies That Changed Psychology: Explorations into History of Psychological Research, 7th Ed. Pearson: (NY) 2013

37. Eckhart, Meister. Quoted in: Booth, Mark. *The Secret History of the World,* Overlook Press (NY) 2008

CHAPTER FOURTEEN: Real Freedom

1. Military's 94% conviction rate -v- civlian rate of 85%: Report of Code Committee of Military Justice. Found at *Incarcerate.wordpress.com.* Jones, Sheri (LtCol). AF.mil/news/commentaries/civilian-vs-mil-justicesystem-how-do-they-compare.afpx Nov 2013

2. Yoshida, Tate. *If You Want Parole, Get Your Case Heard After Lunch.* ARS Thechnica. 11 Apr 2011

3. Dershowitz, Alan.

4. Gardner, Daniel. *The Science of Fear: How the Culture of Fear Manipulates Your Brain.* A Plume Book: (NY) 2009

5. Schauer, Fredrick.

6. Kahneman, Daniel; Slavic, Paul; and Tversky, Amos (eds), *Judgment Under Uncertainty: Heuristics and Biases,* Cambridge University Press: (NY) 1982

7. Purves, E.; Augustine, G.J.; Fitzpatrick, D., et al. *Neuroscience,* 2nd Edition. editor: Sunderland, M.A.: Sinauer Associates: 2001

8. Jampolsky, Gerald DR. *Love is Letting Go of Fear.* Celstial Arts: (Berkley CA) 1979

9. Jackson, Phillip.

10. Mlodinow, Leonard. *The Drunkard's Walk.* Vintage Books: (NY) 2012

11. Frankl, Viktor. *Man's Search for Meaning.* Beacon Press: (Boston) 1959

12. Covey, Stephen R. *7 Habits of Highly Effective People: Powerful Lessons in Personal Change.* Free Press: (NY) 1989

13. Gandhi, Mohandas K. (Mahatma). Quoted in: Herman, Arthur. *Gandhi and Churchill.* Bantam (NY) 2008

14. www.deathpenaltyinfo.org and AmericaAljazeera.com

15. U.S. Disciplinary Barracks, The Passing Times, Vol 10, Is. 6, Jun 2016

16. Orwell, George.

17. Subranian, Ram & Shumes, Alison. *Sentencing & Prison Practices in Germany & Netherlands: Implication for the U.S..* Vera Institute of Justice, Oct 2013. 20 Year Max for Some European Countries (Demark/Sweden): Wikipedia.com

18. Amen, Daniel G. M.D.. *Change Your Brain Change Your Life: The Breakthrough Program for Conquering Anxiety, Depression, Obsessiveness, of Focus, Anger, and Memory Problems.* Harmony Books: (NY) 2015

19. Schenwar, Maya. *Locked down, Locked Out: Why Prison Doesn't Work and How We can Do Better.* Berrett-Koehler Publishers, Inc: (San Francisco, CA) 2014 Per the FBOP website, between &28K-30K per year, as of 3/9/15. www://federalregister.com/document/2015/3/09/2015-0543/annualdetermination-of-average-cost-of-incarceration

20. Ruiz, Don Miguel. *The Four Agreements: A Toltec Wisdom Book.* Amber-Allen Publishing: (San Rafael, CA) 1997

21. Waitley, Denis.

22. Mlodinow, Leonard. *The Drunkard's Walk.* Vintage Books: (NY) 2012

23. Frankl, Viktor. *Man's Search for Meaning.* Beacon Press: (Boston) 1959

24. Jampolsky, Gerald DR. *Love is Letting Go of Fear.* Celstial Arts: (Berkley CA) 1979

25. Stanford, Chuck (Lama). *The Basics of Buddhism: A Twelve Week Course.* Self Published: (KS) 2014

26. Swindall, Charles. Attitudes.

27. The Dali Lama. *How to Expand Love: Widing the Circle of Loving Relationships.* Atria Books: (NY) 2005

28. Pirsig, Robert. *Zen and the Art of Motorcycle Maintenence.* HarperCollins Publishing (NY) 1999

29. Lickerman, Alex. Dr. *The Undefeated Mind: The Science of Constructing an Indestructible Self.* Health Communications, Inc.: (FL) 2012

CHAPTER FIFTEEN: Prison is Tough; Why Not Give Up?

1. Gardner, Richard A. M.D.. Legal and Psychotherapeutic Approaches to the 3 Types of Parental Alienation Syndrome Families: When Psychiatry and the Law Join Forces. Court Review, Vol 28, Num 1, Spr 1991, p14-21

2. Winter, Mary. Parental Alienation: Syndrome Being Considered for Inclusion in Therapists' Official Catalog. Denver Post:

3. Ibid.

4. Mulane, Nancy. Life After Murder: Five Men in Search of Redemption. Public Affairs: (NY) 2012.

5. Ariely, Dan. The (Honest) Truth About Dishonesty: How We Lie to Everyone--Especially Ourselves. Harper Perennial: (NY) 2013

5. Gardner, Richard A. M.D.. Legal and Psychotherapeutic Approaches to the 3 Types of Parental Alienation Syndrome Families: When Psychiatry and the Law Join Forces. Court Review, Vol 28, Num 1, Spr '1991, p14-21

6. Winter, Mary. Parental Alienation: Syndrome Being Considered for Inclusion in Therapists' Official Catalog. Denver Post: DATE??? 2010

7. Stanford, Chuck (Lama). Transcending Fear and Hope: Talk Given: 27 Dec, 2015

8. Frankl, Viktor. Man's Search for Meaning. Beacon Press: (Boston) 1959

9. Peale, Norman Vincent.

10. Twain, Mark.

11. The Dali Lama.

12. Dweck, Carol.

13. Kristnimurti. Quoted in: Selby, John. Seven Masters, One Path: Meditation Secrets from the Worlds Greatest Teachers. HarperSanFrancisco (NY) 2003

14. Einstein, Albert.

15. Salimbene.

16. Hirshman, Albert 0. The Principle of the Hiding Hand. Quoted in: Gladwell, Malcolm. The New Yorker: The Gift of Doubt. 2015

17. Knost, L.R..

18. Rousseau, Jacques.

19. Gladwell, Malcolm. The New Yorker: The Gift of Doubt. 2015

20. Frankl, Viktor. Man's Search for Meaning. Beacon Press: (Boston) 1959

21. Stricktland, Bill (Manchester Craftsman Guild Founder).

22. Osborne, Tom (Congressman).

23. Park, Crystal Dr.

24. Koestenbaum, Peter.

25. Tolle, Eckart.The Power of Now: A Guide to Spiritual Enlightenment. Namaste Publishing: (Novato CA) 1999

26. Gladwell, Malcolm.   Blink: The Power of Thinking Without Thinking. Back Bay Books: (NY) 2010

27. Frankl, Viktor. Man's Search for Meaning. Beacon Press: (Boston) 1959

28. Anderson, Norman B. Dr. Emotional Longevity. Viking Books: (NY) 2003

29. Sogyal Rinpoche. The Tibetan Book of Living and Dying. Harper San Francisco. (SF) 1993

30. Suzuki, Shunryo. Zen Mind, Beginner's Mind: Informal Talks on Zen Meditation and Practice. Weatherhill: (NY) 1970

31. The Dali Lama. How to Expand Love: Widing the Circle of Loving Relationships. Atria Books: (NY) 2005

32. The Prince of Mito.

33. Lao Tzu. Tao Te Ching. Book-of-the-Month Club: (NY) 1997

34. Gandhi, Mohandas K. (Mahatma). Quoted in: Herman, Arthur. Gandhi and Churchill. Bantam (NY) 2008

35. Ibid

INDEX